POT PLANET

POT PLANET

Adventures in
Global Marijuana Culture

✳

Brian Preston

Grove Press
New York

The names of certain people in this book have been changed, sometimes at their request. Parts of chapter 10 first appeared in *Saturday Night* magazine. Part of chapter 11 first appeared in the *Vancouver Sun.*

Published simultaneously in Canada
Printed in the United States of America

FIRST EDITION

Library of Congress Cataloging-in-Publication Data

Preston, Brian, 1957–
    Pot planet : adventures in global marijuana culture / Brian Preston.—1st ed.
    p. cm.
    ISBN 0-8021-3897-7
    1. Marijuana. 2. Cannabis. 3. Subculture. 4. Preston, Brian, 1957—
Journeys. I. Title
    HV5822.M3 P74 2002
    306'.1—dc21   2001058499

Design by Laura Hammond Hough

Grove Press
841 Broadway
New York, NY 10003

02 03 04 05   10 9 8 7 6 5 4 3 2 1

To everyone who
gave me a light

CONTENTS

He had discovered a great law of human action, without knowing it—namely, that in order to make a man or a boy covet a thing, it is only necessary to make the thing difficult to attain.

—*Tom Sawyer,* by Mark Twain

There! there is happiness; heaven in a teaspoon; happiness, with all its intoxication, all its folly, all its childishness. You can swallow it without fear; it is not fatal . . . You are now sufficiently provisioned for a long and strange journey; the steamer has whistled, the sails are trimmed; and you have this curious advantage over ordinary travellers, that you have no idea where you are going. You have made your choice; here's to luck!

—*The Poem of Hashish,* by Charles Baudelaire

POT PLANET

1 : MY HOMETOWN

Four years ago *Rolling Stone* magazine assigned me to write a story about the marijuana culture of Vancouver, British Columbia. Vancouver had been my home for nine years, and although I was a moderate toker by local standards, I had something of a reputation with my stressed New York editor: I was the West Coast stoner dude.

Until then I hadn't considered myself part of any kind of pot community, any more than someone who picks up a six-pack thinks of himself as part of the beer community. I was a consumer, that's all, and pot was a product, a form of euphoria that came to me in convenient little plastic Baggies, in eighth or quarter ounces at a time. Sometimes it was good, sometimes it was mediocre, but I smoked it all regardless and never really worried too much about what variety it might be, or who had grown it, or where, or using what methods, any more than I would wonder about the dairy industry when buying a quart of homogenized milk.

Though I've smoked it on and off since 1976, I only really started thinking about marijuana seriously when, researching that magazine story, I ended up in a store called the Little Grow Shop in Vancouver. The shop sold hydroponic and other indoor growing supplies, and marijuana seeds over the counter, from the basement of a larger store called Hemp B.C., an upscale head shop selling bongs, books, rolling papers, pipes, hemp jeans, and tie-dyed T-shirts on West Hastings Street. Downstairs in the Little Grow Shop I had the strange feeling of being in some urban mutation of the rural farm supply outlets I'd known as a kid—comfortable places where farmers stood around and swapped talk about the crops. Even the manner of speaking was the same—a clipped, minimalist farmer shorthand. The five staff members had varying experiences growing marijuana outdoors in swampy lowlands, dry prairie, hillsides and valleys; some had grown indoors, in soil or hydroponically, using chemical fertilizers or going totally organic. I learned a lot about growing pot just by eavesdropping at the counter:

"We can't guarantee which are females. It's normal to get two or three males in ten seeds."

"You're giving them way too much nitrogen."

"Sativas grow taller than indicas as a rule."

"You need a light, an exhaust fan, a reservoir to hold your water, soil, pots, nutrients, a good fertilizer, and good seed. For about a five-hundred-dollar start-up you can grow four ounces of pot every two months."

"Absolutely everybody grows it differently, which tells you it's real easy to grow."

Surrounded by super-enlarged photo posters of richly resinous buds from strains like B.C. Kush, White Rhino, and Pearly Girl, the store's staff dispensed advice, while the owner, Marc Emery, held court from his desk in the back corner of the open room. He wore his hair in a dated, parted-down-the-middle cut that showed too much of a spacious forehead, and had a habit of squinting as if he were trying to keep his glasses from slithering down his nose, yet somehow Emery managed to exude a kind of charisma. Likely you remember someone from high school who was smarter than the teachers and took pleasure in letting them know it. Emery would be the forty-year-old version of that bratty kid.

He toked from a huge fattie consisting of a variety called Shiva Skunk, then lit up a personal favorite, a cross of two varieties, Northern Lights and Blueberry, but smoking huge quantities of reefer didn't seem to mellow him at all, as pot does most people. He kept up a caustic, funny patter—he doesn't so much talk as crow—and since he was the boss, no matter how obnoxious or abrasive his opinions became, no one could tell him to shut up.

"American farm boy types come in here often," he told me, "and they'll stand there at the book rack, taking in the room over the top of a magazine for the longest time. Then suddenly a big smile comes over their face, and they'll burst out, 'Ah cain't buleeve what ahm seein' here!'"

His desk was a clunky old wooden schoolteacher's model with three cubic feet of drawers that contained the most intense concentration of marijuana genetics in North America. There were about three hundred little black film canisters in Emery's desk, each holding seeds of a unique marijuana strain, some back-bred to stability, others a first-generation hybrid. Many of these strains were local varieties that have given Canada's west coast a reputation for some of the world's best pot.

He wore a headset to take a constant stream of phone calls, and he was filling some of the $20,000 worth of mail orders he received each and every week, inlaying seeds in cardboard flats that he slid into envelopes bound most often for California and Australia. "Our Commonwealth brothers in Oz are really into pot," he said. "They're at the same stage of marijuana acceptance as Canada."

✳

Listening to the staff chat to customers, I felt humbled, and a little intimidated, to be so thoroughly enlightened: growing pot can be approached with all the dedication and attention to horticultural science that any serious farmer gives his acreage, or any prizewinning gardener her rose bed. Beyond that, the fruits of these labors, the harvested flowers, can be damned or praised with the epicurean subtlety, the *gourmandise,* that the French or Italians bring to wine and food. Producing and imbibing the best marijuana can be elevated to an art form.

✳

Researching the story gave me an excuse to keep hanging out at the Little Grow Shop. I really did enjoy the no-pretense General Store ambience of the place, plus there was the promise, or I should say the guarantee, of getting totally baked. By chance I met Jorge Cervantes, American author of *Indoor Marijuana Horticulture* and other outstanding grow books. "This is like a farmer's co-op," Jorge said as he took in the scene, "where you can meet growers and ask them what works for them. Europe is still much more advanced than here, but I think Vancouver's following in the same footsteps as Holland."

Jorge had come north for a research tour. "As an author, I cannot and will not go to a grow room in the United States," he said. "I could go to jail for the rest of my life. If a grower gets arrested and they have evidence of me being there, then I'm an accomplice and I'm equally guilty under the RICO statute." The Racketeering Influenced and Corrupt Organizations Act is a federal law from 1970 intended to fight organized crime, on the theory that planning to commit a crime, or even having knowledge of a crime, is the same as committing the crime, and should carry the same punishment. "I've been all over the world, and the U.S. is one of those Gestapo countries when it comes to marijuana laws," Jorge said. "Here in Canada I can visit people who are growing, do it carefully and quietly, and not have any troubles. And it's nice here."

Many Americans think of Vancouver as part of the Pacific Northwest, but for Canadians it's the extreme *south*west. In winter it's as warm as you can get and still be in Canada. It's like Seattle, only rainier, if you can imagine that. Vancouver's a great town. One point eight million people, and you can still say, as a friend did lately from a sidewalk chair outside a pleasant cafe, "Let's get out of this cultural contrivance and into the beauty of nature." Nature, in the form of clean beaches, or spectacular temperate rain forest, is twenty minutes away. That makes Vancouver my pick as best city in the world to smoke a doob and go for a walk.

Jorge drove me east to the Vancouver suburb Coquitlam to visit the home of Mike, one of the five growers who at that time made up the Spice of Life seed company. We sat with him in the living room for a while, watching the local hockey team, the Canucks, take on Carolina on the tube.

The house was a labyrinth of white-walled grow rooms, some no bigger than a closet. Jorge happily snapped pictures of me sniffing bud, pictures that Mike was careful to stay out of. Things are cool in Canada, but not that cool. Jorge said, "I can't believe the attitude in Spain right now. When I take pictures there, the growers want to be in them."

Mike wished he could be that free. "As far as I'm concerned I'm not doing anything wrong at all," he said. "It's a crime that pot's illegal. It is. How dare they come in here and bust my ass, get the fuck out right now, that's how I feel about it. Turn around and don't break any lightbulbs on the way out."

Jorge said, "You'd make it about a week in the U.S. with that attitude. You'd be kissing the floor with your hands behind your back, a big boot right on your neck"—he made a choking sound—"and every time you'd squeak they'd stomp you a little bit more."

The plant names were labeled on white plastic knives stuck in the soil: Shishkaberry, Sweet Skunk, Purple Hempstar. The Shishkaberry, like the currently popular Bubbleberry, is a hybrid developed from a strain called Blueberry. Blueberry comes out of various crossings and recrossings of three strains: Highland Thai, also called Juicy Fruit when it was first bred in the 1970s in the American Pacific Northwest; Purple Thai, which was itself a cross between Chocolate Thai and Highland Oaxaca Gold; and a nameless Afghani indica.

This knowledge may sound as though it were difficult to acquire, but truth be told, a ton of information is out there for anyone, for free, on the Internet. This is how Blueberry was described in Marc Emery's Summer 2000 catalogue: "80% Indica, 20% Sativa. Dates to the late 1970's. Large producer under optimum conditions. A dense and stout plant with red, purple and blue hues, usually cures to a lavender blue. The finished product has a very fruity aroma and tastes of blueberry. Notable euphoric high of the highest quality, and very long lasting. Medium to large calyxes. Stores well. Height 0.7 to 1 meter. Flowering 45–55 days."

✳

The genus cannabis belongs to the cannabaceae family, which has only one other member, hops. Indica and sativa are the two major species of the cannabis genus (a third, Ruderalis, native to Russia, is seldom bred for marijuana, although I've seen people attempt it indoors in Canada and outdoors in California).

Cannabis sativa originally grew (and still does grow) naturally nearer the equator than indicas. Sativas tend to be tall, from two to six meters, with long thin leaves and loose flowers. They smell fruity. The high is usually described as cerebral and uplifting.

Cannabis indica is associated with the Hindu Kush region, the cooler, mountainous, more northerly terrain of Afghanistan and Pakistan. It's a smaller plant, one or two meters high, with short, fat leaves and tight, heavily resinous flowers. Almost all commercial strains of cannabis have some indica bred into them, because slow-growing long-limbed pure sativas aren't profitable. Indicas tend to smell more skunky than sweet. The high is a heavier "body" stone.

Smoke a sativa and go for a swim, and you're likely to feel yourself to be a water sprite, splashing on the diamond surface. Smoke an indica, and you'll feel yourself a shark, with an urge to hold long breaths and descend to the murky depths.

Most marijuana varieties have a lineage as complex as Blueberry, but not all of them are as well-documented. The venerable weed is, after all, illegal, and breeding in most places is a clandestine, secretive, risky business. And even if pot were legal, many growers would want to keep trade secrets from their competitors.

Mike pointed to an oddly spindly plant and said, "This one is really interesting, it's called Parsley Bud. It's going through a bit of stress right now, but all the leaves grow that way." Rather than spreading out in the familiar seven-leaf pattern, the crinkly leaves clung in tight bunches. "I'm crossing it with a purple strain to get the color into it, then I'm going to back-cross back, to try and keep some purple color with this leaf structure. It does not look like a pot plant."

"It looks like it should have berries," I said.

"The cops could fly over and look for what they're used to looking for, and not see that one. Great, eh?"

Mike had a new strain called Romulan he wanted us to taste. He was planning on entering it in an upcoming Cannabis Cup in Amsterdam. The Cannabis Cup is a huge smokefest hosted annually by New York–based *High Times* magazine, America's leading monthly devoted to marijuana since 1974.

"We should hire someone to dress like a *Star Trek* character and hand out free samples," he said. "It's like any world-class flower show: you've gotta impress the judges."

2 : BON VOYAGE

Wild and free for countless millennia, cannabis is believed to have evolved in central Asia. Either that or God created it on the third day, and saw that it was good. When human beings started to figure out how to grow plants, cannabis was one of their first choices. It has been continuously cultivated in China since Neolithic times, about six thousand years ago. In ancient China the plant was used as a cereal grain, for medicinal purposes, and especially for its fibers. The rich wore silk, the poor clothed themselves in sturdy hemp. Hui-Lin Li, a botanist at the University of Pennsylvania, states, "From the standpoint of textile fibers, three centers can be recognized in the ancient Old World—the linen [flax] culture in the Mediterranean region, the cotton culture of India, and the hemp culture in eastern Asia."

A fifth-century Chinese medical text differentiates between the plant's "nonpoisonous" seeds (*ma-tze*) and the "poisonous" fruits (*ma-fen*), according to Li. The text states, "Ma-fen is not much used in prescriptions (now-a-days). Necromancers use it in combination with ginseng to set forward time in order to reveal future events." A tenth-century work observes, "It clears blood and cools temperature . . . it undoes rheumatism. If taken in excess it produces hallucinations and a staggering gait. If taken over the long term, it causes one to communicate with spirits and lightens one's body."

From China the plant spread to India, where it was awarded sacred status in the Vedas, the central texts of Hinduism, recorded between 1400 and 1000 B.C. In India's Ayurvedic medical tradition, cannabis is still prescribed for a variety of ailments. In ancient times the plant spread to all regions except the driest of deserts and the dampest of jungles. It flourished from Norway to South Africa, from England to Japan. It was one of the first plants brought to the New World, by the Spanish to Mexico and South America, the French to Canada, and the British to America.

✳

Mankind's ancient relationship with cannabis began when some sharp-witted Neolithic Homo sapien thought, Let's throw some hemp seeds in the soil around the camp here, so we don't have to walk so far to find them next year. From that long-ago moment, lost in the shroud of undiscovered prehistory, an unbroken human-plant symbiotic continuum flows across the millennia, the centuries, and the years, and ever-widening like a river delta near the sea, spreads for a moment to include me smoking a joint on a ferry along the west coast of Canada in 2000 A.D.

I'm on my way to be a marijuana judge, at *Cannabis Culture* magazine's first-ever Cannabis Culture Cup. Compared with *High Times'* Amsterdam Cannabis Cup, this one promises to be pretty modest. In fact, it's supposed to fit into Marc Emery's living room, in a rented waterfront house on British Columbia's mellow Sunshine Coast. Emery is the publisher of *Cannabis Culture,* which has a circulation of about 60,000.

Twenty-eight months have passed since I first met Marc at his Little Grow Shop. The Vancouver police long ago raided the place, along with the Hemp B.C. store upstairs, and seized inventory worth half a million dollars. Charges have never been laid, and the merchandise has never been returned. Emery promptly reopened, but the city government of Vancouver ultimately shut down Hemp B.C. for good by refusing to renew the store's business license. Emery then transformed his seed-selling business into a strictly Internet operation, and relocated to the Sunshine Coast.

To get to his house I need to ride from Horseshoe Bay on a big ferry that can carry 360 cars. It's almost empty on this cool mid-winter day, about 10 Celsius, 50 Fahrenheit. Out of the chilly breeze the sun is warm on my face. Beneath its glinting surface the water looks very cold, black, and secretive. I have a joint to smoke that I've cadged from my stoner niece. I love smoking a joint on the ferry, because all that clean water and fresh air seems doubly sharp and bracing when I'm high. The ferry makes it easy to be naturally high on life, of course, but why not just take that natural high and make it even higher?

On the upper deck I wander outdoors in search of a lighter. On the starboard side two rosy-cheeked blond teenage girls sit cross-legged on a big box of life vests, turning their backs to the too-playful sea breeze and trying to ignite some pot in the little bowl of a brass and wood pipe. One of them lowers her chin to tuck her pipe inside her jean jacket and out of the wind. That works.

She lends me the lighter and I perform the same trick, hiding in my coat like a bird tucking beak under wing. We share the smoke of the blessed burning herb, not exactly hiding what we're doing from the passengers who stroll past us, but pretending we are invisible, as do they. Canada is very civilized that way.

A guy from Nova Scotia with an acoustic guitar invites himself to join us, and we sit on the big life preserver box and sing Leonard Cohen's "Bird on the Wire" together. The girls' shy voices are as beautiful as the snow-topped mountains that fall in a skirt of green forest to the distant shore. Under us the vibrating hull shudders along a serpentine path toward a familiar dock. We start talking about ambition: one of the girls is trying to choose between becoming a helicopter pilot or becoming a chiropractor. We decide she can do both if she wants, combine them even: dangle her patients by bungee cords below the chopper, and give their spines a good jerk.

"I feel better, I feel better, just let me down!"

We're high and happy, all of us. On many occasions marijuana stirs the same impulses in me that make people cry at corny movies. Makes me love the sun, the moon, the earth, and human-kind. It's an alternate state of consciousness that makes life more lovable. How could I not love life when I'm headed to a glorious smokefest? How could I not start bragging? "As a judge I'll be sampling and rating sixteen varieties of top-flight bud, and our combined overall scores will then determine a champion," I say matter-of-factly, as if I do this sort of thing every day.

✳

When the ferry docks I see Barge, a Vancouver photographer specializing in shots of marijuana buds, sucking on an eight-inch-long handblown glass pipe and offering tokes to three of his friends, in full view of people in rows of parked cars waiting to drive onto the ferry.

"Doesn't it make you feel exposed, or vulnerable, to smoke it so openly?" I ask.

He shrugs. "I just act like it's legal, like it's perfectly nor-mal." He offers me a toke, which I take. The other three decline. They're going to be judges too, and appear to be taking the respon-sibility seriously. They don't want to get baked too early. One of them is a twenty-three-year-old marijuana grower named Arthur.

Marc Emery arrives, and we pile into his old International Harvester. Barge scrambles in through the back window with the luggage, Arthur and friends take the backseat, and I get the front passenger seat. I'm being treated like a celebrity.

Marc describes my official judge's sampling kit: "Some of the people at the lower end of the priority list will be smoking less desirable samples. But you've got all flawless buds."

"Geez, you shouldn't spoil me."

"Yes we should, because this has to reflect well in your book."

He knows I'm writing this book, knows I'm planning to fling myself by the slingshot of velvet-comfort modern air travel to a dozen countries around the world, in order that I might experience the dance of intimacy between humankind and marijuana in all its infinite variety and confusion. In corners of our planet near and far, I want to see how cannabis is cultivated, processed, and ingested, not to mention championed or denigrated. Pot lovers, psychologically landlocked by the War on Drugs, need to be reminded there's a big ol' world out there where the DEA doesn't hold sway. I'm the tour guide for a global gourmet-ganja holiday.

"You're not going to find better pot anywhere than what you're going to smoke this weekend," Marc says. "Every single entry was grown here in B.C., and most of them are B.C. strains. One of them is Arthur's, as a matter of fact: Mighty Mite/Skunk. There's Blueberry from Oregon, there's Shishkaberry, which is old Breeder Steve's from around here, plus there's a Texada Time Warp, and a Northern Lights, too. I've had them all grown and harvested under exactly the same conditions."

Marc has been a salesman since the age of eleven. As a boy in London, Ontario, he saved his paper route money to start Marc's Comics Room, a mail-order comic book business that had 29,000 titles by the time he sold it at sixteen. At age twelve he was buying up vast numbers of bound volumes of American newspapers that a local recycler had bought at auction from the Library of Congress, and cutting out the daily comics to sell to collectors. "I met my first celebrities this way," he tells me. "Like Mort Walker, who did 'Beetle Bailey.' He collected 'Moon Mullins' strips from me." At thirteen he was pulling down four hundred bucks a week tax-free. "One of the motivations for making money was to be able to eat in restaurants. My mom was English and hated to cook and just *steamed* the hell out of everything. Eating in restaurants was a revelation."

At sixteen he quit school and started up an antiquarian bookstore. He ran the store for eighteen years, sold it, went to India for two years, then settled in Vancouver in 1994, opened Hemp B.C., and started selling seeds over the counter.

"At that time there were only four or five types of pot around here," he says. "Big Bud, Hindu Kush—it was all good, but very homogenous, very similar. What we did was buy up a few local strains, and brought in some varieties from Holland. Seeds were almost reinvented in that period, because everyone was just growing from cuttings. The market demanded sensimilla pot, and there weren't a lot of males around." Marijuana is one of the few plants (kiwifruit is another) that is either entirely male or entirely female. On most of the world's plants the female and male sex organs, the pistils and stamens, occur on the same flower.

"We started growing some males, pollinating females, and now there are all these strains," Marc tells me. "The consumer is demanding name pot now. They want Juicy Fruit, by the Dutch company Sensi Seed Bank, for example, and they're willing to pay for it. In the U.S. they pay so much for it that the customer is getting sophisticated and demanding it from the dealers."

Marc Emery Direct Seed Sales is now quite likely the largest seed supplier in the world, with yearly sales of more than a million dollars. "We mail anywhere in the world," Marc says. "This week alone, we've sent seeds to places like Poland, France, and Croatia."

✳

The sixteen varieties in competition this weekend are all available from Emery on the Internet. "I've commissioned this one guy to grow them out for me," he says. "They're flushed twenty-one days, so it'll all burn perfectly."

"What do you mean 'flushed'?"

"Flushing is when you just feed the plant water in the latter part of the growing, to get rid of the chemicals from the fertilizers." Commercial growers don't bother with niceties like that, he says. "Most growers just do that for five or ten days because they're anxious to get it to market and pay the rent. Arthur knows all about this."

In the backseat, Arthur just nods.

"What happens is there tends to be a carbon buildup in the plant material, because of the heavy fertilization," Marc continues.

"One of the ingredients of fertilizers, potassium, is actually like asbestos, a fire retardant, and so when you find pot that doesn't burn well it's either wet, which is curable, or it wasn't flushed long enough, which is not curable. You can always tell if you have perfectly flushed pot if the ashes are white. You want the ash to be powder white when you flick it. If it's gray or black or anything like that, it ain't flushed properly."

After the three-week flushing, the plants in competition were harvested, the buds manicured, which involves clipping off all but the tiniest leaves from around the buds, and then cured for a month. "They sit in my grower's cedar box, slowly drying out. So these are all flawlessly dried, at their peak potential. You can't get better. All grown by the same person, with the exception of three strains—so there are no variables. Because some pot could be a great strain genetically, but a bad cure, a bad flush, a bad manicure, or a bad everything can really affect it, you could have the same strain taste completely different and give you a completely different high from grower to grower. All the ones in competition today are in their optimum condition. The only odd thing is, the Afghani seems to be awfully leafy, and I'm not sure why."

While he's been talking and driving I've been looking at all the tasteful upper-middle-class houses tucked back among big trees, mostly well away from the road. Some of them must have amazing ocean views. "Who lives around here?"

"Mostly people who don't need to live in the city," Marc says. "There are a number of potheads, but they're mostly forty-five to fifty-five years old. I'm hoping the sun comes out, because we live right along the ocean."

✳

The sun fails to come through; it's the kind of drizzly misty gray winter day that's typical here. The Sunshine Coast? A Realtor must have invented that one.

The living room of Marc's house has a huge fireplace framed by twelve-foot windows with a view of Georgia Strait between the spaced trunks of tall spruce. The judges gather and sit themselves down shoeless on the thick carpet while Marc lays down the rules: "Each of you will be testing sixteen strains, and each of you will have about two ounces total of bud to smoke. That's about an eighth of an ounce, three grams or so, of each sample for each judge."

"How much should we smoke of each?" someone asks.

"I would suggest one hit in a pipe, until you get high. Just smoke a small amount and assess it."

Each of us recieves an obese manila envelope containing sixteen self-sealing numbered Baggies. Mine all contain flawless buds, as promised. Even the little leaves surrounding the buds glisten with resin. Marijuana's psychoactive ingredient, delta-9-tetrahydrocannabinol (better known as THC), is found in serious amounts in resin glands that occur most densely on the female flowers—the buds—and on the small leaves that cradle them. Some of the buds Marc's given me are so gooey with resin, if I threw them at the wall they'd stick.

In the envelope along with the buds there's a three-page judging form, asking that each strain be rated and commented upon according to six attributes: appearance, fragrance, texture, taste, aftertaste, and stone. The seventh and final category, overall impact, will be used to determine the winners.

We get down to the work of smoking, and the experts start trading opinions:

"I'm going to roll some seven."

"Seven? I just smoked it. Seven is the red-haired extravaganza with the minty ephemeral kind of fragrance, and I gave it a good score for texture, with a smooth taste."

"Do you know if eleven is plum bud? It seems like a lemony citrus bud . . ."

"I'm sure this one is Blueberry. It's got that unmistakable Blueberry flavor."

The conversation at times verges close to sounding like pretentious wine-snob chatter. It's not surprising, really. The wines of the world are made from less than a hundred of the existing five thousand varieties of grape. Marc Emery's seed company alone offers nearly four hundred marijuana varieties. Variations in taste and aroma in marijuana are potentially as ripe for subtle analysis as are variations in wines. In fact, the aroma wheel developed by A. C. Noble for wine tasting (in which basic olfactory categories, like "fruity," "floral," or "pungent," branch out to more specific scents) has inspired marijuana grower and connoisseur DJ Short to create a chart for marijuana.

Short's main cannabis aroma categories are "woody," "spicy," "earthen," "pungent," "chemical," and "vegetative." The more specific flavors branching from these broad phyla can be found in any number of subtle combinations. Obviously the palates (and lungs) of most pot smokers aren't that subtle, and there's one major difference between sampling pot and wine: elite wine samplers take a sample taste and spit it out, so that they don't actually get drunk during the course of testing. Wine experts will discuss aroma, taste, and body till the cows come home, but they don't often write about the *drunk,* the inebriation, about the variation of intoxication between, say, a Bordeaux and a Merlot, although I'd argue that a different feeling of tipsiness from a little, and drunkenness from a lot, does make itself felt among different vintages.

Cannabis connoisseurs are less disingenuous about the ultimate appeal of their favorite mood-altering substance than are their wine counterparts. People drink wine to get tipsy or drunk, and people smoke pot to get high. Cannabis connoisseurs inhale and so get high almost immediately. Beyond aroma and taste, they notice differences in the types of highs from one strain to the next, which relate to variations in the sixty or so known cannabinoids found in marijuana, which act upon the main psychoactive element, THC, in ways still little understood.

❋

Three hits is all it takes. Tiny samples from numbers 1, 2, and 3 of my 16 Baggies. Three good tugs on a pipe, and already I'm too high to tell the effect of one entry from the next. We're smoking them quickly, one right after another. There are always joints lit and circulating. I take a toke of number 8 and think, Wow, what a fantastic, awesome, head-clearing high, but maybe number 7 from five minutes back is a creeper. Or maybe it's the combined effect of 1 to 6 amalgamating into a fireball of shivering joy playing hot and cold fingers up my spine. Or maybe I've just smoked too much dope to do the job. That does happen. That's why it's called a recreational drug. Turning it into a job is ridiculous. The effect of cannabis is to free the mind, not focus it.

Rising from the carpet to the middle of the big circle of cross-legged stoners, Marc Emery teases me about my dilettante's palate. Nodding toward a woman busily scissoring up some number 6, he says, "You'll be giving everything eights and nines out of ten, while she'll be giving things threes and fours."

He's right. Everything seems like a nine to me. This is pure organic smoking pleasure. No chemical headache aftereffect. Each toke a gift.

✳

Even a seasoned smoker like Dana Larsen, the editor of *Cannabis Culture* magazine, admits, "After a joint or two, you're only really able to judge for taste and flavor, and for how well it burns, as opposed to the effects. Unless it's really spectacular and cuts through everything else." He intends to judge the psychoactive qualities of each strain by smoking a different strain each morning for the next two weeks. I decide to do that too. It turns out to be a better way to separate the differing qualities of each high and select favorites.

But my appreciation is inevitably affected by how the world and my responsibilities to it impinge on my day. You could say the difference between good pot and bad is the difference between being in love and having a gastrointestinal disorder, because being in love has moments that feel like a gastrointestinal disorder.

Of my sixteen samples, some buds are covered in clusters of fine red hairs, others wear a shaggy green-blond wig. Some buds are tight and dense, others loose. Some smell like citrus, others skunky, musky, still others like fresh-mown hay. I'm talking smell before lighting. I'm talking sticking your snout in the Baggie to inhale the pungent perfume of the herb. There is a huge variation at that point. And the scents can tantalize. Pot advocates keep telling me cannabis was a major ingredient in nineteenth-century perfumes. I have no trouble believing it.

However, once it's rolled up and ignited, I find it impossible to rate pot smoke in terms of flavor, as some pot smokers claim to be able to do. Cigars I can tell apart. Good pot from bad I can tell apart. But when all the pot is excellent, as at this intimate coastal competition, it pretty much all smells alike to me.

✳

Barge and I stay overnight at Dana Larsen's house, and in the morning we eat blueberry pancakes fried in hemp oil. They have a greenish tint but taste delicious. After breakfast Barge is ruthlessly taking the scissors to his samples, pruning every little leaf to reveal nothing but the essential bud. Whoever manicured the buds for the competition has left them way too leafy for his taste. "I'm doing the job someone else should have been doing," he complains.

Dana sees positives in unmanicured buds. "It's a good thing, because with all those leaves to protect it, there'll be fewer trichomes busted off in transport." When magnified the THC-laden resin glands on the bud look like oily little blobs called trichomes. The most THC-potent of them are called capitate-stalked trichomes, and they look like little gooey mushrooms.

I hesitate to admit it to them, but the way the tiniest leaves wrapped around the bud entered into my appearance ratings yesterday. Some cradled the bud like five perfect little fingers round a softball.

"That's a personal preference," says Barge. "I don't like to see any leaves on it when I smoke it. The calyxes and the hairs and the crystals are far more important when I smoke." The calyxes and hairs are part of the female flower, and crystal is yet another word for a resin gland. In Holland the terminology gets even weirder, because they call the resin "pollen," although pollen has nothing to do with it. Cannabis pollen is produced by the male plant, not the female, and the buds we smoke are the females, horny girls denied their pollen and overproducing the sticky resin in the hopes of catching some.

Barge trims off every single leaf and sets them all aside to make butter or cooking oil. "It's better to make a concentrate form than to smoke all that green leafy matter," he says. "Anytime you're smoking, it's not the best for your lungs."

He finishes rolling a joint, using the absolute minimum of paper. The joint looks taut as a stuffed sausage skin. He brings it to his lips unlit, and inhales it that way, an act he calls a dry hoot. Dry hoots are the best way to savor the flavor, according to Barge. "Sweet, sappy smell," he says of this one. He yells to Dana, who is playing with his young daughter in the living room. "Hey, Dana! Number seven. Smells sweet and sappy!"

✳

Marc Emery takes me back to the ferry in his big blue International Harvester. Along the way he stops to buy a massive bouquet of fresh-cut flowers from a roadside stand. It's the honor system; just a little metal box with a slot for your money. Canada is very civilized that way. We stop for brunch at the Gumboot, a funky restaurant up the coast at Roberts Creek. As he parks, Emery points to the local hemp store next door. "When a community of two thousand people can support one of those, you know you're in eco-hippie central," he says.

The Gumboot is packed with dreaded, barefoot, tied-dyed, twenty-something neohippies. Emery is wearing a *Stranjahs in da night* baseball cap, which is about as countercultural as he ever looks. Stranjahs is a semi-underground Vancouver restaurant that cooks with cannabis. Their slogan is "An All You Can Eat Buffet to Make You Hungry." They use donated shake, not bud. "It cleans you out, plus you get a mild body buzz—great for arthritics," says founder Cherise Mitchell.

Outside the Gumboot the woman who runs the little juice stand that sells organic drinks of the beet-carrot-ginger type is plugging an upcoming outdoor rave in the woods, proceeds going to save some nearby old-growth rain forest. By her cash register there are postcards hand-lettered with "Gumboot Rules," a list of mostly too-cute aphorisms like *No rain, no rainbows.* Emery underlines one with a finger: *Goals are deceptive—the unaimed arrow never misses.* "This rationalizes a lot of layabout behavior here, though," he says. "I've always been very goal-oriented. Every day needs to have some sense of accomplishment."

Over brunch we run through the list of places I don't want to miss on my pot pilgrimage. Nepal, Southeast Asia, Australia, California, Morocco, Spain, France, Switzerland, Holland, and Britain are on the A list. I run out of breath just rhyming them off. My lungs are tender from two days of solid smoking. No stamina.

Marc tells me I cannot leave out Jamaica—no book would be complete. Or India.

"Go to Jaisalmer and find the guy who owns the bhang shop there."

"Where?"

"Jaisalmer. It's in the middle of nowhere between Pakistan and India, a wonderful old fortress town built in the fourteenth century in the desert, where nothing deteriorates because it never rains out there," he says. "You can tell the tourists who've been to the bhang shops because they're the ones taking close-up photos a foot from camels' faces. There are lots of great places in India. The problem for you is the same as for me—you won't get approached. If you look straight, no one tries to sell you anything. But look like a dreaded hippie, like these guys"—he surveys the unaimed-arrow crowd at the tables around us—"and they all want to sell you stuff."

"But is it good pot?"

"Oh yeah. The quality of pot is really good everywhere. I remember in Mysore, India, I hadn't scored in four weeks, and I'm in the market. A guy looks at me and says, 'Peter Tosh? Legalize it?' And I go, 'Yeah, I like Peter Tosh, and I believe in legalizing it,' and he goes, 'Okay, follow me.' Of course, it's always going to take a lot longer than they tell you, it's going to cost a lot more, they'll say for extra expenses. But you know what? If you give them money in advance in India they will always come back, they will not rip you off! It's really cool that way."

"Unlike here at home," I say, "where every adolescent learns the hard way there's no legal recourse."

"Yep. Thailand has good pot, but the paranoia factor is high. The concept of bribery—once you have to start bribing people it gives you an uneasy feeling, it reminds you you're doing something wrong, and if something doesn't go right they could just throw you in the brig. If you want to score anywhere in Asia, just find a place where they're playing Bob Marley music. Malaysia has nothing, it has the death penalty. And pot is like twenty bucks a joint, which is just ridiculous. I remember buying two pounds in Indonesia in 1993 for five hundred dollars. Of course, the paranoia kicks in when you're wandering around with that much pot in a backpack."

"I don't just want to buy and smoke the pot," I say. "I want to go where they grow it."

"In Thailand that's the north, and you'll have to bribe people for sure," he says. "That'll double the paranoia factor. That'll be a theme of your book, I bet. First of all because it's something you know about yourself, that you get paranoid easily. And then the sellers are going to magnify the paranoia just because it's profitable for them."

I start thinking about something a Vancouver Drug Squad cop told me a few years back: that except for a few timid souls, everyone who wants to smoke pot is doing it already. No one worries about the consequences around here, because it's a slap on the wrist. But in foreign countries, it's another matter. I can't even picture where I might end up, but I can picture myself being Timid as Hell over there. The Timid Toker Abroad.

"You'll do fine," Marc says at the ferry dock. "Keep your eyes open, be a little brave, and have a good time."

3 : NEPAL

"Tomorrow is the day of puffing," Rajiv says. "It is part of our religion. Shiva used to puff hashish, so in the name of Shiva, those who wish to can puff also. Tomorrow everyone is free to puff all through the day, through the night until morning, and the police will not interfere."

The streets of Kathmandu are crowded with Indian pilgrims who have streamed north from the plains into the mountains of Nepal for the festival—rural people, confused, frightened, and fucking up the traffic flow by not knowing how to get across the roundabout above the temple. Nepali cabdrivers are mellow, usually. This is the only time of year you'll hear them curse. Fronting the circle across from the police station is the Siva Shakti Fastfood Cafe, and we are eating a lunch of momo, a Tibetan dish of fried meat and vegetable dumplings similar to Japanese gyoza. Rajiv is one of four Nepalese schoolteachers, unmarried guys pushing thirty, who are taking me to the temple at Pashupatinath, on the western edge of the city. They are all nonsmokers of cannabis, but they have befriended me.

Pashupatinath is named for one of Shiva's incarnations, Pashupati, the Lord or Guardian or Protector of Animals. It is one of the holiest Hindu shrines. Tomorrow night is the culmination of the festival Hindus call Mahashivaratri—Shiva's Great Night— or more often just Shivaratri, Shiva's Night.

The Indian scholar Shakti M. Gupta has written that to keep vigil on Shivaratri "is reckoned so meritorious that every orthodox Hindu keeps awake by engaging himself or herself in pious exercises, and Shivaratri in common parlance means a sleepless night . . . Those who keep vigil on Shivaratri are promised, in the Puranas, material prosperity and paradise after death; the indolent who sleep on this night are destined to lose their worldly goods and go to hell on death."

Earlier today I asked one of the owners of the school where Rajiv teaches to explain to me the religious significance of Shivaratri. "Well, you sit around a fire with your friends, smoke hashish, and talk all night," he said. So much for pious exercises. Add some vodka and it sounds like camping trips I've been on. But on camping trips you're out in the woods where you won't bug the neighbors, while in Kathmandu bugging the neighbors is unavoidable—the fires will be lit on street corners and in the weedy patches between suburban apartment blocks.

Kathmandu is a desperately polluted city. Little Indian-style black and yellow diesel auto-rickshaws hiccup and sputter their noxious exhaust in competition for street space with belching buses, children large and small, bicycles, brightly painted trucks, white foreign-aid SUVs, and the occasional sacred cow. Once upon a time Kathmandu had an earthly reputation for mystical serenity on a par with the fictional Shangri-La of James Hilton's *Lost Horizon,* but the only time you are reminded of Shangri-La nowadays is in billboards for Shangri-La "luxury filter tip" cigarettes, a local brand.

Most Nepalis I've been talking to seem to have only the vaguest idea why Shiva's Night requires the faithful to stay up from dawn to dusk. Sanskrit literature exalts Shiva as a multifarious deity under 1,008 names, and he's had multiple adventures under each alias, so it's not surprising people have trouble keeping track. The explanation favored by my teacher friends concerns a long-ago hunter who climbed a bel tree. He knocked some of the bel leaves from their branches, and they fell on a lingam hidden in the bushes below the tree. A lingam is a smooth squat stone penis, and is the symbol by which Shiva is worshiped. Shiva was extremely pleased by this offering, and the hunter, who stayed up all night in the tree, was rewarded in the morning with divine status and taken up to heaven by Shiva.

The Pashupatinath temple, which is near the airport in Kathmandu, contains the most sacred and revered of all lingams, a three-foot-high black rock with five faces carved on the top. Non-Hindus aren't allowed in the temple to look at it, but I'm told it has four faces around and one face on top. Some Nepali Buddhists believe the image on top portrays the Buddha's face. I'm not an expert on Buddhism, so I can't say why they think the Buddha would be pleased to have his likeness carved on the head of a lingam. I had thought Buddha was all about renouncing the caste system and the idolatry of Hinduism. But in Nepal what's Buddhist and what's Hindu are hard to separate. When Nepalis need to pray it's any temple in a storm, and some temples even cater to that—they're decorated half Buddhist, half Hindu. Some are 70–30, some 20–80. The Buddha was born in Nepal, and his influence is great among Nepali Hindus too, who worship him as the ninth incarnation of Krishna, who is in turn an incarnation of Vishnu, who is at Shiva's right hand in the triumvirate that puts Brahma to Shiva's left. Which is to say Shiva is front and center in the ranking of Hindu Gods, and especially in Nepal. There are lingams big and small all over Kathmandu, shrines to Shiva that are washed daily by the faithful, but washing the lingam at Pashupatinath on Shivaratri and sprinkling on some leaves, or better yet flowers, from the bel tree is the ultimate offering. Hundreds of thousands are coming to honor Shiva tomorrow.

This is my third day in Nepal. I'm staying in Thamel, which has long replaced Freak Street as the budget hotel zone for tourists. "Trekking" companies line the street, selling complete Himalayan expeditions featuring hiking, bungee jumping, and white water rafting (one company is called Wet Dreams) to young Westerners looking to buy an experience. Ragged Kathmandu kids have been tailing me every step in Thamel, peddling trashy Nepali knickknacks and cheap Chinese Tiger Balm brought in via Tibet. Bent women carrying kids beg on the streets with a tug on the sleeve and an open palm. Older kids and men have been trying to sell me hashish. But it's tough arriving in a new town, knowing no one, and trusting strangers to sell you illegal drugs right on the street. Plus there are a lot of cops around in Thamel, operating out of a little booth just up the street from my nine-dollar-a-night hotel.

My first day in town, three hours after landing, I drank beer with three Brits at a little two-table Tibetan-run snack stand. One of the Brits was an old alcoholic who'd been in Nepal since the 1970s. Pouring rum from a pint bottle in a delicate trickle into the mouth of his bottle of Coca-Cola, he introduced himself as Swami Swingalingam, and wanted me to know his favorite "American" expression, which I'd never heard in my life: "I'm on the Jersey side of snatch." Likely it had been years since his swinging lingam had nudged itself into the sweet enclosing lips of the yoni. To compensate, he drinks. He warned me not to buy hash on the streets, insisting that the local dealers would shop me—turn me over to the police for a cut of whatever the cops could extort from me.

Obviously dealers can't be shopping every naive foreigner who says Yes to Drugs, but maybe a certain percentage do get shopped to feed the poor underpaid cops, who live on the wages of corruption. They stop cabdrivers and bicycle rickshaw peddlers all the time, demanding to see their "list." The list lists the cops they pay protection money to, so that other cops can't hit on them. But what about dope dealers? Do they pay their list off by pointing the cops to some dopey foreigner who, under duress of the threat of jail, can be squeezed for what's left of that hundred-dollar American traveler's check he just cashed? Maybe. It was enough to scare me into taking my time to enter the market. One of the others Brits said, "Don't buy in the city. Wait until you're in the hills. You'll see marijuana growing everywhere there, and people will give it away. They don't even want money for it."

Yesterday I met a Nepalese guy who works at a Western embassy who assured me that the police wouldn't touch me for buying or possessing trifling amounts. "They don't want the hassle that goes with arresting a foreigner," he said. "They can't beat you and mistreat you the way they're used to doing with Nepalis." The mainstream guidebook I brought says discreet possession carries virtually no risk, but flagrant (or fragrant) use could get you shopped by an innkeeper. Still, I'm a timid toker. Before I start buying I like to be really and truly certain that I'm not stumbling jet-lagged into some stupid setup. Now it's day three, and I'm ready to buy. But I'm with schoolteachers who have no interest in cannabis at all. Oh well. "Tomorrow is the day of puffing."

With my new friends I'm reconnoitering Pashupatinath, figuring out the layout. Within twenty-four hours there will be a throng of pilgrims a hundred thousand strong, and I'd like to be sure I know where I'm going before I wade into that. After lunch the schoolteachers and I walk down a curving tree-lined street, closed to motor traffic, toward the complex of temples, passing sadhus on the way. These are holy men, mendicants dressed in tatty saffron robes, some with bodies and faces flamboyantly painted with ash and paint. "Some of them are cheaters. But no doubt some of them are saints," Rajiv says. "In some way I might prefer their life. No worries, no anxieties, no fears." Sadhus live without possessions, mostly wandering, mostly begging. Some fast for long periods. Others smoke a lot of dope. Shiva accepts almost any form of worship you care to perform for him.

Someone on the staff at my hotel has been smart and thoughtful enough to write descriptions of local festivals and post them on the bulletin board by the stairs. One warns guests not to take taxis on a certain day, as the Marxists will be staging a citywide general strike, and you, your driver, and the vehicle could have rocks thrown at you, or worse. The writer always tries to put a positive spin on things, though: if the Marxists shut down the town "it will be a perfect pollution-free day to walk or bicycle." The page about Shivaratri ends with this: "No sadhu gathering is complete without the customary puff of marijuana. Surely this will be the experience of a lifetime."

✳

The sacred Bagmati River that dissects the complex of temples at Pashupatinath is incredibly filthy. It's a sewer, essentially. Old people come here to die with their feet in the Holy River, so that on expiration they head straight to Nirvana and avoid any more incarnations on this painful, dreary planet. You would need to be pretty nearly dead to agree to dip so much as a toe in the fetid black soup of the sacred Bagmati. Ready to let toxic shock finish you off.

We cross the river downstream and walk up on the side opposite the main temple. There are monkeys living off trash and donations. One of them, all crippled up, is trying ever so painfully to climb some stone stairs above the water. He hasn't given up yet, but death is near, and it's pretty painful to watch. Like imagining a senior living alone, falling in the tub and breaking a hip. We watch the monkey and get very sad. "A monkey sadhu," says Rajiv. "Life is like this. Someday we will also grow old."

There's a sadhu on a hunger strike in a tent, starving himself to draw attention to his contention that the polluted river is a physical manifestation of the corrupted minds of the temple's administrators, and that both must be cleansed. Nearby we enter a little stone building, just one thick-walled square room the size of a suburban bedroom, with a ladder to a windowless loft. There, cross-legged, sits Milky Baba, another sadhu, a local from a moneyed Brahman background who makes this spot home, contributes to the running of a school for orphans on-site, and acts as the spiritual master and father figure. He wears his hair in dreadlocks that hang to his knees, but at this moment they're wrapped around his head like some huge fantastic turban. He's called Milky Baba because he has lived on nothing but milk for the last twenty years. "Austerity life," he explains. That's the extent of his English, apart from asking if I want tea. Sure, I say, and he snaps his fingers once, sharp and loud, causing a kid to go running off to get water for the kettle. It seems a selective austerity, that he can snap his fingers and make lackeys jump.

The next day, back at Pashupatinath without the schoolteachers, I step out of the multitudes flowing toward the temple.
Time to smoke a last cigarette. It'll soon be too crowded to smoke
without burning someone.

A Nepalese kid named Robin comes over, and we start talking. He's sixteen, still very boyish, with a thin mustache that has
never seen a razor. He's watching my cigarette in a way that says
he'd like a cigarette, but won't beg for one. I offer, some kind of
ritual of sharing has taken place, and he's my friend. In his mind,
he's more than a friend, he's my guide. Friends get cigarettes,
guides get paid is how Robin looks at it. I won't figure this out till
later.

Robin calls over his friend Santosh, who looks fifteen but
claims to be eighteen, resplendent in a spotless salmon-colored
outfit of loose, light, almost transparent oversized pajamas that
looks almost formal. It's a gift from his grandparents for Shivaratri.
By way of introduction, Robin says of Santosh, "He is my best
friend. He has seen my troubles."

Off we go, making a few false starts down alleyways that end
in an impassable crush of sari-clad humanity. We back out and
circle around to the east side of the river, which is fine because I
want to go back to talk to Milky Baba again. Why'd he choose milk,
anyway? Robin and Santosh go to the Baba's school for orphans.
They also smoke pot. I ask them what the Baba thinks of his charges
smoking pot. "He doesn't care about that," says Robin. "He's more
interested in a person's character. His morals and ethics."

When we get to the Baba's place there's eighty people lined
up for an audience with him, wanting to sit with him and take his
blessing. The staircases that run up and along the hillside are
completely choked with pilgrims and tourists, so like a lot of people
we are climbing over the stone walls that serve as banisters. Sometimes a three-foot wall has a nine-foot drop on the other side. The
two boys are agile—they descend these things like monkeys. The
real monkeys I saw yesterday have all gone into hiding. I'm not as
nimble, and now there's a complication: I'm having the inevitable

gastrointestinal emergency. Day four. At least I'm getting it over with early in the trip. It's hard to scale walls using tree roots as handholds and footholds when you're squeezing your sphincter tight, trying to keep the dam from bursting. Robin leads me to toilets twice. Both locations are shut for the day. Finally we find a latrine, dug specially for Shivaratri, with burlap curtains to screen you and ankle-thick bamboo poles laid across a hole in the ground. There's a gap to squat above and aim for, but people have been shitting all over the bamboo. A single glance down is plenty, but I do feel better about one thing: from the evidence, lots of other people in Nepal have the same loose, runny shit I do. I am not alone. Blastocystis hominus, unite.

We head to where the sadhus have gathered to perform, or worship, depending on how you look at it. Some seem devoutly off in their own search for a higher place, others look like they're trying to make a buck. An old man is smoking something that doesn't smell anything like cannabis to me, keeping it burning with a glowing coal pried from a fire log and plopped on top of his red clay chillum. He offers it to a hesistant European tourist woman. Oh, why not, dear? It will definitely take the edge off the crowds and dirt and noise.

Another sadhu, hiding from the heat under a beat-up black umbrella, sells what looks to be dusty, brownish, crushed leaves to some Indian pilgrims in their best polyester shirts and leather shoes. (They'll have to check the leather at the temple door. Shoes, belts, and jackets. The schoolteachers checked theirs yesterday, and came back with reports of naked men dancing in the inner sanctum. Not just sadhus, but wealthy businessmen who fly in from Bombay for the weekend.) For ten rupees the pilgrims buy enough for maybe two cigarette-sized joints. I ask Robin to help me buy some but he says no. "This is not good marijuana. It's for the tourists," he says. "Come with me to our house, and we will smoke the good one."

We gradually work ourselves upstream against the flow of pilgrims still arriving. In a tight crowd there's a scuffle, as a woman accuses a man of trying to pick her pocket (do saris have pockets?). He slinks away, body language betraying him: guilty and making himself scarce. The crowd thins beyond the roundabout at the top of the hill, which is closed to traffic; the nearby streets too. We have a half-hour walk. Robin says, "Do you know Bob Marley? All the sadhus and all of Kathmandu are fans of him. Do you know his colors? Red, yellow, and green. Do you know that his first love was the game of football? It was only through force of friends he started singing."

I didn't know that.

We haven't even smoked and he seems high, a delighted sixteen-year-old having an adventure. He tells me, "We are only on this earth one time, so we must enjoy as much as we can."

"I thought you believed in reincarnation," I say.

"People of my country believe in reincarnation, but to me that is rubbish," he says. "I like the rules and regulations of Christian people." We end up turning into a curving, shoulderwide alley off a side street near Dili Bazaar and come out in a big courtyard with a few small plots of spinach growing in neat rows. There's a stone house tucked to the side. I have to duck through the five-foot-high door and stoop again to climb a stairway steep enough to be called a ladder. Then we are in his friend's room, and I'm presented like a trophy. Look what we brought home from Shivaratri!

The four guys already there, eighteen to twenty-three, are in the middle of rolling. One of them squeezes and kneads the tobacco out of a filter cigarette. No damage to the paper. He keeps half the tobacco and uses his fingers to make it more powdery in the palm of his hand. Now he adds the pot, which looks not much better than that stuff the sadhu was selling, but smells good at least. Smells like pot. He keeps mixing for a bit, then puts the hollow cigarette between his lips, brings his palm up within range, and scoops up the pot using subtle lip action to control the cigarette like a little shovel. This is the favored Nepali way of rolling pot. They possess amazing lip dexterity. They scoop it all up, stopping at intervals to tap the joint on the wrist or a tabletop to make sure it's packing nice and tight. Top it off with a pinch or two placed by fingertips, fold up the end, and voila, you are ready to smoke, and you've kept that industrial-strength filter in place to take care of the tar. Though it's nice to watch the filter turn from white to brown as the joint is smoked down, and think, *Thank God that brown shit isn't in my lungs,* you have to wonder how much THC is lost in the process.

At the first toke, that strange bodily sense of eagerness and impatience takes hold, a longing for the remembered indolent happiness of being high. The mere taste of it in mouth and lungs brings on the longing. Then comes the payoff—that great *whoooooooooosh* of feeling uplifted, like some unseen force is tucking its hands into your armpits and whispering, Come fly with me. I feel light, giddy, high. We are all high.

"How do you say that in Nepali: I am high."

Jaab.

"How would you spell that? *Jab* or *jaab?*"

"Both are better."

Okay. Whatever.

"It means relax, freedom, 'in trip.'"

I'm thinking I better write that down, or I'll never remember. Instead, Robin commandeers my notebook.

THE GUIDE:
I was born in 1982. In 1st November. I am poor guy. We are poor so our lifestyle is full of marijuana. I have much friends, and you also know it. My friends are also frank. Our lifestyle is very freedom. I pass my time by going here and there.

There are now ten of us in the tiny room. We're using a chillum, cupped upright in the hands, with a little square of torn cloth—red, yellow, and green—as a filter over the bottom end. A chillum has to be loaded, held, and smoked upright. I have a hard time figuring out how to cup my hands around the bottom so that it's sealed airtight. It's trial and error. The boys have a radio alarm clock for music. It's a mix of local music with some 'N Sync, Tom Petty, and other Western stuff. A Nepali rock song comes on, a Bob Seger-or BTO-style rocker driven by a cowbell. The room starts to percolate, the little one-speaker radio is cranked to hideous distortion, but the power chords sound good that way. Santosh is jumping up and down in his shiny new dhoti, dancing in one spot because ten is a crowd in here. Another kid, with two pieces of white adhesive tape in a cross at his scalp line (he was in a street fight yesterday), plays air drums.

"What are they singing?" I ask.

"In the morning the cock sings,
Why is the cock singing?
The hen laid an egg,
That will grow up to be a chicken . . ."

Eventually it's time for me go make a phone call. "Best of luck with your project," the kids tell me. Robin and Santosh come with me and we shoot two games of pool—the school's residence building has a pool table, so they're sharks. Robin takes me to a little store that sells photocopies, faxes, and has a phone for hire so I can make my call, and I end up making two calls: as a measure of how stoned I still am, and of how polite Nepalis can be, I have a five-minute conversation with a Nepali before he has the heart to tell me I've got the wrong number. Everyone in the store speaks enough English to find this funny. We then discuss whether Santosh's oversized pajamas should be called a dhoti. Apparently I've been wrong. Someone teaches me the right word. I repeat it, nod as if I've learned something, and immediately forget it. Robin, unasked, has started to help a high school teacher sort newly photocopied chemistry exams. He's a good kid.

This little phone-and-photocopy store has a poster by the counter featuring a cartoon of an anthropomorphized horny, macho rooster hunting down a frightened, wide-eyed young chicken while a matronly old hen looks pleased with herself as she sits on an egg. The slogan: "We run after new business but leave old customers satisfied." Somewhere in my cannabis-heightened consciousness that actually seems profound. Earthy, sexual, and eternal. City or country in Nepal, you do wake up to the sound of cocks crowing.

Robin and Santosh walk me over to Dili Bazaar, on this national holiday as tranquil as it ever gets but still crazier than any street in my hometown. Now comes the money part. They don't have any and want some of mine. Suddenly I'm thinking, *Am I just Another Tourist? Did I just buy an experience?* I give them every-thing I have except cab fare to Puran's place.

Puran is the part owner of that school I went to yesterday, and I promised him I'd come to dinner tonight. He's a journalist, fortyish, who smoked hashish in his student days at university in India and remembers how it aided his understanding of Western philosophy. Then he went back to his little village in eastern Nepal and taught school, where he quickly became super-depressed. He thought the exciting part of his life was over, that he would teach school in the backwoods for forty years and then die. So he started smoking dope daily. After about a year he kind of slapped himself in the face and decided to get his shit together. He stopped smoking, went back to university to become a journalist, and has never smoked pot since.

His father was a peasant farmer who earned money in the season between harvest and planting by carrying salt on his back through the mountains from India into Nepal. For years his father smoked ganja to ease the pain and monotony of manual labor, until the family prevailed upon him to stop. According to Puran the long-time ganja smokers of his village all suffer strokes. "Life in the village is subsistence, a struggle. No one has time to look after a victim of stroke," he says. "Who's going to feed, dress, and clean the shit of such a person? They die quickly of unavoidable neglect."

After a meal at Puran's place, we go out to see what Shivaratri looks like in a suburban neighborhood of unpaved alleys, weedy vacant lots, and four-story apartment blocks. In the dark there are bonfires about every hundred yards or so. Drums beating and people swaying. I see only men. Puran keeps us at a distance.

We end up at Puran's school, pass through a gate to a bare-earthed playground. The teachers are there, having a couple of San Miguel beers each around a modest campfire of discarded planks. Only the caretaker, of a lower caste, has been smoking hash. He has been drinking some kind of cheap whisky too. He's pretty looped and talkative, overfriendly to his superiors, at least until Puran barks something almost under his breath, and the caretaker jolts in the direction of sober. The school is in a bit of a valley, and around us we can hear the drums and whoops and hollers of livelier parties. Puran cocks his ears to what suddenly sounds like voiced anger and the shouts that precede a fight, people cursing each other.

"Shivaratri used to be a festival of hashish, a time for intro-spection and quiet talk," he says. "Now you hear the effects of al-cohol. This is new in Nepal, in the last twenty years. People get intoxicated on liquor, and even though it is a religious holiday, it is sometimes dangerous now."

✳

Nepal is the big Himalayan tourist destination for young adven-turers. They gather in the resort town of Pokhara, clad in Gore-Tex and sporting Oakley sunglasses, clutching their Lonely Planet guidebooks, where they prepare for their "treks" into the moun-tain. Pokhara is four hours from Kathmandu, nestled in a high valley at the end of a lake called Phewa Tal, in the shadow of the spectacular snowcapped peaks of the Annapurna range. Along the lakefront the King of Nepal has a summer palace. The narrow street that winds past it to an array of tourist restaurants, shops, and E-mail parlors gives it the impression of being a small waterfront village, but stretching back away from the water, where the tourists seldom go, is a modern Hindu city of four hundred thousand. My hotel in Pokhara is full of Japanese twenty-somethings who have come to smoke pot, hike in the hills, and attend a music fest that includes Japanese pop bands. These Japanese are nice, harmless kids, trying to play bongos but lacking a certain soulfulness.

On the first morning I decide to walk to the World Peace Pagoda, a modern Buddhist stupa across the lake on top of a hill. To get there you go down past the dam, where a small river spills from the lake, and look for a little suspension footbridge. In a small park by the dam I pass four locals sitting on top of an old stone wall, similar to the ones that terrace the mountainsides into rice fields. This one is part of a chotera, a raised platform with a tree planted on top. The tree is tall, broad, and leafy. "The ancestors thought we would like shade" is how Keshav puts it.

Keshav and four friends, all in their twenties, are sitting in the cool that is a gift from the ancestors, smoking pot. I first noticed them from fifty yards—people just don't pass tobacco cigarettes like that—and walked over to say hello. It was kind of an awkward moment. The joint had just been finished and there was none for me. I asked what variety they were smoking. "Local variety," said Keshav. He showed me a film canister of green buds, squished in so tight you had to pick bits out with a thumbnail. "This is from my tree at my house. I grew two, but now there is only one left."

One of the other guys wants to show me his pot, too, in a worn and weathered Baggie. It's pretty seedy, but the bouquet is lovely. Lemon-lime. I make appreciative noises of yum yum yum, and he smiles. "It's not as good as Keshav's. Keshav has the best pot in Pokhara." He takes enough of his stash in his palm to sort a joint, flicking the seeds and twigs onto the ground.

"If you look around here, you'll see the seedlings sprouting in the grass," Keshav says.

I hop down a couple of levels of terrace and search for them. Keshav comes down too. He finds the first one, just four little leaves on a two-inch stem. When we've done a census, we climb back up, where a Rizla paper now encircles a tapered joint, with not exactly a filter but a couple of extra wraps of rolling paper in a half-inch band around the end.

"Just for extra strength," someone says.

The joint and a disposable lighter are offered to me. First toke. I take a dry hoot. Now that is good.

Keshav has long, thin hair with a slight gold streak in it, tied in a ponytail that ends between his shoulder blades. He looks a bit like Bob Marley, and from the way he shrugs when I tell him that it's clear he hears it all the time. He's got some kind of lazy eye, or may even be blind in it.

I start telling them about Vancouver, the varieties available on the Internet. "None of our varieties even have names here," says Keshav. "We just go into the hills and find a plant growing wild, and if we like the taste, like the feeling it gives, we keep the seeds. The one at my house took a year to grow. I cut it back in January, but it still has a few branches left."

"Can I come and take a picture of it?"

"Sure. Tonight."

✷

Keshav and his brother live with a childless aunt who owns a business in Pokhara. Their mother is dead, their father works in India and seldom comes home, which is fine by everyone because he is an alcoholic. The brother married at nineteen and now has three kids, and is planning to head off to Korea to work in construction. Keshav is expected to assume the responsibility of running his aunt's restaurant, which is not successful. A family strategy has been formulated in preparation for the brother's departure. First, Keshav will stop smoking pot. Second, he will get serious about the business. Third, and most important of all, he will get married. Of the three, the third has proven the easiest to enforce.

He married six weeks ago. His bride is nineteen and he is twenty-six. It was a marriage arranged between families, but the bride and groom did meet a couple of times to look each other over, and had agreed to it. His wife was never introduced to me, but I caught glimpses of her watching us from doorways from time to time. A pretty girl from a mountain village, still just thrilled to be in the Big City of Pokhra, according to Keshav. Prior to the marriage the two of them had met for one serious talk intended to ferret out any major incompatibilities that might threaten conjugal happiness. During that talk she had asked him directly if he used any drugs. Her family knew he was a pothead, but didn't tell her, and they advised Keshav not to tell her either. So he lied to her and said no, he didn't use drugs.

"Now she's unhappy," he tells me. "She cries a lot. I've never cried in my life."

"So what do you do when she cries?"

"What can I do? I just hold her, stroke her back, tell her it's going to be all right."

"Do you love her?"

"Yes. There's no divorce here. We have to be partners. She loves me and I love her. But the situation is very hard. The family. The business."

He has a gesture he makes often in these kinds of moments, opening his mouth wide and sticking out his tongue, as if to say, Life is overwhelming and scary.

His cannabis plant must have been fucking huge. It's still eight feet tall, and the stalk is an inch and a half thick where he's cut it off at the top. Keshav says it was six meters tall before he hacked it back. And it's growing in plain view not twenty feet from a public sidewalk in Pokhara.

"Don't the police come and harass you about this? Or want a bribe or something?" I ask.

"They don't make problems for me, because I'm not selling," he says. "I just grow for me to smoke it. This is a very poor country, and the police have a lot bigger problems to deal with than me."

I've been thinking about his family's business, trying to figure out what could be done to rescue it. I'm thinking Keshav should use his pot in cooking and convert the restaurant into more of a coffee shop, offering cakes and cookies and yogurt shakes, all THC-loaded. A bhang shop, like they have in India, only more like a Dutch coffee shop. Tourists could come and eat and get high.

Keshav doesn't like the idea. "Some customer might freak out," he says. "The police would have to be involved all the time." He's not really a people person. He's young still, and restless, and not business- or money-minded. To the despair of his family, his favorite thing to do is to go hiking in the hills, then smoke dope on the mountaintops.

Hey, me too.

*

The next day we go hiking in the hills. First we smoke up in a side room at Keshav's restaurant, under the disapproving eyes of his brother. Keshav's friend Bijay joins us, and we take the bus north a couple of hours. All the seats are full. I'm sitting on the floor in the aisle near the back because the ceiling is too low for me to stand straight. The guy in the seat at my elbow is teaching me how to say "How are you?" in Nepali.

I definitely need to add to my meager two phrases, *namaaste* (the all-purpose greeting) and *daanyabaad* (Thanks). I learned *daanyabaad* by word association with the English phrase "Tonya Harding is bad." Drop the middle two words. "Tonya Bad." *Daanyabaad.* When the ticket-taker reaches the back of the bus he and my new teacher get into a hot argument. Later Bijay gives me the translation:

"I'm the assistant superintendent of forests for this region and as such I am entitled to ride this bus free."

"Where's your ID?"

"It's at home, but I'll be glad to show you when we reach there."

"No ID, no freebie. Pay up."

"But I insist I am the assistant superintendent of state forests for this region!"

Various passengers join in a simultaneous shouting match, all of them on the ticket-taker's side. Variations in Nepali on the phrase "Get the fuck off this bus, freeloader!"

He finally does depart, growling ominously, "You'll be hearing from the authorities!"

Afterward it's agreed by one and all that the guy was scamming, and that he'll likely wait for the next bus that comes along, climb aboard, pull the same stunt, get kicked off several miles down the road, and keep repeating this until he reaches his village.

We disembark in a tiny village in the hills—one little store, a few livable-looking stone houses, and a few frail peasant shacks. We buy some *roxi,* the local moonshine, in a large beer bottle. The store owner takes a cob of dried corn and twists some of the kernels from the end. They fall into a tin cup with that pebbly sound familiar to anyone who has ever made popcorn on the stovetop. Then he reveals his purpose by chopping off the end of the cob to make a cork for our bottle.

We walk up and up, climbing shadeless hills on a dry windy day, and our shirts are soon soaked in sweat. We come to where the edge of a cliff falls away to jungle down below, a canopy of trees out of the wind. The sound of birds and the echo of one lone axe rise to our ears. There's a forest ranger sitting up here, surveying his domain. Bijay says that recently the forests have been returned to local communities to manage. Previously forested land had been managed by the central government, and as a result no one gave a shit, and would go in and chop the trees down without a second thought. "Now that it is theirs to manage, they take better care of it," he says.

The forest ranger is dressed in rags so dirty they are the color of his skin, and a loose turban on his head makes him look from a distance like a squatting bird of dull plumage. We sit with him and Keshav begins his ritual for smoking on mountaintops, which we will repeat five times through the day, walking from peak to peak. He lights three sticks of incense every time, and commences with the sacramental hollowing-out of a Khukuri, the cigarette brand that is the favorite of Nepali tokers. Khukuris are stubbier and thicker than other brands, and so easier to restuff. A *khukuri* is a Nepalese dagger; the package design shows two blades crossed to look like scissors, which only adds to the stoner symbolism.

I ask Bijay to ask the forest ranger if he ever smokes marijuana. They talk for a while.

"No, he doesn't smoke," Bijay reports. "None of the hill people around here do. Maybe once or twice a year as a religious rite, but otherwise they don't like it. They have to work too hard just to survive, and it makes them lazy. But they all keep it around as an herbal medicine for the cows or the water buffalo. When cows get sick they feed it to them, and it improves their appetite."

We leave the ranger squatting on the precipice above his domain and continue our climb. On a narrow field that's a bottleneck between two steep drop-offs, we come face-to-face with a big water buffalo. These creatures are not nimble, not native to the mountains, but they cope. It's funny, the difference between city and country buffalo. The ones in Pokhara lope along unspooked by the chaos of the crowded streets, while this four-legged country bumpkin is rattled enough to turn tail in terror when Bijay tries to approach with an offering of a banana peel.

"You're missing a treat!" he yells after it.

Later we're sitting beside a tiny mountaintop temple where members of a local caste worship. There's a pierced stone tablet to which they tie the sacrificial goats. I've got my notebook with me. I read them Robin from Kathmandu's page: *The Guide*. I'd thought they'd admire his sentiments about frankness and friendship and freedom, but Keshav disapproves of something. "They start them young in Kathmandu. I never give marijuana to children or smoke with children. I think eighteen is the time to first try. But some fucking guys don't care. They'll sell to sixteen-year-old kids."

Bijay wants to know if it's true that in my country if you have no job the government gives you money. Yep. "It's good to have a social safety net, as long as people don't start thinking of it as a hammock," I say.

Keshav asks about marijuana culture in the West. I tell him there are activists working to get their lifestyle legitimated, and that I think it should be legalized. "I'd like to see it like U Brew beer laws. Grow it at home, consume it at home, no problem."

"But what of the ones who don't like to smoke? Do they think the activists are foolish people?"

"A lot of them do, yeah. A lot of them think the activists are evil. But who has most to lose if it's legal? The criminals, the police, and the jailers who profit from its being illegal."

"Maybe in a hundred years it will be legal," says Keshav. "But not soon, I think."

We stop to give marijuana, tobbacco, incense, oranges, and candy to a hilltop sadhu. The real thing, not a Kathmandu poser. He's the local priest, a soothsayer, advice giver, calmer of hysterical women and the men who make them that way. He's got a certain clarity. He looks into my eyes very deeply and lets me look into his.

Bijay says, "He has devoted his life to God."

I ask him what this means.

"Never married. No family. No greed."

The Baba's eyes are sharp, but a layer of dirt can't hide the fact that his feet are swollen and purple. The toes look about to burst. "That's all right," he says. "They are not my feet."

He wants to pose for a photo with his prized possession, an iron trident painted bright orange. "He doesn't actually *use* it," Keshav explains. "It's just a symbol. For rituals."

✳

Last stop is at the little stone shed—eight feet by eight feet—of a friend of Keshav's. He's not home. We finish off the bottle of *roxi,* which is weaker than I was expecting, more like mead than whisky. A third of a bottle hasn't altered my high much. We leave the empty for his friend, plus half a dozen cigarettes. Keshav has a chillum and before we depart we get higher, the highest of the day, sitting on the stone wall of a hilltop rice terrace.

The soil is dry and hard in the spring heat. Summer will be cooler, and wetter, and these terraces will flood. Now we can sit and hang our feet out over the wall, and imitate the kites and vultures that circle over the valley at our altitude. We are birds. We've taken off our shoes and socks and are pretending our dangling toes are eagles' talons. We are free as birds. At least for the day.

✳

By the time we are back in town it's dark, Keshav has missed most of his shift in the restaurant, and his brother is not happy. I ask him what he thinks of Keshav's smoking pot all the time and he's a bit taken aback by such a direct question about sensitive family issues. Not willing to say anything negative about his brother, he avoids an answer. I sense a bond of love and respect between them.

Later Keshav says, "We have compromised very much. But I know he hates it when I smoke this."

✳

On the morning I leave for Kathmandu Keshav gives me (free, just as those Brits had predicted) a generous supply of his finest. Back in the capital I feel it's time to make a tourist buy in Thamel, just to compare. I get Ted to come with me to translate. Ted's an American who has been studying Nepalese attitudes toward mental illness by wandering alone into isolated villages and asking to speak to the craziest person in town. His example will later inspire me to head to Mechi, a distant zone where few tourists go.

We stroll and trawl the narrow lanes of Thamel, waiting to be approached by someone selling hashish. It's typical: when you're not looking for it every third guy is whispering to you, calling you "My Friend," offering "For you special price!" As soon as you actually want to buy some shit, they evaporate.

Thirty years ago we could have just gone to any number of cafes in Kathmandu selling ganja or *charas* (the Nepali and Indian word for hashish) legally. By the early seventies the Nixon administration, paranoid that too many young Americans were abandoning junior sales positions at Kmart in favor of smoking weed and making love not war in Kathmandu, gave the Nepali government four million dollars to outlaw cannabis. Foreign aid money to solve our problem, not theirs. In his great little book called *Hippie Dharma,* still in print in Kathmandu, Indian journalist F. D. Coolaabavala wrote at the time, "The shopkeepers ask: 'Why stop charas? It has not corrupted our people and earns valuable foreign exchange.' The charas-growers are even more angry with the outside world . . . They argue: 'We consider beef-eating as the biggest crime but we do not go about asking beefeaters to stop slaughtering cows.'" Thirty years of prohibition later a THC high is no less available in Kathmandu than it was then, or than it is in America today. Prohibition has just made it much more expensive, not least because the police expect a cut to look the other way.

It's ten o'clock. Kathmandu is under curfew: no women are allowed on the streets after nine. Tourists, of course, don't count. The rules give the cops an excuse to harass "loose" Nepali girls, and families an excuse to lock their daughters up at home. So there are only men on the street. Finally a man of the one-legged variety, propelled by sturdy, well-used wooden crutches, says the magic word. Hashish.

"Look for the one-legged guy!" says Ted, delighted. "It's perfect for your book."

The one-legged salesman tells us to wait, disappears for a long time, reappears, and says, "It's coming." We're all standing on the street, feeling awfully conspicuous. A kid delivers it, moves off to wait on his own. The three of us go down an alley to a dark alcove in front of the locked doors of a business. It's too dark to see anything properly. The hashish is moist, soft enough to tear easily, and smells only faintly of anything, and therefore smells only faintly like hash. He wants 1,000 rupees for about ten grams. We settle on 600 for two thirds of it. Ted asks him how he lost his leg. A truck ran over him when he was a kid. There can't be many employment opportunities for an illiterate one-legged man in Kathmandu, so we feel we've done him a favor.

✳

So I have some good hash for my journey to Mechi, easternmost of Nepal's fifteen administrative zones. The next day aboard a bus circling the ring road in Kathmandu, not even out of the city, I can already see little semiwild foot-high cannabis plants growing everywhere in the trash along the road, unmistakable even under a coat of fine brown dust. It's three in the afternoon, the bus is not air-conditioned, and some of the windows don't close. Our destination is Ilam, a town in the middle hills of Mechi less than 200 miles to the east. Five hours of travel later we are 70 miles west of Kathmandu, and therefore 270 miles from Ilam. It's the mountains—to get through them we go west before we can go east.

We arrive in Ilam at eight the next morning. It's a hill station tea plantation, a tough little town. The view to the east is across a valley, where the road disappears into the hills of India. That's the shortcut to Darjeeling, but it's closed to foreigners.

Having a chunk of hash spares me the chore of scoring cannabis in Ilam. I'm using Keshav's technique: hollowing out Khukuri cigarettes, breaking the hash into tiny mouse turds, mixing it with tobacco, and repacking. Ilam is a nice town to wander into the hills from, but there's not much else going on. Schoolteachers want to practice their English with you in the coolness of the evening. One tells me, "I've heard Darwin's theories are very seriously applied in Western society and one must work very hard to survive there." Another wants to know all the English dirty words.

From Ilam I head north by local bus to the town of Phiddim, which is as far as you can get into the hills of eastern Nepal by bus. I've read an article in a hemp magazine about Nepali villages where hemp is still used traditionally—the seeds for food, white bast fiber from the stems to make fiber for cloth, and the thickest stalks for all kinds of uses where thin poles of wood or bamboo would be useful. The article suggested that this might be the last place on the planet where peasants wear down their teeth chewing the hemp stocks to separate out the long fibers, which are eventually woven into cloth on preindustrial backstrap looms, a millennia-old, extremely time-consuming technology that was once common in nearly every agricultural society. With a roof covered in bags of rice which serve as pillows for a dozen young men, the ancient bus groans up the steep mountain passes. Another schoolteacher wants to befriend me. I have a hard time convincing him that ganja is what I'm going to Phiddim to find. Maybe I'm pronouncing it wrong. I'm calling it hemp, cannabis, ganga, bhang, all kinds of names, hoping to get my point across. When we reach the town, after a four-hour trip to cover less than ten miles, he takes me to a bookseller who operates a sidewalk counter. There are maybe fifty titles for sale, including a Nepali-English dictionary. He searches in it, then writes on a slip of paper: *Cannabis/hemp = ganja, bhanga.* I knew that. Now he does too.

"It's not legal here," he says. "The police will destroy it." Then he leads me around the town, which feels like a medieval village in daylight and even more so in the evening, when the power shuts down and everything is lit by candles. We stop in at a sweetshop, my teacher friend making an exaggerated excuse about being really thirsty all of a sudden. While tea is prepared he draws my attention to a platter of green dessert squares among the sweets in the glass cabinet. These greenish confections are kept discreetly out of the line of sight of passersby on the street. I ask if I can have one, and he orders it. The counterman brings over our glasses of tea and a ganja cake on a little square of wax paper, and my new friend holds it before me in one palm. With the other hand he makes a finger-spinning gesture of being intoxicated and falling down. "If you eat." That'll be me if I eat it, spinning out of control. His eyes go wide as it dawns on him I'm actually going to eat it. I take it and pop it whole in my mouth. It's basically flour, oil, sugar, and ganga. He's shocked. "Now you know where to get more. Have a nice stay in Phiddim." He gulps down his glass of tea and scurries away quick as he can.

The next day is a holiday called Holi, the Hindu Festival of Color. I'm sitting in the shade at the only guesthouse in town, peeling an orange, when some local government official comes by to read the morning papers. Another local comes by and they fall into discussion. I hear the word "bhang." When there is a lull in the conversation I ask the official if he'll be celebrating Holi. He says, "People are putting on the colors today, but I don't like it. The colors are very dark, and not easily removed."

"I heard you mention bhang."

"Yes, bhang and alcoholism." He makes a face of great distaste and disapproval and gestures toward the little corner storefront counter here at the guesthouse, behind which are bottles of San Miguel beer and Nepali hard stuff—ubiquitous Nepali brands like Mount Everest blended whisky and Ruslan vodka, and rarities like Red Rider (with a label showing the silhouette in red of a nude woman on a rearing horse) and Shree's Bullet, a red wine in a clear glass bottle with a label that would have looked right at home in an Arizona saloon circa 1910.

The labels look so bright and cheery to me that I realize a bhang stone is creeping up on me now. I ate bhang about half an hour ago. The one square I had yesterday was nice, but I could have handled being higher. Today I've already been back to buy three more, and have eaten two for breakfast. Now I can feel a cool all-over body tingle that hints at big highs to come. I'm sitting in the shade, eating oranges, eggs, and rice for breakfast. A young laborer trudges past with a sturdy wicker basket on his back, full of bricks. It's held in place by a strap across the forehead. Two older men work alongside him, lugging bricks up the street on their backs, walking back empty to start again. All day. Every day. Humans of burden. The young one is maybe eighteen, not yet deformed by a poor diet and having to carry bricks all day, like the other two twisted, prematurely aged little runts.

I'm thinking if I were the young one I'd be only too glad to run off and join the Marxists in the hills. The Marxists control huge patches of the country. If he did escape and join them at least he'd have some adventure instead of this drudgery. I was reading in the papers that the cops have adopted a new strategy for ferreting out potential Maoist sympathizers. They go into remote villages posing as guerrillas, gathering the menfolk and making rousing speeches castigating the corrupt, caste-ridden society that is responsible for the misery of the poor. And in a country with a per capita income of 200 bucks, there's no shortage of miserable poor people. "The elites must be overthrown, equality must reign! Join us in the struggle against tyranny!" That's what they're told. Think Mel Gibson in *Braveheart:* "Freeeeeeedom! Join us and win your freeeeeedom!" Anyone who agrees to fight for freedom is promptly arrested when the meeting ends. From the government's point of view, those peasants are a threat to the existing order. From my point of view, they're a threat to the existing disorder.

*

A man with a face powdered red as the devil is walking by, the whitest of white cigarettes dangling unlit from his lip. There's a kid who works at the guesthouse named Tikka. He's fourteen, stunted, illiterate, and he likes to come to my room and just stand there and look at me, likely because I smile at him, try to make conversation, and never tell him to get lost. Now he's pointing to the red-faced man and shouting with excitement. It's festival day! "Holi! Holi!" I get up and walk toward the street, and he looks at me as if I am completely insane to be heading out into Holi.

Kids are throwing colored powder mixed with water at each

other, or just pure powder, trying to scrub it like paste into each other's faces. At the police checkpoint at the beginning of a path down to the river in the valley floor, rowdy young cops, kegs of time-to-party testosterone, have painted each other pink and purple pretty much from head to toe. Head and shoulders solid, the rest is collateral damage. Now they see me coming. So white. So untouched. Such fair hair. I try ducking at first, but there is really no point. Better just to accept the blessing. One of them cups my face in his palms, rubbing powder into my cheeks. "You are welcome in Nepal!" he shouts, and a crowd of kids and old women howls with laughter at me.

I leave town behind and start to descend the steep path of switchbacks down to the river. Suddenly it's Limbu country. The Limbus are ethnically similar to hill tribes that run all the way from here through Burma and down into Thailand. They're the famous Gurkhas, legendary fighters for the British Army. The last vestige of their formerly exalted place in the British Empire is that five thousand of them still work as cops in Singapore. Retirees from the Gurkha regiments build houses in their villages and live on British Army pensions, which in Nepal amount to more money in a month than many people see in a year. Down the slopes are other tribespeople. Some of the women wear this strange nose ring that hangs down all the way to their chin. It's like a bit of flattened gold, in the shape of a pineapple, hanging from a hinge just under the nostrils. The little pineapple prongs seem to protect the lips against unwanted kisses. That's about the only purpose I can imagine.

I scrub my face in the first stream I come to. The ganja cake has added to my paranoia that the powder might be permanent, and using my sandals, as kneepads, I'm kneeling in the cool stream, madly submerging and scrubbing my face with my T-shirt. The first scrub has left the purple-pink pattern of two perfect handprints on my soaked shirt, and my paranoia subsides a little. The problem with eating cannabis, as opposed to smoking it, is you feel far less in control of your high. I can only imagine what the local Limbus are saying to each other as they pass me by. The men grin, the women tend to laugh throatily at the purple-painted white guy kneeling in their irrigation canal. Out of town, the festival of Holi has no meaning. The Limbu people aren't Hindus. They're animists.

At the bottom of the valley the stream collects in a little reservoir that feeds a pint-sized hydroelectric station. I swim with some kids, then eat my other ganja cake. On the steep trek back to Phiddim I meet women tending cows and a man whose job is carrying medicine on ice packs in a camping-style plastic cooler on his back, from the town out to the villages. I meet ten-year-old girls who carry firewood up the mountainside in baskets on their backs, held in place by a cloth strap across their foreheads. I can barely lift one of these baskets. These tiny girls lift theirs and lug them from river's edge to hilltop up the steep mountainside without complaint.

Back at the guesthouse I clean up, relieved to find the paint has mostly come off, and sit down for dinner with Bhawani, an English teacher at the local college who has contracted with the guesthouse for two meals a day. It's dark because there's a power outage. Bhawani, his hands casting huge shadows by candlelight against the walls, asks, "So what do you think of this life, Brian? What is life all about?"

"I really have no answer for this question," I say. I'm starting to talk like him. "The more I see of this world the less certain I am of anything."

"Well, it certainly is a drama," he says warmly.

"Shakespeare: All the world's a stage, right?"

"I prefer the statement in *Macbeth*," says Bhawani. "Life is a tale told by a fool or an idiot, he said so, and full of sound and fury, but signifying nothing else, only that."

I just nod.

"Life begins in zero, goes somewhere, and ends in zero, is it not so?" He's reading *The Great Gatsby*, in preparation for teaching it to his students. "What is the lesson for this work of literature, please?"

I tell him it's been twenty-five years since I read it, but I think it might be Money can't buy happiness.

He bobs his head in that Indian way that could mean yes, could mean no. "I think from what I've read so far, the moral is, Love is a dangerous, corrupting force, because Gatsby is willing to sacrifice his life and everything he has for Daisy. For the sake of love. Is it not?"

He's been eating his *dhal baat,* the rice and bean staple of the Nepali diet, with his right hand. Now that he's finished he's pouring water from his glass onto his hand, to clean it, and the water is dribbling into the leftover food on his stainless-steel plate. I'm staring. He's got bits of uneaten rice and *dhal* right up to the crotch of his fingers. He sees me staring and stops.

"Oh, pardon me. This is rude. We have a superstition that if we wash our hand on the plate like this, it results in trouble. It makes the plate appear like the pot where we vomit when becoming sick." He changes the subject. "What do you know about Keats? What of his love of Fanny?"

I'm rummaging around in my mind for the opening line to the poet's ode "To Sleep." "I used to know it by heart," I insist, buying time while I wait for my mind to retrieve it from some arid, long-unvisited mental desert. "Wait a minute, wait a minute . . . O soft embalmer of the still midnight! Shutting, with careful fingers, uhm . . ." I mangle a few phrases, but nail the ending: "Turn the key deftly in the oiled wards, And seal the hushed casket of my soul . . ."

Bhawani is politely unimpressed. A great poem half remembered is like looking at the scraps of a fine meal someone else ate— what might have been delicious is now only scraps. I've failed to quote Keats, but I can sing Bhawani my favorite Beatles song: "Please don't wake me, no don't shake me, leave me where I am, 'cause after all, I'm only *sleeeeeping* . . ." I know the words to that one, and in the candlelit room it goes over quite well.

"Lennon and McCartney are the Keats and Wordsworth of their age," he says. "The foreign music we hear is always in English. Is it not inevitable that the language of the most powerful country should also be the lingua franca of the world?"

"Maybe it would be better if the language of a small and insignificant country was the world's linguafranca," I suggest.

"Yes, yes. Ethiopia! Then all the Ethiopians would have employment, as the language teachers of the world."

"And we wouldn't even have to change the initials of ESL."

"But Brian," he says seriously. "In the Ethiopian language those initials would most probably be completely different." Of course. So logical. He's not stoned, and I am.

My room is separated from the next by only a single layer of thin planks. Someone has made a number of peepholes. It's possible to lie in the bed and see the bed in the next room, when their light is on. It's a young Nepali couple, who turn the light out, relieving me of the temptation to peek. In the dark I hear the cooing of lovers. They might as well be in the same room. They are very much in love, whispering, snuggling, talking at times in soft voices, maybe comparing impressions of the events of their day. Then they make love, quietly and sweetly. I miss my lover's touch, and no amount of marijuana can substitute for it.

4 : SOUTHEAST ASIA: THAILAND, LAOS, AND CAMBODIA

The Atlanta Hotel squats next door to a Baptist church at the very dead end of Sukhumvit Soi 3 in Bangkok. It was built by a German in the 1950s, in a style already twenty years out of date, and hasn't been renovated since. The swimming pool was the first private pool in Thailand, according to a plaque beside it. Another plaque on the entrance door to the lobby reads:

THE ATLANTA DOES NOT WELCOME
THE FOLLOWING:
1) *Badly behaved people*
2) *Dirty and dirtily dressed people*
3) *Ill-mannered people*
4) *louts*
5) *hooligans, drunkards, and drug addicts*
6) *other socially objectionable characters*

That's essentially the same list of people who are not welcome in my house. At the Atlanta, on a laminated plastic sheet of paper at the front desk, and again on the first-floor landing, where you can't miss it coming up the stairs, this notice is posted:

> *Guests who are engaged in illegal activities, including pedophilia and the use of narcotics, will be reported without advance warning.*
> (i) *to the Thai police*
> (ii) *to the prosecuting authority of their home state*

(iii)   *to the newspapers of their home state. In addition the Atlanta will file its own charges against such miscreants for bringing the good name of the Atlanta into disrepute.*

There are many places which tolerate, connive at, or even encourage illegal activities. The Atlanta is not one of them. The staff may be sweet, and rather ineffectual, and can appear quite incapable of enforcing anything, but in matters of zero tolerance the director will take charge.

It sounds a bit daunting, but after checking in I find half a pack of unused hypodermic needles in the strongbox in my room and, taking them down to the front desk, manage to make the staff look terribly embarrassed, although a German tourist couple on my side of the counter thinks it's quite funny. All this verbose Atlanta signage has a subtext: be discreet. And since my room has a balcony, that's easy enough.

But finding pot in Bangkok is not easy.

The city is huge, new, centerless, and laced with major highways, like a tropical Los Angeles. Local middle-class people pile into the family car and drive half an hour to eat on the sixth floor of a mall. So in some ways it's almost like home. First World in big chunks. But in other parts it's pure Third World, whole huge neighborhoods that are just shacks on stilts, with terrible sanitation, too many people, sick-looking dogs padding limply from one piece of shade to another. Below the rickety wood-plank sidewalks you catch glimpses of a netherworld where humans never go. On the swampy putrid surface where the stilts sink into the garbage heaps, it's Rat World.

There's a large English-speaking expatriate community in Thailand. Brits, Australians, Americans, and Canadians, working hard, most making good money by Thai standards, the rest making good money by any standard. As a well-scrubbed Westerner in khaki cargo pants and a clean, collared shirt, I fit in with them fine. The thing is I want to meet Thai people. Thai people who smoke pot. None of these expats I keep meeting seem to know any. In Thailand the drug of choice is a methamphetamine called Yao Baa, or the horse drug, because the pills used to be imprinted with the image of a horse head. The Thai news media portray speed as the current Number One Evil Scourge Threatening Our Youth. Thai critics complain the DEA spends piles of money to try (and fail) to stop heroin from Burma getting on airplanes or ships bound for America, but gives nothing to stem the flow of cheap methamphetamine into Thailand from Burma.

"There are ten thousand *sois* [side streets] in Bangkok. You can buy amphetamines on every single one of them." That quote, from a Bangkok cabdriver, is the introductory remark in a lecture given by Daniel Rey Lewis, an American academic who has been studying the methamphetamine problem in Thailand for the United Nations Development Program. Lewis calls Thai speed "a social drug used in combination with drinking, motorcycle racing at night, dancing in nightclubs, playing cards, and playing sports." Likely his conclusions will fail to please his UN patrons: "Thai amphetamines are not addictive, not very dangerous, and much more mild than those used in the West," Lewis says. "The government is using a noncredible story—they're telling people that these drugs are really dangerous, and they are not. I think they're a fad. There seems to be a five-year cycle with new drugs, where everyone tries it, then it dies back down." Unfortunately, at Thammasat University his message is delivered to only a handful of his academic peers, this pot journalist, and a couple of students more interested in staring out the windows at the barges and the speedboats churning up the choppy waters of the Chao Phraya River. "The greatest problems that amphetamines cause are probably the result of their being illegal, rather than the dangers from the drugs themselves," Lewis says.

Marijuana use among young Thais seems to be out of vogue. Nualnoi Treerat, an economics professor at Bangkok's Chulalongkorn University and coauthor of *Guns, Girls, Gambling, Ganja: Thailand's Illegal Economy and Public Policy,* tells me, "It used to be that young people began with marijuana, but now marijuana is more and more associated with rural people, who grow for their own use, put it in soups and things. Now the young urban people start straight with amphetamines."

Even among the expats, it's tough to find potheads. Opium is around and everywhere, of course. In a hiply but not happily decorated bar that everyone takes to be an important sign of Bangkok's cosmopolitan sophistication (I guess you're supposed to like a bar that wants you to feel like you're sitting around the coffee table in a stockbroker's office), an expat complained to me that back home in America, smoking dope had been a pleasant ritual of talking, giggling, and getting silly with your friends. "But the local grass here is laced with opium," he lamented. "You smoke it and you just feel real heavy and quiet, and then you fall asleep. It's not even fun at all in a group. The only time I smoke is if someone has Nepalese hash."

Later in Chiang Mai an American expat will insist to me that slathering opium onto pot is standard Thai practice, and go into elaborate detail about how, in the process of milking opium from poppies, the less opiated first liquidy ooze is set aside to be spread onto the famous Thai sticks, to give them that extra kick. I'd thought it was an old wives' tale of the pot world, that Thai sticks, long sativa buds wrapped by bamboo strips around a sturdy central stick to make for less damage in transport, were laced with opiates. But in Thailand no one doubts it.

✳

There is a bar in Bangkok called Barbican, in a Japanese *soi* off Silom. When I say Japanese, I mean most of the street is taken up with whorehouses catering strictly to Japanese businessmen. For most Westerners the girls are way too pricey, but even rich Westerners aren't allowed. The Japanese have this thing about AIDS. They think AIDS is something Westerners give to Thai prostitutes. So as long as the girls never fuck Westerners they are safe for Japanese guys to fuck.

On this otherwise all-Japanese *soi* the Barbican is an oasis for Westerners and Thais, a kind of upscale English pub that's evolved into a "second wives" bar for Japanese girls who have become the mistresses of wealthy Thai men. They gather in groups to drink and kill time while their men are preoccupied with business, or wife and family number one, or maybe even third wife. The second wives perch together on stools at tall tables, giggling occasionally but looking rather understimulated. It must be boring to be kept women. I was not bored looking at them, as they were quite leggy and gorgeous in short skirts on those high bar stools. After the lock-up-your-daughters puritanism of Hindu Nepal, I was having a hard time getting my mind around a new set of sexual mores. Bangkok reeks of sex. In a different way Nepal does too, I guess: it reeks of frustrated young men not getting any. Thailand reeks of men of all ages getting it, and addicted to getting more.

At a table beside the second wives, two expats named Ian and Dennis are trading Thailand pot stories. Dennis has a Thai friend who lives in the countryside. For fun he likes to smoke speed and creep around all night in the rice fields, trying to catch poisonous snakes. He brings them into the city to sell, in a big burlap sack, and as a precaution he fills the bottom of the sack with fresh cannabis branches and leaves. "It mellows the snakes out completely," says Dennis. "You can pick them up with your bare hands."

According to these two, and most other expats I talked to, marijuana cultivation in Thailand is controlled by the army or police, and most of the major plantations have crossed the border into Laos and Cambodia, where it's easier to hide them. They both recommend I check those places out. Dennis tells the story of a friend of his who came to Bangkok via Phnom Penh, where pot can be smoked casually almost anywhere. Forgetting himself, he had sparked up a doob in a sidewalk restaurant on Khao San Road, Bangkok's noisy, party-hearty backpacker booze, pill, and STD mecca. Lighting a joint in public is a brazen Bangkok faux pas; he

[57]

was immediately scooped by the cops, who demanded 30,000 baht to let him go. Several hours of friendly bartering from Dennis got the price down to 5,000 baht, or about 150 bucks.

In Thailand you are expected to bribe your way out of possession offenses. Even major offenses. While I was in Bangkok the newspapers announced a "record haul" of 4,354,000 methamphetamine pills from a van heading toward Bangkok. "Police say the suspects, who had offered a bribe that was turned down, escaped while going to the toilet," reported the *Bangkok Post*. There seems little public questioning of actions of the authorities in Thailand— all part of the Thai culture of knowing your place and saving face. It's reflected in the attitude toward the monarchy: the King and Queen are untouchable, worshiped as near-perfect beings. But the monarchy is like any kingship that can bestow real favors. Sycophants surround the monarch while honest people bristle. You might hear that whispered privately by a Thai, but it never seems to get said publicly.

✳

Bangkok is not pot-friendly. There are a couple of reggae bars in the alleys off Khao San Road, places with big sloppy amateurish Bob Marley portraits painted on the walls, where you'll be offered ganja, but in the guesthouses nearby you can buy speed, ecstasy, or ketamine easier than pot, and why not? In a crowded city, where privacy is virtually impossible (thank God for my balcony at the Atlanta), it's simply much less hassle to conceal and consume a little pill than to light up and smoke that telltale stinky old weed.

The only pot I score in Bangkok is from a whorehouse Ian takes me to, a Bangkok special with a huge pink neon sign out front, valet parking, and a plushly carpeted but chairless lobby inside where you stand at the observation window and pick and choose from fifty girls sitting in loose gauzy robes behind the plate glass. To score pot you walk right past them to a restaurant in the back and ask for a Fanta and special Krongthips. Krongthips are a local brand of cigarettes. (The Thai government has a monopoly on tobacco, and makes only two brands, Krongthips and Marlboros.) A package of cigarettes is duly delivered with your orange soft drink and you are charged the exorbitant price of 600 baht. The package is perfectly sealed, right down to the little pull string on the cellophane. But inside the filter cigarettes contain pot, not tobacco.

Now, I smoked a good many of these cigarettes in Bangkok, and never experienced the giddy rush, the sudden *whoooooosh* up the mental mountainside that marijuana usually brings me. Were these smokes laced with opium? All I know is I would light one up before heading out on the town, expecting that THC buzz to pick me up and propel me out the door into the chaos of Sukhumvit, but instead I'd end up flopped on the bed, lying on my back listening to the air conditioner hum. I'd be thinking, I don't really feel great, in fact a little queasy, and numb, and I have no interest in getting up off my bum. Is that all there is, or is this opium?

❊

Vientiane is the capital of Laos, but with a population of less than 150,000 it's hardly more than a town. In the cool of morning even the rush-hour traffic seems serene. Immaculate, lovely schoolteachers in ankle-length skirts glide by on bicycles, and motorcycles putter along at nearly that same sedate pace. The boulevards in the older districts are tree-lined, and in the shade Lao ladies sell breakfast sandwiches, minibaguettes stuffed with lettuce and cold processed meat slices similar to Spam. The Lao people use the French word, paté, for this meat. Laos, like Cambodia and Vietnam, was once a part of French Indochina.

The name Vientiane was what the French came up with when they tried to reproduce the Lao name for their capital. It means Sandalwood City, and "Wieng Chan" would be how an English person might have done it. Wieng Chan would have been a little less pathetic than the French try, but still misses out on the whole tonal aspect of the Lao language, which is also spoken in most of northern Thailand.

I was told in Bangkok that you could buy cannabis in the open-air market in Vientiane. "Just go to the market and start sniffing the tobacco. People will figure out what you're after pretty quick." But first you have to find the right market. The market west of the bus terminal is crammed with hardware, dry goods, and cheap electronics. Then there is another, shabbier market east of the bus terminal where vegetables are sold, and meat. At the farthest eastern edge are the tobacco sellers, baking under low tin roofs, surrounded by big open bags of shredded brown leaf.

I pick up a pinch. Sniff, sniff. The vendor offers me some filterless prerolled cigarettes in a clear cellophane pack of twenty.

"Tobacco?"

"*Tabac.*"

I buy some rolling papers with a little rooster on the red cover. Maybe he'll figure it out: I'm buying papers, but not tobacco. A woman from three stalls over comes sidling up in a worried hurry.

"*Gansa?* Opium?"

"*Gansa,* yes, *oui.* Opium, no."

She gestures me to follow her back to her stall. The guy I bought the papers from shoos me away dismissively.

The *gansa* seller looks ill at ease. Scanning the market to make sure no one's paying undue attention to us, she bids me sit on a low stool behind a pile of big bloated sacks, so that I'm nearly hidden from sight. She reaches into a deep recess between the sacks for her stash, a shopping-sized bag of ganga. With exaggerated haste she stuffs handfuls from it into a similar-sized transparent pink bag for me. Three, four, five ounces. "Whoa! That's way too much." I take out a few stalks from what appears to be mostly a big bag of leaves and look for some signs of buds. Yes, there are some, but they've gone to seed. The seeds, stems, and leaves are extremely green, yet brittle. I apportion myself about two ounces and gesture to her that's enough. She wants 20,000 kip. That's the name of the Lao currency. Four 5,000-kip notes. Less than three

American dollars. The 5,000-kip note is the largest denomination they print, and it's worth 70 cents.

Now I have a big bulge in the thigh pocket of my cargo pants. I wander around the market, gradually satisfying myself that people are totally indifferent to me. The market at this hour seems to be mostly barefoot old women stepping gingerly under heavy loads. I'm a foot taller than everyone else, and I feel very white, obvious, uncertain, and exposed. I haven't even smoked the stuff yet and I'm getting paranoid.

Back in the air-conditioned splendor of my room I pick out the seeds and roll up a big fat one with my new Rooster papers, which are glueless and oddly shiny, like glossy magazine paper. Then I head up to the rooftop to smoke. It's about ten in the morning and the sun is burning hot. It'll reach 40 Celsius today. Double it and add 30—that makes it 110 Fahrenheit. Nothing to do but hide in the shade.

Back in my room I feel the high hit me. It's powerful but not all that pleasurable. "Neither stimulant or depressant, pharmacologically it is classified by itself." So says Joan Bello of the marijuana effect in her essay "The Physical, Psychological, and Spiritual Benefits of Marihuana," which I came across in a great little book called *Psychedelics Reimagined*. Pot heightens whatever mood I happen to be in, and at the moment I'm feeling alone and isolated in this town, driven indoors to an air-conditioned cell.

At two in the afternoon the streets of Vientiane are deserted. Everyone's hiding from the dizzying heat, except mad dogs and cannabis smokers. One of them, anyway. Maybe it's cooler by the Mekong.

Five outdoor restaurants line the banks of the river. No walls, dirt floors, rickety tree branches serving as poles to support patchwork roofs of woven palm and tin. Here there is a faint breeze. The river flows wide and low, three hundred yards away across a dry, sandy floodplain. By the time the breeze reaches us across the baking sands there is no coolness in it.

The waitress is sitting with three transvestites. The bunch of them are quite obviously appraising my looks, my handsomeness, my virility. The "girls" fan themselves to keep the sweat from bubbling through their pancake makeup, bat their eyes at me, and say things in Lao that sound like backhanded compliments, in that exaggeratedly arch feminine tone that's common to drag queens the world over.

I order beer, the local brand, Beer Lao. A German girl comes along, sits at a nearby table, and I invite her to sit with me. She tells me to go north to find marijuana, to Luang Nam Tha, and from there farther north to Muang Sing. "The women of the mountain tribes will try to force it on you," she says. Sounds like the right place.

We are joined by a young Lao couple who speak good English. They are working to create a local cyber-business, finding it hard to please the bureaucrats, the old-fashioned, change-averse communists who've been running the Lao People's Democratic Republic since 1975. The government, army, and police seem oddly invisible in this place, except that there are several bland Stalinist-style buildings in town, and the only English newspaper is state-controlled and full of nonnews, with headlines like "Vietnam attaches importance to cooperation with Laos" and "Irrigation remains a priority."

Change is in the air here, though. The communists are opening up to tourism, hoping to follow the development model of the Thais. That's Thailand there, just across the Mekong. "We live across the border from this economic powerhouse, and watch on television all the slick images that go with it," says Noi, the female half of the Lao computer couple. "Everyone dreams now of owning a car, and everyone is willing to work really hard to own a car." I contemplate that while droplets of condensation run down the sides of our drink glasses and sweat runs down my forehead into my eyebrows.

"But how can we ever stop being poor in this heat?" she sighs.

An alcoholic squats nearby, crouched in the shade under a derelict table along the path between the terraces and the river. Whenever people get up and leave any of the five little restaurants he rushes over to their table to consume the last traces of alcohol in the melted ice water from the bottom of their glasses, or sucks on the straws that disappear into green coconuts bigger than his head.

After 4 P.M. the inhabitants of Vientiane begin to emerge from their cool hiding places and stroll along the riverbank. A young Buddhist monk passes, his saffron robes the color of the weakening sun, which can now be stared at without strain as it settles into the haze above the horizon. Crossing into Laos from Thailand yesterday morning I saw twenty monks in a line, waiting their turn to receive uncooked rice from a storekeeper. The Buddhist idea of merit is met this way—you earn it by giving, and little gestures count.

A young man named Kham joins the conversation, eager to practice English. I buy him a drink. He wants Ovaltine. "It's a food supplement." We're waited on by one of the transvestites, and Kham does a double take at the sight of her. "Is that a man or a woman?" he asks.

"A man who wants to be a woman."

He makes a sour face of disgust.

"How do they make love?"

"Love is a feeling that comes from the heart."

A few hours later, after dark, I see the same transvestite hooking on a street corner a few blocks away.

The next day Kham takes me on the back of his little Honda motorcycle to the airport so I can fly to Luang Nam Tha, north into the hills near the Chinese and Burmese borders, to escape the heat and mediocre pot of Vientiane. On the way to the airport we pass a checkpoint. A soldier in fatigues waves his machine gun barrel for us to stop, but Kham just drives on, yelling over his shoulder that we're in a hurry to catch a flight.

"Won't you get in trouble for that?"

"I'll just take a different route home," he says with a laugh. In ten days in Laos, it's the only time I notice police or military men.

✻

Luang Nam Tha is a strip of new guesthouses and restaurants along a narrow highway. At the morning market, tribeswomen come down from the hills into town and sell what they've collected from the forest: live bats, all manner of bugs and maggots, and barbecued rat on a stick. They don't waste any protein. Poor people, but honest. The old lady who sells me bananas insists that I take 200 change on the 500 kip I try to give her for a bunch. Five hundred kip is seven cents.

At the biggest building in town, the office of a development project funded by the European Community, I find a translator. Ken says there is no marijuana being grown around Luang Nam Tha, but plenty of opium, and offers to take me to a village where they grow opium. The villagers might know about marijuana too. So we climb onto Ken's 100cc Honda motorcycle and head for the hills.

"There were tigers here once," he says over his shoulder as we climb through hills covered with scrubby-looking second-growth forest.

"How long ago?"

"Fifty years. See on that hill over there? An American air base was there. Thirty years ago. Local people still go there for scrap metal."

During the Vietnam War America conducted a secret war on Laos, dropping 1.9 million tons of bombs on this country between 1964 and 1973. That's more than 25 tons per square mile. The North Vietnamese ran the Ho Chi Minh Trail as a supply route through eastern Laos and took control of great chunks of the country in the process. In response the Americans trained an army of locals, mostly ethnic Hmong tribesmen, to harass the Vietnamese. With the victory of the Vietnamese-backed Pathet Lao in 1975 many of the Hmong kept right on fighting, and some still do.

The dislocation of shell-shocked peoples is still being sorted out today. The village Ken takes me to visit, Swan Ya (it means Open Garden), is new, set in what look to be unproductive steep hills with little farmable flatland. Swan Ya was created on the orders of the Lao government, which combined and relocated three villages from the east, each village peopled by a different tribal group. Lao Huay, Yao, and Hmong are forced to mix together here.

"Are they happy about that?"

"Not happy," Ken says curtly. "But last year they managed to celebrate New Year's together for the first time. And they are starting to intermarry."

A big school is being constructed with European money, and the schoolyard is busy with kids, pigs, and ponies. The ponies used to carry rice down from the higher paddies. We ride Ken's motorbike behind the school up into an ever-narrowing valley, past the comic sight of twelve water buffalo crammed together up to their necks in a tiny mud hole, and in the end find a small Hmong cluster of shacks along a nearly dry stream.

It's the hot, dry season, a month before the monsoons. In front of the village is a three-acre field covered with the brown, headless stalks of opium poppies. In one corner of the field there's a pile of leftover waste from a successful opium harvest: stalks and dried-out poppy heads with their telltale slits down the sides. "All the evidence of opium production is just lying around," I say to Ken. "What do the police do?"

He just shrugs. "What can they do? It's one thing to arrest a criminal. It's another to take away the livelihood of a whole village. Are the women and children to starve?"

Inside the biggest of the huts an old woman tends a huge metal bowl of corn mash and rice husks simmering over an open wood fire, making slop for the pigs. A bunch of kids and teenagers crowd inside to gawk at the foreigner. Against the wall farthest from the smoky fire lie three addicts. Two, virtual skeletons, use opium three times a day. The third is younger, healthier, but he had an accident a few days ago and crushed two fingers into a purple swollen mess. He's smoking opium for the pain. I ask if it's only men who smoke, and a teenage girl pipes up. Everyone laughs.

"She says boys and girls of courting age use it too," Ken translates. "Would you like to see some opium?"

I'm presented with a brown ball the size of an orange, very soft in the heat. There's some paper stuck to it like the wrapper of a melting chocolate bar. "They sell it to Chinese traders for 2.6 million kip a kilo," Ken says. About 340 bucks.

They're not getting rich, but it's worth so much more than any alternative crop. Really in this isolated valley it's the only crop they could grow that's valuable enough to cover the cost of getting it to distant markets. I take in the squalor of this smoky, filthy hut and ask Ken to ask them, as delicately as possible, why they don't use the money to build themselves better houses.

"The money is saved for medical emergencies," Ken says. "In case they need to send a village member to Vientiane for surgery."

"And marijuana? Do they grow it, or use it at all?"

"They used to grow some in the old place," Ken says. "But when they were relocated to here they lost the seeds."

One of the addicts asks Ken something, and they talk for a while. Ken sums it up in translation: "They are disappointed. They were hoping you might be an opium expert, and be able to tell them how to improve their yield. Their crop is getting smaller and less potent every year."

✳

Back in Luang Nam Tha, Ken and I eat dinner at my guesthouse, a cheap place where at night you can hear rats in the walls. A girl from California tells me she and her friends were in Muang Sing, the next town north, for a month. "We were just, like, *totally* into the hill tribes."

"Is there pot there, or only opium?"

"They'll sell you pot, but opium is sooooo cheap."

Then she and a couple of her friends head upstairs to her room for a "sesh" before bed. An opium-smoking session. "Go up to Muang Sing, rent a bicycle, go out to the villages, try it out," she urges. She thinks I'm uptight because I'm sticking to pot.

It takes four bouncy hours in the back of a pickup truck to reach Muang Sing. The road rises through hills clad in jungle to a flat valley next to the Chinese border. I'm barely out of the vehicle before a half dozen Akha tribeswomen, in elaborate headdresses covered in old coins, surround me, tugging on my shirtsleeves, wanting to sell trinkets, necklaces of tiny shells, opening the lids of little grapefruit-sized woven baskets filled with marijuana, and discreetly displaying little balls of opium in cupped palms. The pot is fresh-picked and mostly leaf. I pass. I take a walk around town looking for Mr. Pun, who Ken has told me is the only English speaker available as a guide. There are photocopied papers newly posted in the restaurants and guesthouses around town, in Lao and English:

Important announcement: Lao nationals and foreigners, tourists, foreign aid workers, businessmen and relatives of Muang Sing inhabitants should act according to the following:

1) *Everybody must respect the culture and traditions and religion of the people of the different ethnic groups of Muang Sing.*

2) *Newcomers must check in at the local police station, showing all required documents.*

3) *If spending the night, one must stay at a guesthouse. It is not allowed to stay at local homes with other individuals, or at other places. The guesthouse owners must look after their guests and ensure that their belongings will not get lost.*

4) *Visiting the area and trekking to villages is confined to the lowland area of Muang Sing, and one should be back in the guesthouse at 17.00 pm.*

5) *At 21.00 pm the guesthouse owners should advice their guests to go to sleep.*
6) *It is forbidden to bring any documents that oppose to the Buddhist religion.*
7) *It is forbidden to use, buy or sell any addictive drugs such as opium, heroine, marijuana or others. It is forbidden to secretly marry or secretly establish oneself in the district or to secretly cross official borders to other countries.*
8) *It is not allowed to use bicycles to get around in Sing District. Instead people should rice a tuke-tuke or pick-up truck.*

Too many tourists have been wandering out to the hill tribes and smoking that opium. Apparently an Englishman recently died in the process.

I track down Mr. Pun, who is twenty-five years old, self-taught in English, and quite ambitious. He was raised in Vientiane but has settled here and married a local girl. He's not aware of marijuana's being grown in this area, but his wife seems to think it is, so he wanders off down the street to ask around. He comes back and says he knows of a village. It's along the road west of town that leads to the upper Mekong, the border with Burma. A village of two hundred souls, made up of Tai Li, Tai Dam, and some recently arrived Hmong. We hop in Pun's flatbed van and drive out.

The first house we visit is the head man's, raised up on poles five feet off the hard-packed earth. An old woman goes inside and emerges with a blue plastic shopping bag that looks like it might contain a pound of pot, until I see how loose and dry this cannabis is.

Pun sternly says to me, "You can look at it, smell it, touch it, ask questions about it, take a picture of it, but you can't buy it or smoke it. That's illegal, and as a licensed guide, I can't allow you to do anything illegal."

Fine by me, as it looks even less appealing than the pot from Vientiane I've been smoking. It's last year's crop, mostly brittle brown leaf. At this time of year, April and May, the villagers are not farming any crop, but will soon be planting. For now they are occupied with timbering and with building or repairing their houses.

These villagers have been cultivating cannabis for a mere three years. It was brought by the recently arrived, relocated Hmong. "First they saw the Hmong grow it. 'May I have a little bit?'" Pun translates. "They like it. But it's not a cash crop for them. It's just for friends coming over, and to make the taste of soup better."

I'm warned to be careful in Lao restaurants. As in Cambodia, pot is often added to noodle soups to give flavor. So it's primarily an appetite enhancer? Yes. Do they ever feed it to cattle or other animals for that purpose, as is done in Nepal? No, it's too expensive for that. They plant in May, harvest six months later, or seven if they let the plants go to seed. In good soil the plants are three meters tall. The patriarch says something emphatically. "He says if the government allowed us to, we would grow big amounts. But it is illegal, so we only grow a little," Pun translates.

"Opium is illegal too," I say. "And people are growing it all over the place around here."

"Yes, but the people believe opium is a medicine given to them by their ancestors," Pun responds. "They believe the government has no right to stop what the ancestors have bestowed."

The ancestors have also bestowed Lao Lao, the local moonshine, and a bottle is produced, along with a dish called *paasam,* made with fish caught in the stream that runs below the village. It's salted and spiced, then packed raw into bamboo tubes for ten days.

"This is food you can never find in a restaurant, real food of Lao people," Pun tells me. I tell him we call that "home cooking" in English, and he repeats the phrase back to me several times over the course of the afternoon, just to make sure he's got it: "Lao home cooking, correct?" Correct.

Raw river fish sounds risky to me, even more so when I realize they haven't bothered to gut the little suckers. Raw heads, bones, organs, guts, and bladders, all to be eaten with the hands, along with some sticky rice. I choke the first mouthful down, only to discover it's actually pretty good. In this heat a body craves salt. In this heat Lao Lao hits the head pretty quick. After one sip the patriarch excuses himself to go bathe in the stream, but I'm expected to keep drinking with the two young men. The youngest is fourteen and more than ready to get shitfaced. So we do.

✳

Seven kilometers north of Muang Sing, near the Chinese border, is a guesthouse called Adima. Photocopied advertisements for it in town said, *We are not in the Lonely Planet yet . . . you better come before the rest of the world finds out about us.*

Right. And get the T-shirt: "I Helped Ruin Laos." I did buy the *Lonely Planet* guide to Laos—it was the only book in English I could find in Vientiane. Here's the guilt trip author Joe Cummings lays on the opiate seekers who trickle into Muang Sing:

"Opium is traditionally a condoned vice of the elderly, yet an increasing number of young people in the villages are now taking opium and even heroin . . . If you are tempted to experiment with a little 'O,' keep in mind the effect your behavior may have on the local sociocultural situation—you may smoke once and a few weeks later be hundreds of kilometres away while the villagers continue to face the temptation every day."

Does supplying the tourists turn more locals into junkies? Could be. Rather than selling the lot to Chinese traders, they have to keep more on hand for the foreigners, and they have to show the foreigners how to use those funny little long-stemmed pipes.

Although new, Adima feels like an old-style lodge from the colonial era. In the cool of the evening, while peasants trundle past on a path to the hill villages, we tourists relax on a terrace overlooking tethered water buffalo in the rice paddies. The beasts wear little wooden boxes around their necks as cowbells. The sound they make is a hollow *tap tap tap* like horse hooves on cobblestone.

With a Swiss woman, Natalie, as a companion, I head in the morning to the hills. In the very first village, a kid, all of eight years old, comes running out offering opium and *gansa*. I bite. Junior takes me home and pulls out a half dozen little half-ounce pink Baggies for me to examine on the porch. Nearby a man hand-planing a log for a house beam watches our transaction sullenly. I take one bag and give the kid 15,000 kip. Two bucks. There are some buds in there among the leaves, and although it's seed-laden there's at least an encouraging glint and shimmer of abundant resinous trichomes.

Natalie's already tired of waiting for me. "They resent us looking at them like animals in a zoo," she says of the villagers.

So we climb farther into the forested hills. The heat, the exertion, and a joint smoked Nepali style, in a hollowed-out cigarette, combine to make me momentarily dizzy. Then I feel that *whoooooosh* up the mental elevator to a blissful high, a high that the Vientiane pot has never properly delivered. Natalie doesn't smoke, but has nothing against it. Her brother in Switzerland is a pothead and grows it openly on his apartment balcony.

We walk the shaded jungle path along a ridge, and soon there are great bursts of raucous laughter in the distance. We hear the village before we can see it. And there's a party going on.

In the center of this dusty little village stands a big communal hut, open on one end, where the men have gathered. They drink Lao Lao and play cards. In the back a couple of guys are laid out on mats. One lifts his head, and with a spacey grin removes the opium pipe from his mouth and tilts it toward me with an offering gesture.

Natalie is very much against it. "You can see the consequences of it in the addicts, and I don't want to contribute to it," she says. "For us it's a lark, an experiment. For them it's a constant."

"You've been reading *Lonely Planet*."

As we leave the village three bare-breasted Akha tribes-women gesture for us to come over to their porch. The kids are all shouting "Sabadee!" (the Lao greeting) and "Opium, opium!" On the porch the women show us some beaded bracelets for sale, and offer opium, then one starts making gestures, pointing at herself and at me and rubbing two fingers together. Seems like sex is for sale. They are all three somewhere between thirty and fifty, but have not aged well. From my shallow, consumer-culture perspective, they have not an ounce of sex appeal. They're saggy-titted old broads.

"Just pretend you don't understand," Natalie suggests.

I try to make it clear I'm not interested. Then they offer a younger girl, a teenager in a T-shirt sitting alone on the far end of the porch. The girl keeps her head lowered. The ladies go back to offering opium. They can't believe we've come all this way for nothing.

"*Gansa?*" I ask.

They seem to have no idea what I'm saying. I pull out my little Baggie from village one to play show-and-tell. "*Gansa.* This is *gansa.*" I hand the bag to one of them.

She gets very excited, pulls a seed from it, and asks by gesture if she can have it. Of course she can. The three of them take turns going through the bag, digging and poking around with their rough peasant fingers until they've pulled out every last seed. They're all smiles. One makes a gesture of plants growing and points to me as if to say, "When they grow, you come back, I'll give you as much as you like."

Now isn't that odd? I'm supposed to be the journalist, making my pilgrimage to the tribespeople in the hills, studying and reporting on how they traditionally grow their cannabis, and instead I'm bringing it to them. Western culture intrudes once again. Cannabis got here first, Coca-Cola will be next.

✳

They were fighting a war on the outskirts of Phnom Penh as recently as 1997. Who? The Cambodian Army. And who else? The Cambodian Army. Makes it very tough to tell who's winning. Soldiers taking orders from commanders aligned with FUNCIPEC, a political party, were fighting soldiers taking orders from commanders aligned with the CPP, another political party. Now, three years later, the prime minister, Hun Sen, maintains a private security force of a thousand soldiers at his compound, just to be on the safe side. He's a former Khmer Rouge himself, running a country that has endured most of the last thirty years as a battleground, overseeing a population now made up of three kinds of people: those who watched as a quarter of the population was brutally exterminated, those who did the exterminating, and those who were born afterward.

How to explain the Khmer Rouge? They had a fantasy that a twentieth-century country could be returned to Eden. To them Eden was an insulated, self-sufficient classless agrarian Maoist peasant society. For forty-four months, beginning April 17, 1975, they had a chance to create their version of the perfect world. To get there they banned money, banned mail, banned newspapers, and killed two out of every seven citizens. Many of those who survived stayed alive by picking the corn out of each other's shit. Death from starvation was that close for millions.

After all they've been through, little wonder no one in Cambodia trusts anyone. You can feel it on the streets.

It's Saturday of the weekend of Khmer New Year. From the airport I hop on the back of a motorbike and take the six-dollar ride into the city. The place feels deserted. Decaying, rotting French colonial architecture and some socialist apartment blocks thrown up in the era after the Vietnamese liberated the place in 1979. Dust blowing in a dry wind. The smell of garbage. In the city center a giant piss-yellow art deco building like an upside-down colander, slatted to let the heat out, houses the central market. I'm headed for the north of town, where a string of guesthouses perch on stilts over a tiny lake called Boeng Kak.

My guesthouse has a long deck that stretches out over the lake, where a young American guy and a Nigerian are rolling joints and passing them around. Until very recently pot was legal in Cambodia. It was a drug for old people to smoke in the evenings or use in soups as an appetite enhancer. It was a weed. You could buy it in the market for a dollar a kilo. Thanks to American diplomatic pressure it was made illegal three years ago. And now that it's illegal it's worth something. The price is around seventy dollars a kilo in Phnom Penh, which means in three years cannabis has gone from worthless weed to the most profitable crop a farmer can grow. So everyone's growing it. Once again market forces have made a mockery of Prohibition.

The pot this American and Nigerian are sharing is very leafy, dry, and powdery. You need to smoke quite a bit to get high, but the high is light and heady. The American has just spent a week on a deserted island off Sihanhoukville in the Gulf of Thailand. Locals from a nearby island came by every day with fresh fish, fresh fruit, beer, bottled water, and pot. Unbelievable. The whole package for five bucks a day (only the beer was extra). The pot was a toss-in, on the house. It was on a par with this Phnom Penh pot, he says. The stuff we are smoking costs about five bucks an ounce, although the guys on the street ask ten from tourists, and often get it.

The American is planning to cross into Vietnam next. He's been there before, has even visited the Museum of American Atrocities in Saigon, now called Ho Chi Minh City. "Good to get another perspective on the things your country does," he says. I tell him I'm planning on taking a high-speed ferry up the Tonle Sap River to Siem Reap, the town nearest the legendary ruins of Angkor Wat and Angkor Thom. In the twelfth century Angkor Thom was the richest city in the world, center of the Khmer empire. After years of political instability Cambodia's ancient masterpiece has reopened to tourists.

"One of those speedboats was hijacked a few weeks back," the American says. "Thirty tourists were tied up and robbed."

"Not killed?" asks a white South African woman who's been listening to us.

"No, not killed."

"That's not so bad, then. That's nothing, really."

Apparently the carjackers of today's South Africa are not so merciful. A siege mentality now pervades the lives of the privileged whites of Johannesburg, and she's happy to be away from it.

"Turns out the speedboat hijackers were all students at a college here in Phnom Penh," says the American. "They were studying to work in the hospitality industry, believe it or not. The papers are saying the ringleader was the brightest student in the class, and he's still at large."

The South African insists I absolutely must include Africa on my world pot tour. "Durban Poison? The best!" she proclaims. She rattles off a few other strains she grew in her day in her backyard.

Now it's Gabby the Nigerian's turn to lobby for his homeland as an essential cannabis destination. Another African, Bembo, from Ghana, rolls out of a hammock near the water's edge and comes over to sit with us. "We have great pot in Ghana, too," he says. "But if you smoke it everyone knows about it, and you are ostracized in the community. You're shunned. It's like you're a murderer."

Gabby says it was the same for him in Nigeria. "When I tried to explain to my father that I like the way it makes me feel, that I don't think it's harmful, he just looked at me and said, 'You are not my son.' Many people smoke it, but often they do it secretly, so that not even their family knows."

✳

I feel bad about wasting my first day in Phnom Penh sitting in the shade talking to other foreigners. I'm nicely stoned, and itching for a little walkabout. Time to head to town and see how the Khmers celebrate New Year's.

Two hundred yards from the guesthouse I realize I have my passport and wallet in my shorts. Not good. But it's too oven-hot to want to walk back just to lock them in the dubious-looking wooden box at the guesthouse bar. Onward. In the first restaurant I pass the television is broadcasting a live outdoor holiday concert of Khmer pop music. It has a distinct plaintiveness—the voices of the singers rise and fall like plucked strings—but in some ways it's quite Westernized, slick.

It contrasts with this restaurant, where the owner is lying in his underwear on a patch of tiled floor below the television screen. He's staked out the coolest spot in the place. I order what everyone else is drinking: iced tea. They bring you the tea steaming hot in a chinese porcelain six-cup pot, with a glass of ice cubes. The tea melts nearly all the ice, and in doing so is made cold. Then you drink it quick before it gets warm, and when you finish the glass they bring more cubes.

When I tire of tea and TV and Khmers staring at me, I go over to the little counter where they make the tea. Six people converge to see what the foreigner's going to do. I pull out my wallet and show them some money. I have no idea what a pot of tea with all-you-can-melt ice cubes might be worth. All my money is in my hand, maybe 100,000 riel, which sounds like a lot, but is actually less than thirty bucks. But thirty bucks is enough that my little audience lets out this amazing collective gasp of shock. I've never heard six people collectively suck in their breath like that. It's the sound a crowd makes when someone falls off the high wire, and here they are making it at the sight of thirty bucks' worth of their money. The woman in charge is sweet and honest; so many Cambodians seem to be. They're good to foreigners—they just don't trust each other. I offer her a 5,000-riel note for the tea, figuring she'll make change. No. A 1,000-note? No. A couple of 200s? She takes one. Two hundred riel. Six American cents' worth of tea.

From there I wander toward the center of the city, still vaguely high but mostly just headachy from that pot I smoked at the guesthouse and the sugar I put in the iced tea. Farther into town the streets fill with people. They all seem to be wearing short-sleeved white shirts. Men and women, boys and girls, all in white shirts.

Under the shade trees around Wat Phnom, a huge Buddhist stupa on a hill near the river, the crowd is converging, seeking shelter from the sun. Kids are squirting water at each other with cheap water pistols and dousing each other with talcum powder from little plastic bottles. Part of the ritual of the water festival. In a crowd of thousands, I'm the only tourist. Some of the braver teenage boys douse me with talc powder. Once I'm baptized in this way it breaks the ice, and everyone else decides it's open season on the foreigner. It seems good-natured fun at first, but having talc powder ground into your cheeks on a stupefyingly hot day soon loses its appeal.

Rescue comes in the form of a local named Yophirun, who is capable of making the kind of menacing noises that cause Cambodian teenage boys to think twice. I get my new friend to teach me how to say "Happy New Year" in Khmer. I have it down cold in no time. Yophirun is twenty-four and desperate to practice his English, which is truly terrible. Hideous accent, near-zero vocabulary.

"Big cock," he says to me. "I show you big cock."

I follow him through the crowd to a garden on a slope facing south. The bushes form the shape of a clock face, and there's a working mechanism in the center to drive two arms fifteen feet long around the dial.

"Big clock," I correct him. "'Cock' is something else altogether."

Below us by a statue an elephant is causing the crowd to surge forward and back as its trainer struggles for control. I say to Yophirun, "Let's go look at the elephant."

On closer inspection the elephant looks sickly, with a ragged, sore-looking ear and a rope chafing a back ankle. On the other end of the rope twenty Khmers are preparing to battle in a tug-of-war with the beast. Someone yells, the Khmer for "One, two, three, heave!" They tug on the rope with all their might. The elephant's owner whips the flank of his two-ton slave. No contest. Let me tell you: an elephant is a powerful force.

In order to be a tugger in this war you need a string necklace with a number attached to it on a sheet of paper. Yophirun says the right things to the right people to get me one. "You!" is all he can say to me as he offers it. The rest is pantomime, a gesture to put on the number and take the rope. Why the hell not?

So I'm in there with the rest of the boys, sweating enough to soak through the layers of talc on my face, holding on to a big rope, and thinking, Hmmm, this is not good, my passport and wallet are in the front pocket of my saggy shorts and my hands are occupied elsewhere. Better cut this short before bad things happen to good people. Then they're yelling "Heave!" in Khmer and we all do as instructed.

We are winning! The elephant is being tugged backward against his will—and guess what? Elephants don't take kindly to that. The colossal beast turns and starts stomping toward us, and we drop the rope, scatter, and tumble, people are losing their sandals and tripping over each other, the elephant handler is screaming, the elephant is calmed before he's trampled anyone, and as the dust settles I'm checking my pockets and thinking, *In all that chaos some fucker had the presence of mind to pick my pocket.* Passport, credit cards, ID. It's all gone. I am an idiot.

Yophirun takes it even harder.

"I'm story, I'm story," he keeps repeating.

I don't even have the spirit to correct him. He's nearly crying. We keep checking the sidewalks and the trampled grass under the swirling crowd, hoping my stuff just fell out of its own accord and will be lying there waiting to be discovered, like a perfect little seashell on a sandy beach. As I'm circling around with my head down, obsessively scanning the earth between Khmer feet and legs, kids continue to soak me with talc powder and water, thinking it's hilarious. This is a party! Happy New Year!

We give up. Yophirun takes me to the fringes of the crowd, to a road where motorcycles weave their way between kids loading squirt guns in dirty puddles, to where some cops stand on the flatbed of a truck, watching the crowd. There is nothing they can do, of course, but it seems to me, just from their body language as Yophirun reports the crime, that they are taking pains to empha- size their indifference to the sad-sack tourist under the talcum- crusted hair. Some punks on a motorcycle whizz up, and one of them pitches a water balloon that explodes against my chest and showers me with dirty water. Not only does it hurt, but the act was clearly meant malevolently and is not at all in the spirit of holiday hijinks. The cop beside me checks himself to make sure no splat- tering muck landed on his crisp uniform. He says to Yophirun, "Tell him to report it on Monday to the tourist police. No, go Tues- day—Monday's a holiday."

At least I left some cash in my room at the guesthouse. With five bucks of it I buy an ounce of pot on the street outside, and pre- pare to wallow in my misfortune for a few days. But wallowing is difficult when others have it worse. Gabby the Nigerian is also without a passport, having just served three years in a Cambodian prison for drug smuggling. He's out of jail, but not free to leave the country. No passport, no exit. Stuck in godforsaken Cambo- dia. He seems defeated, without an idea to get enthused about or a plan to put faith in. The plan is more like a wish: get a passport, get to Thailand, get some money, get a ticket to Nigeria. That sounds highly improbable.

Bembo from Ghana saw similar troubles not too long ago. When he lost his passport in Phnom Penh, it took him a year to get a new one. In that year he found a job as a DJ at a radio sta- tion, then moved onward and upward to local television as a VJ, the cool black dude who introduced the hip-hop videos to Cam- bodian kids. He became a local celebrity, and rich too, making six grand U.S. a month organizing ravelike dance parties. Then the son of a major Cambodian politico, one of that class of people you just do not fuck with, announced that he was now Bembo's man- ager and would henceforth be entitled to 40 percent of everything

Bembo earned. Bembo chose instead to go into retirement, and is keeping a low profile, hiding out at the guesthouse, waiting for a visa to Japan. He's married to a Japanese tourist girl, and she's back in Japan, where she recently gave birth to an infant son he has never seen.

"The Japanese come here to smoke pot," he says. "Two weeks in Phnom Penh, and they don't do any of the tourist things—they don't go to Angkor, they don't want to see any killing fields—they just want to sit in their room, all day and all night, blowing clouds of smoke."

It drives Bembo crazy with exasperation that Gabby lacks the spirit to get off his ass and make things happen. Prison has done something to Gabby, not broken him exactly, but deflated him. Both in spirit and body. He keeps talking about how heavy and muscular he was when he went in. You sense that he had once been powerful, an arrogant son of a bitch. Now he's gaunt as a desert-dwelling ascetic, and reduced to mooching off tourists. He can tell you what he wants from life—a wife, children, and a decent, honest job. He just has no clue how to make it happen. "I'm sick of hustling" is as far as he has formalized his future.

The three of us nurse a few beers on the deck, and Bembo gives Gabby the now well-practiced lecture about how he, a fellow African who has known the same dire predicament of being exiled in corrupt, incomprehensible, rat-infested Phnom Penh, rose above it through sheer hard work and determination. But Gabby just wants to smoke another joint and feel sorry for himself.

To change the subject, he says to me, "Brian, how can we get Canadian girls to have sex?"

A couple of weeks back they met two girls at the guesthouse and had gone out for a night on the town in Bembo's little white Toyota. The girls had hot-boxed the car for them, rolling up the windows and chain-smoking fat reefers until the interior was white with smoke. "I never coughed so hard in my life," says Bembo. Gabby still thinks one of the girls was a junkie, but Bembo figures they were just messing around with opiates while on vacation in the Exotic East. Anyway, the girls were beautiful, but refused all attempts to bed them.

"We thought they were Australians at first," says Gabby. "We thought it was going to be easy."

"Be gentlemen" is my advice. "With the accent on 'gentle.'"

"I knew that. We were trying to act macho, tough," says Bembo. "By the time I figured out they thought that was bullshit, it was too late."

❋

Next morning I'm on the deck, stretched out in a hammock, rolling a spliff with the last of those glueless papers I got in Laos. Gabby appears, and I pass him the bag. He's got his own papers. We each roll one. It takes a full, fat one each to get high. We lie there in silence for a while. I turn to see if he's sleeping. No, just watching big swan-necked water lilies drifting across the lake.

To make conversation, I ask him, "What words of wisdom do you have for me?"

He smiles like a shy boy. First time I've seen that smile— his face is usually set tough. He takes a big breath, exhales slowly, thinking. Finally he says, "Faith in yourself is the only thing that can save you. Your faith in yourself, the faith of your friends, and your mother's faith. That's all."

We contemplate that in silence while the lilies drift by. It's noon. I've made up my mind to sit in the shade until four. Until then it'll be too damned scorching to be out in the sun.

"Hello, Brian."

I have to turn in my hammock to see who it is. It's Yophirun, face dripping sweat. His clothes are soaked too, like he's just run five miles in the heat.

"Hey. How are you?"

"Let's go meet my parents, right now."

"It's too hot right now. Maybe tonight."

"Let's go meet my parents, right now!"

"It's too hot, Yophirun. It's like a furnace out there."
"Let's go meet my parents, RIGHT NOW!"
"It's like fifty million degrees!"
"LET'S GO MEET MY PARENTS, RIGHT NOW!!!"

So I cave. He's borrowed a motorcycle to take me to his place. No helmets, of course. The apartment is just east of the center of town, on a broad, busy thoroughfare lined with identical four-story apartment blocks and businesses on the ground floor. The alley to the courtyard reeks of urine. There's piles of garbage rotting on the landings of the stairs.

The layout and quality of materials is typical Soviet housing. You enter the family apartment by a back door, beside the kitchen. The kitchen walls are black with soot. They're cooking with kerosene or some other stinky sooty fuel. There's only a small window for the smoke to escape through. Nasty. The rest of the apartment is one big room, with dark hardwood floors and high, pocked plaster walls. It's home sweet home to Yophirun, his parents, and two sisters, ten and fifteen. There's a little blackboard on one wall, with two sentences chalked on it: *Let's go meet my parents right now,* and *Don't forget me when you go in your country.* Haven't heard that one yet. But I'm certain it's coming.

Yophirun shows me his little desk in the corner, with its English grammar and two dictionaries. My shirt is soaked in sweat from the ride over and from climbing the three flights of stairs. I can feel sweat dripping down out of my hair and catching on my eyebrows. Yophirun's dad is lounging around in shorts and no shirt. Soon he'll put on a collared white shirt, blue pants, and black shoes and go back for the afternoon to his job managing an open-air market. He knows no English but can manage a few phrases in French. Those are soon exhausted. Well. Now what? The entire family watches me wipe the sweat from my eyebrows with the back of my hand. His dad asks him to ask me if I would like to take a shower. Yes I would.

The shower is attached to the kitchen. The walls are also utterly black, and there is no lightbulb. When I close the door I cannot see a thing. There is a little letter-slot-sized slit at eye level in the door, so I can look out and see the kitchen, but the black walls in here completely absorb the sliver of weak light that penetrates in through the slot. I take off my pants and shirt, then step out into the kitchen in my underwear to find a place to hang my pants. Fourteen bucks and no ID in the pants. I'm actually worried about the fourteen bucks. The fifteen-year-old sister is in the kitchen, alone. This is strange. She's squatting washing dishes in a tub of water on the floor, looking at me as if I am supposed to do something. Back in the shower, I hang my underwear up over the shower pipe, behind the nozzle, along with the tiny dish towel they've given me to dry myself with.

On this scorcher of a day the shower feels amazingly good. From overheated to goose bumps in twenty seconds. Then Yophirun is looking at me through the slit in the door, cackling like a maniac. I'm thinking it would be very easy for him to lock me in here. My high has worn off but left me paranoid. Bastard Cambodians killed two million Cambodians, some bastard Cambodian stole my passport, and maybe this bastard Cambodian is capable of locking me in here and murdering me for the fourteen bucks in my pants.

This moment of hysteria passes, thank God. Yophirun goes back to the front room, and I never do figure out why he cackled like a maniac. Is it because there is a light in the shower that I've failed to notice, and he thinks it hysterically funny that I'm showering in the pitch black? When I emerge from the shower in my underwear it's just the sister in the kitchen again, scrutinizing me as I put on my pants and shirt. Is she making eyes at me or is that my imagination? In the living room we all fail to have a conversation, but the mother seems nice, and the ten-year-old too. Kids are easier to relate to; you can just clown with them. I'm staring out the balcony door at one point, looking over the rail at the traffic on the street below, and Yophirun says, "Brian, would you give money for my sister?"

"No."

He seems surprised that I didn't even hesitate.

Yophirun's English is very bad. Did he mean the question innocently, begging for a small amount to buy her some school supplies or a computer lesson? Or was he offering his sister for sale? My abrupt answer means the subject gets dropped, and I'll never figure that one out. The parents don't seem like the kind who would agree to that kind of sleaze. But on the other hand Phnom Penh is the place for pedophiles these days. In a bar called Martinis, pretty much the most popular tourist dance club, I was offered a child for sex by a mother on a bar stool, her daughter, who looked twelve, maximum, leaning against her awkwardly with her elbows on her mother's knees. Mom claimed the shy, clinging kid was eighteen.

✳

Monday is a holiday, but it also happens to be the twenty-fifth anniversary of the Khmer Rouge takeover of Phnom Penh, and the papers are all trying to make sense of the horror. The *Phnom Penh Post* has asked Hun Sen for a quote suitable for the occasion. The prime minister's reply: "History remains history that cannot be changed." No one in power is interested in war-crime trials. Everyone in power today has seen and done horrible things to get ahead. The threat of justice might be enough for some warlord to take his army back to the bush, in effect declaring, "If I'm guilty, come and get me." And no one wants more blood spilled, even in the name of justice.

Peace. Peace is what is needed. Cambodians all tell you so. No one wants to stir up the barely stifled emotions created by unspeakable horrors witnessed and endured. Meanwhile the *Phnom Penh Post* lists the names of major Khmer Rouge criminals living at large: "Thiounn Theoun, the guy who may have been responsible for the order to evacuate Calmette Hospital of all its infirm patients on April 17, 1975, now shops at Lucky Market wearing a natty baseball cap and Day-Glo windbreaker.

"Keo Pak—a man steeped in blood—lives comfortably in Siem Reap, and blames others, notably Pol Pot, for all that went wrong.

"Others who pulled the trigger, followed orders willingly, or participated in sending up to a million souls to the thousands of killing fields all over the country, still give fright to the survivors who remember the details of the crimes they committed. Many of these aging monsters live side-by-side with the relatives of their victims."

When you're in Phnom Penh you have to go to S21, the elementary school in the heart of the city that was transformed by the "Pol Pot clique" into a torture prison. Thousands were tortured here before being sent to the killing field at Cheong Ek. The steel-frame beds and iron shackles are still in place. On the walls are poster-sized photos of bloated corpses strapped into these selfsame bed frames. The flesh of one prisoner's face appears eaten to the very skull by acid. I've been to Auschwitz and Birkenau, and those are bleak museums, but believe me, at S21 in the heart of Phnom Penh, you don't linger. You feel the torture as if it's still going on, you feel like something could happen in a heartbeat and they'll decide to lock you in.

That night I go to a sleazy bar full of pretty, dainty young Vietnamese whores, to meet up with Adam Parker, an Australian expat who publishes an irreverent local magazine called *Bayon Pearnik*. The most recent issue covered a staged-for-the-media marijuana bust east of Phnom Penh, designed to show the Americans and Japanese that the Cambodian government was dutifully toeing the line in the War on Drugs.

"The absurd thing was, the police were burning the stalks and stubble for the photo op, but very carefully putting as much of the high-grade buds as they could into the helicopters to take back to Phnom Penh," Parker tells me. "The cops thought it must be worth something if they were going to all this trouble to seize it, and tried to sell it back in town, but pretty much ended up giving kilos of it away."

✳

At the guesthouse I hear the story of a Kiwi—a New Zealander—who had lost his passport and fallen to pieces. When he reported it to the police, the cops picked up on his vulnerable emotional state, took him in a back room, yelled at him for a few hours, and made him cough up 200 bucks just to be allowed to leave the station. "But he was an idiot," I'm assured. I'm prepared for the worst, but on Tuesday morning at the tourist police my cop turns out to be a bureaucrat who, rather than trying to extort anything from me, just out and out begs. "Look, I make thirty dollars a month. I'm poor. I have a wife and two children. Can you please give me fifteen dollars to process your document? I have to split that with my boss, too."

"Sure, okay, whatever. You want it now?"

"No, no. Pay when you come back."

Fool.

When I go to my embassy, my passport, ID, and credit cards miraculously appear at the gate while I'm inside. My faith in humanity restored, I take back all the times I've linked the word "Cambodian" with "fucking" and "bastard" in my mind lately. But I leave town as soon as possible. On the speedboat upriver to Siem Reap next morning I remember I meant to go to a famous Phnom Penh landmark, Happy Herb's Pizza on Sisowath Quay. Ask for your pizza extra happy, and they pile on the pot. Oh well. Can't cover every base.

Turns out there's a Happy Herb's in Siem Reap anyway. The waiter asks me how happy I want to be.

"I wanna be able to walk home."

The little bits of leaf and bud are clearly visible in the melted cheese, but they don't give me even the slightest buzz. I spend an hour waiting for it, drinking beer in a bar around the corner called the Angkor What? The waitress, from New Zealand, insists to me that kung fu legend Bruce Lee died the first time he ever smoked hashish, because he had zero body fat to absorb the THC. Where do people get these crazy ideas? Another drinker down the bar claims Bruce Lee was a chronic hashish smoker, to control back pain from a lifetime of stunt injuries. That at least sounds plausible.

Later I go back to Happy Herb's to dis the potency of their product, and they give me a joint, which I smoke at a little patio table along the sidewalk, but it doesn't do much either. It gets me just light-headed enough to become sentimentally choked up at the loving, delicate way a father from the shop next door carries his son across the street. In that cradling, tender gesture, I feel hope for Cambodia. The child has seen no horrors. Let's pray it stays that way.

5 : AUSTRALIA

The first piece of graffiti I saw in Sydney said, "Karl Scully is a bludger."

It's for certain the Aussies have a distinct dialect. When an Australian says, "I gave him a serving," he doesn't mean cake and ice cream, he means roughly "I beat the crap out of him." Also, in everyday speech, many Australian males use the word "cunt" in any situation where we would say "person," or "guy," or "dude," or the suffixes "-body" or "-one." For example: "Some cunt phoned for you." "Anycunt could do that." "I gave the cunt a serving." Which is not to say all, or even most, Australians are louts. Loutish behavior is found among them, but mostly among the men who drink "piss" (what they call beer), not those who like pot.

In Sydney the people who like pot are well-hidden to the newly arrived tourist. The easiest place to buy marijuana is at the Amsterdam Cafe, a coffee shop off King's Cross, but the Amsterdam is the kind of place that makes you feel a little bit dirty and sleazy for taking part in something illegal. You go to the manager and set an Australian twenty-dollar bill on the permanently empty table he stands beside. He picks up the twenty and drops a tiny inch-square resealable Baggie containing a gram of grass onto the table. So you never directly pass anything hand to hand. And as far as getting any information out of this guy goes, if you're writing a book about pot you're shit out of luck.

"What kind is it?"

"Hydro."

"Okay. But what strain is it?"

"Look, you want it or not? You're asking too many questions, mate."

Here was evidence to confirm something I'd read by Australian hippie historian Neil Pike: "The psychedelic, sacramental dealing circles of the sixties have long ago been replaced by more commercial, well-oiled interests."

Did I want the pot or not? I did want it. It was your classic hydroponic commercial product. A chemical taste and a poor burner, a bit of a headache, but a powerful high. Stonger than anything I'd smoked since Nepal.

The Amsterdam Cafe is very cramped—claustrophobic or cozy, depending on your outlook. They'd applied that kind of black film on the windows that lets in some light but doesn't let any out. An all-very-clandestine feeling. People were rolling joints Australian style, mixing the pot with tobacco and using three papers when one would have done. Nearly every customer was male, everyone seemed slightly edgy about the whole exercise, and no one ever glanced at anyone else's table except for me.

If I felt shunned, I couldn't entirely blame people. In Cambodia I'd had a reaction to malaria medication and sunburn—after the five-hour ride on the roof of that speedboat up the Tonle Sap to Siem Reap, my bottom lip swelled up to three times its normal size and then split, cracked open, and refused to heal, so that by the time I hit Sydney a week later, from one corner of my mouth to the other it looked like a giant, oozing herpetic swamp. Who in their right mind would want to share a joint with Mr. Pus Lips?

"People who are in much hurry will not be served at the Amsterdam Cafe," said a sign on the wall. People are in much hurry in Sydney, because Sydney is essentially Americanized. Everyone drives too fast, reads too many fashion magazines, and talks incessantly into cell phones—they call them mobiles—in public places. The only thing I really liked about Sydney, apart from the ferries zipping around the harbor, were the giant bats that came out at dusk in the parks. There were surveillance cameras everywhere, all over town, in the parks and on street corners, freshly installed on the pretext of security for the Sydney Olympics. It was pointed out to me that the Jim Carrey movie *The Truman Show* was directed by an Australian.

"We're living the Truman Show."

✼

I hitchhiked along the Prince's Highway from Sydney to Melbourne. It took three days and two nights, through beautiful green rolling hills, thinly populated farmland, and a coastline of undeveloped, deserted sand beaches. Two thirds of the way I rode with Gypsy George, a beer-soaked Queensland prospector heading south to Tasmania to see an old flame. George drank and drove all day, every day, and it was so natural a state for him that he was no danger on the road. In fact, he was a good driver. He lives in his van with his dog, a Blue Heeler whose name was Shit for Brains, I kid you not. George yelled "I'll bash you!" at it a lot, and occasionally did. The dog seemed to love him anyway.

In his youth in the 1960s George had traveled in a nomadic boxing exhibition, playing small towns on weekends, fighting all comers, taking on up to ten locals a night, five dollars a fight. He told me a bludger is a lazy cunt who does fuck-all. Wanting to educate me further into the mysteries of Australian English, he told me, "You're on the wallaby." That meant I was wandering around.

While he drove I rolled him cigarettes from a pouch of White Ox tobacco and he outlined the various conspiracy theories to which he wholeheartedly subscribed. The Port Arthur mass murder, in which thirty people were gunned down? It wasn't the act of a madman, as the papers would have you believe. The Australian government's own secret service had been ordered to carry out that atrocity, because the politicians wanted to increase public support for gun control, in order to take guns out of the hands of citizens and make it easier to impose a dictatorship. "Fucking power-crazed cunts are capable of anything!"

Thanks to Gypsy George I had an entree into the world of redneck small-town Australia, because we stopped for a schooner of VB in every bar along the road. Draft beer comes in two sizes, a middy and a schooner, and VB is short for a brand called Victoria Bitter. In a town called Orbust I listened to a local barfly mutter ominously how he was burning with the urge to take his truck up a nearby hillside and crush under his wheels all the aboriginals who lived up there. A bunch of stoic-looking white Aussies listened and gave tight-lipped nods of approval. Scary, or as the Aussies would say, *sceeery*.

George had been a small-time outdoor cannabis grower himself for many years in Queensland. His herb of choice had been something called Sumatran Tripping Grass, a legendary strain originating on the Indonesian island of Sumatra. Then he forgot to grow seed one year. Although on that occasion he'd been "a fuckwit," he considered himself something of an expert on pot. I told George my plan: I'd eventually be heading to the annual Mardi Grass celebration in the town of Nimbin, a big music and cultural festival that is also Australia's largest cannabis law reform rally. "The Nimbin hippies made money and built grass palaces," he told me. A grass palace is a house paid for with the profit from growing commercial quantities of pot. "They were hippies; now they're middle-class," George continued. "And their kids don't share the hippie ideals. Then some cunt in Sydney had the bright idea that the hippies might get tired of smoking their own shit all the time, and they might like the hammer."

"The hammer?"

"Heroin."

"Goddamn it, everywhere I go people want to clutter up my pot story with opium or heroin or speed or something!"

Soon I'd be adding nutmeg to that list. In Melbourne I split the purchase of a half-ounce of pot with a young stoner named Spliff and his raver friend Damien, whose favorite drug experimentation story featured a two-day coma and a near-death experience overdosing on that common kitchen spice. Whatever happened to good old ganja?

✳

The answer, in a word, is Nimbin, the epicenter of Australian cannabis culture. A quiet little town with a population of 700, it's tucked away in the foothills of subtropical rain-forest parkland in the Northern Rivers district of New South Wales. I hitch into town and get dropped off along the single commercial street, and find myself in a hippie time warp. The strip of storefronts, restaurants, and coffee bars is decorated with sixties-style psychedelic murals. The sidewalks are Old West–style wooden boardwalks, and on benches and stools along them, stretching and coming to life in the early morning sun, lounges an odd collection of aboriginals, neo-hippies, "ferals" (back-to-the-land types who have reverted to a semiwild state of nature, indicated usually by matted dreadlocks, permanent deep sunburns, and unkempt hippie garb), and even a few small-townish-looking regular folk. Some of these people are smoking joints quite openly in public. No furtiveness, no fear, no fuss.

"The police attitude is, Okay, we've got hippies in Australia," one Nimbinite will tell me. "But to attack them in Nimbin is like putting poison down a drainpipe—the cockroaches will scatter everywhere. Sometimes it's better just to leave things alone." Not that the police have always taken that hands-off approach. They put poison down the drainpipe for years, but the cockroaches of Nimbin didn't scatter, and didn't die.

The Nimbin HEMP Embassy (HEMP in this case is an acronym for Help End Marijuana Prohibition) is the most prominent building on the main drag. It's part meeting hall, part office space, part head shop. Tucked in one corner is the HempBar, a recently opened coffee shop run on the Dutch model: a friendly place to buy a cappuccino and a joint of (hopefully) consistent quality.

The HempBar is where I've arranged to meet Gary John Gray, who will turn out to be my host and guide to the complicated interwoven network of cliques and freaks that make up the Nimbin cannabis community. Gary is nearly forty and in a previous decade was a hot young car salesman in Dallas, where his Australian accent, along with his gift of gab, paid dividends. He made big money, but most of it he snorted up his nose in the form of cocaine. Now he's a born-again hippie, a pot purist, with a full red beard and Jesus hair, and a little too much hubris when it comes to how unwashed and ragged he allows his Salvation Army thrift store clothes to get. They're meant to externally represent his inner rejection of materialism. But bragging about it negates the ascetic effect.

Apart from that, Gary's great, and days and hours spent with him in the HempBar are times of great happiness for me. Unlike in Nepal or Southeast Asia, here I can just sit on my ass, get baked on fine weed, and let the story come to me, in the form of locals and tourists wandering in for a doob and a chat. Sometimes stories can be found right on the very walls. Two newspaper clippings from the *Manly Daily,* for example. In the first a little old lady complains that thieves keep stealing segments of her garden hose to make homemade bongs. In the second a Nimbinite, a former member of the HEMP Embassy named Binna Powell, proclaims, "Bong use is dopey." That's the headline, anyway. "Bong use was proven in causing lung diseases including emphysema because unlike tobacco smoking the technique uses a person's entire lung capacity," states Powell.

Next door to the HempBar, a character named Rob with long black hair and a nasal voice seems to run the HEMP Embassy, controlling the purse strings in a way I'll never exactly understand. "I'm really glad that Gary's done so much for the cause, but I wish the Embassy could get behind his Big Bong thing more," Rob tells me one day. Gary has a website called the Big Bong Burger Bar whose goal is to franchise pot restaurants in the shape of a giant bong. "But we can't because of the health risks of bongs, the dangers of getting water in the lungs."

Gary's reaction: "There are differences of opinion in this movement, but when they crop up you can't take it personally. We're not doing this for the gratification of our own egos—we're doing this because innocent people are being wrongfully put in jail."

Gary and his girlfriend, Paris, are very harried the week of Mardi Grass, busy pulling together a webcam network to send live streaming video of the latest edition of the annual Cannabis Reform Rally around the world on the Internet via a couple of computers on the counter of the HempBar, all the while keeping up a running conversation with the real flesh-and-blood noncyber patrons who wander in off the street for a cappuccino, a joint, or a space cookie. Looking after their needs is a short semitoothless fellow who has legally changed his name to Dave Cannabis. Most people called him Cannabis Dave. "I think a name should reflect who you are," he says by way of explanation. Regarding space cookies, his advice is the same to every potential customer: "Eat half, wait half an hour, see how you feel. There is such a thing as too much of a good thing."

*

If bongs are dangerous because they can overload the lungs, I think chillums are even worse. Cannabis Dave hauls out a chillum regularly and stuffs it with his namesake biomass. After a massive sucking intake, he looks like a cartoon teakettle about to blow, holding his breath as long as possible before disgorging a cloud of smoke huge and heavy enough to show up on a satellite weather shot. Then comes a massive body-racking fit of hacking and coughing. You'd think poor Dave is tubercular or something. One time he hands the chillum to Paris, who takes a long hoot and overinhales, as is so easy to do with bong or chillum. She doubles over, spits out a panicky cloud of smoke, and coughs for five minutes straight, I swear, her face turning red as a beet. "I think I burnt my lungs," she says, when she can finally speak.

"All that hideous hacking suggests to me that chillum lung burn is not healthy," I say.

"It's not really coughing, it's lung aerobics," suggests Dave through his handlebar mustache. "To exercise your lungs, cough regularly."

Paris says, "No more of that. I'm off chillums. I really think I hurt myself."

I like Paris a lot. She has long straight black hair, wears jeans and men's shirts, and has a smooth yet weathered, wise, noble face, like those iconic photos of 1930s Dust Bowl mothers. She has three kids under the age of fourteen, and is raising them in the countryside with proper values. Articulate, TV-free, bareback horse-riding outdoorsy Huck Finn types all three, they are very refreshing to see.

Paris takes a hand sometimes in giving a proper education to other people's kids too. She tells me, "Whenever I see a small child terrorizing their mother in a supermarket or somewhere, if I can get them out of sight of the mother, I like to take them by the shoulders, look them straight in the eye, and say, 'Listen, you be nice to your mom! I can always tell the little girls or boys who aren't nice to their mom by how tired the mom looks, and your mom looks very tired. You think your mom was put on earth to take care of you, but it's you who was put on earth to take care of your mom.'"

"Wow. What do the kids do?"

"They get real wide-eyed and scared. And they hurry back to their mother." She laughs. "I think they get the message."

There's a sign prominently displayed in the front window at the HEMP Embassy. It's titled "BEFORE YOU GET BUSTED." It reads, *Be aware that in New South Wales it is an offence to possess even one seed or leaf of cannabis. This includes cookies. Don't get casual. HARSH PENALTIES APPLY!*

I ask Gary what exactly the penalties are in New South Wales. Gary sends me to Rob at the HEMP Embassy. "There's a cautionary system up until fifteen grams now, but the police aren't trained in it," Rob says. "Any more than that, it really depends on the magistrate. One woman in another district recently got a twelve-hundred-dollar fine and a criminal record for four plants. Here the magistrate is more likely to give you a twenty-dollar fine and a discharge."

Many Australian politicians have confessed to smoking marijuana in their youth, and several have admitted they still smoke occasionally. With role models like this, it's not surprising that possession has been decriminalized in practice in many parts of the country. In the state of South Australia, for example, penalties for possession of up to ten plants for personal consumption are less than what you get for driving ten miles an hour over the speed limit. On the other hand the state of Queensland, a mere hour's drive north of Nimbin, is noted for corrupt, brutal, redneck cops, stiff penalties for possession, and American-style zero tolerance. Flipping through old newspapers one day in the HempBar, I come across an article that says Queensland undercover cops will soon be granted legal permission to take illegal drugs while working undercover, so as to "retain the confidence of criminals," as the newspaper put it.

"They'll be allowed to take them, but will they be allowed to *enjoy* them?" Gary asks.

One afternoon in the HempBar a new friend named Jab, a wiry ball of energy with an elfin face and a tiny goatee gathered in a braided point, comes rushing to the couch in the back corner where I'm trying to decide if I have ever been as high in my life from THC alone. I think it was the cookies. Although I'm passing up bongs and chillums, I keep losing track of how many cookies I've munched. And I never turn down an offered joint. At times this makes me incapable of speech. Jab opens a wrapping of white tissue paper under a reading lamp near my lolling head, and cackles excitedly. "Look at these little lovelies! From seed to flower in six weeks!"

These buds are the gooiest, most resin-soaked things I've ever seen, and they stink. A whiff of them carries me back to the Lemon Pledge my mother used to polish the coffee table I crawled under when I was a kid.

"What are they?"

"Tasmanian Tiger."

"What's the genetic heritage of that?"

"In Auckland it was called New Zealand Green," Jab says. "It was a local name for a strain that had once been called Thai Buddha, then went to Hawaii for a while and came back with the name Hawaiian Head. Then I took some seeds to Tasmania and got someone to grow these for me outdoors in a sunny little microclimate there. And now they're back! My little beauties are back!"

※

The story of Nimbin, the great citadel of cannabis culture Down Under, really begins with Graeme Dunstan. Graeme is a gray-beard, an elder, and a lifelong political activist. Before introducing us, Gary said of him, "Did you know he once dove under LBJ's car?"

In 1966 Lyndon Baines Johnson, thirty-sixth President of the United States of America, and first ever to visit Australia, arrived Down Under to drum up support for the Vietnam War. During the motorcade in Sydney, Graeme and several other hippie peacenik activists slipped from the crowd lining the street and zipped under the front bumper of LBJ's limo. Hard to believe, but the cops merely dragged them out from under and threw them back into the crowd, whereupon they immediately made another dash for the limo. Graeme managed to slip past the cops and crawl under the car three times in all.

It would take six years and five hundred dead soldiers before Australia disengaged from Vietnam. "That LBJ action was a turning point in popular resistance," Graeme told me. "We were the generation who turned our backs on the Cold War and made friends with Asia. I still meet people who were there under LBJ's car with me, or know someone who was there. But mostly it is another moment forgotten. Many heroes are dead and forgotten. Just to be alive is a victory!"

※

With the end of the war Dunstan and other radicals in the Australian Union of Students, in the spirit of the times, felt that some kind of ecology-based pacifist communitarianism was the logical alternative to greed-based corporate capitalism. Graeme was the creative force behind the Aquarius Festival, a celebration of war's end that was intended to pull the radical peace movement out of the cities and transplant the seeds of the counterculture back to the land. The first festival was in 1973, and Nimbin was chosen as the site pretty much by chance. At that time it was a stagnant farming town, crippled by the Australian dairy industry's loss of traditional British markets to the European Economic Community.

Australian hippies flocked to Nimbin for the annual Aquarius festivals, and many stayed on, joining communes, intentional communities, and various other alternative-lifestyle groups that sprang up in the area. To this day Nimbin continues to attract the kind of people who flee corporate conformity for a chance to reinvent themselves.

Some get pretty damn creative about it—for example, Judy Canales, founder of the Star Earth Tribe. At the same bunkhouse where I've found a bed for Mardi Grass, Judy's staying for a week, to be close to town for the festival. Crinkly-eyed and dreamy-smiley-stoned, she's at the computer in my dormitory-style room when I wake up on the first morning. "Don't mind me, I'm just writing the labels for cannabis cookies," she says. "Does this sound right? *Dosage: no more than one cookie or one part cookie every two hours. Warning: overdose will not cause death but overintoxication may induce paranoia.*"

Judy was living in Melbourne in 1991 when she made headlines: "Yoga teacher on drug charges." She'd been busted for selling pot. "My lawyer told me, 'The law says you are guilty, so the only way to regain your innocence is to change the law.' I said, 'Right. I'm closing up shop, I'm moving to Nimbin, and I'm going to form a religion.'"

So began the Star Earth Tribe. They own a big acreage about six miles from town, where they grow "yarndi"—she uses the aboriginal word for cannabis. "We're not hiding it at all," she says. "We grow it quite openly, for spiritual use. I show it to the cops. 'Here it is!' It's a bit wild at the moment, but it's good. It just *grows.*" Cannabis is, after all, a weed, and despite millennia of domestication by man, it goes back to happy, thriving weedhood as soon as it's set free from human constraints.

An incomplete copy of the Star Earth Tribe's official handbook is lying around the bunkhouse. I sneak peeks at it.

> The sanctuary is where we learn to live together as a family, to share and not to judge, to communicate without dominating, to offer without expecting, to enjoy, to create with love and to learn self-reliance and the importance of patience. The basics of Tribal and Wild Lifestyle living is expressed in the Buddhist meditation:
> Before enlightenment, chop wood, carry water.
> After enlightenment, chop wood, carry water.

The Star Earth Tribe seems to consist of Judy, her lover, Diego; Judy's twenty-six-year-old son, Paul; his partner, Lisa; and their infant daughter. They're all in town for Mardi Grass. They also need to be near a phone, because they're taking care of the details of renting their lands to a promoter from Sydney, who's going to put on an outdoor "doof" on the Saturday night of Mardi Grass weekend. (A doof is Australian for a rave, as in "You know: *doof, doof, doof doof doof-doof-doofdoofdoofdoof . . .*")

An outdoor doof on the Star Earth Tribe's lands is not without serious potential consequences. Paul tells me that the last time they allowed a rave to be put on, it took two years for the owls to come back. "They'll eat, but not nest anywhere near. They remember."

He's sitting on our bunkhouse porch in the morning sun rolling a big joint with some of the tribe's semiwild organic pot buds. I'm rolling some pot that Gary gave me, mixing it with tobacco and repacking a filter cigarette, Nepalese style.

"What are you smoking that thing with five thousand chemicals in it for?" Paul spits.

I explain I like having a filter.

"But you don't know what it's made of. Could be fiberglass. Breathing in fiberglass is one of the worst things you can do."

Meanwhile his mother is on the phone to the promoter, and getting quite exasperated.

"You're just throwing a party, and that's the difference," she insists. "It's not just a party with us. The money we make has a purpose." They plan to donate their rent to fight uranium mining in northern Australia. "Now, another thing. For fifty thousand years the only people who went to our land were elders," she's shouting into the phone. "Real elders. So it's a sacred space. So we've got to do a ceremony before, to tell all the aboriginal spirits to go to sleep or to go away and come back in a few days. Some of them will take years to come back, but—" She's been interrupted, but of course we can't hear the other half of the conversation. Only her response: "Last time we had a doof, they did a ceremony to let the light in, and we were left with the aftermath. All kinds of demons tried to come in."

She hangs up and comes out to the sunlight to report the deal that's being offered: the promoter wants the first $4,000 of the gate to cover costs, and will split anything beyond that fifty-fifty. The Star Earth Tribe goes into a four-adult group hug, chanting a long deep "Om," while the baby cries and stands unsteadily by, clutching her mom's pant leg. When they break apart consensus is quickly established: they will agree to terms.

Judy has seen Nimbin through years of struggle against police harassment, the era in which helicopters regularly buzzed low over the communes in the surrounding countryside. A turning point came in 1997 when a bunch of hippies chained themselves to the police helicopter overnight. The Australian press and public largely agreed with the protesters' assertion that this chopperful of gung ho cops on overtime was a waste of taxpayers' money.

The Australian press is also largely sympathetic to Mardi Grass. The festival presents marijuana as the centerpiece of a weekend of harmless fun. Judy has been part of making Mardi Grass fun from the start. A few years back she attempted a costume of caked-on mud, along the lines of a Papua New Guinea tribesperson look. "The mud was moist and thick when I applied it," she remembers. "But then it all dried out and cracked and fell off, so that I was naked and faintly orange. The HEMP Embassy took a picture of me and turned it into a postcard. I pleaded with them, 'Please, if you make it a postcard put what I was chanting on it, so that people know it was a spiritual ritual, and not just some old broad with floppy tits,'" she says, laughing.

It's impossible not to like her, although she says many people have a hard time looking her in the eye. Must be people who have something to hide, because her gaze feels open and accepting to me.

"Nimbin's okay," she says. "There used to be more of a culture of abundance here, and in Nimbin that meant you could arrive and fifteen minutes later it was 'Here's a joint, here's some food, need a place to crash?' But in the last few years that has changed. The younger kids coming in have this attitude that you have to take care of yourself first, you can't just give. But people only do the wrong thing when they're brokenhearted. You just show them the love. A lot of people need to learn that God isn't some magical fairy flying around in the sky. God is responsibility, and it emanates from inside you."

✳

On the Friday before Mardi Grass weekend really kicks into gear I go for a schooner or two of VB at the Lawn Bowling Club, the last bastion of old-guard, nonhippie, nonalternative Nimbin citizenry. The club will be serving breakfast, lunch, and dinner to nonmembers over the weekend, and the barman is on the phone to Sydney, trying to figure out how to program a new debit card swiper so that they can dispense cash to the masses. "It's the big festival—the Mardi Grass is on this weekend," he bellows into the phone. A pause. "No no, it isn't gay and lesbian. This is 'Smoke some dope and go full on!'"

The Mardi Grass isn't all partying, though. On Saturday seminars are presented, one by a local doctor, David Helliwell, regarding a proposal to open police-sanctioned Amsterdam-style coffeehouses. That's essentially what the HempBar is, but it operates without official approval, following the axiom that if you're creating something new that the authorities can't fathom, it's usually easier to beg forgiveness after the fact than beg permission before.

Another seminar highlights the nascent Australian industrial hemp business. The speaker, Dr. Andrew Katelaris, came to Nimbin three years ago preaching hemp, and received a cool reception from the local guerrilla growers, who worried about potential pollination of their budding females by hemp males. This time Katelaris gets a big laugh when he mentions that he has produced five hundred kilos of hemp seed, making him the second-largest cannabis grower in Australia, "after the New South Wales Police." Later Katelaris tells me, "I'm for the legalization of marijuana, not just hemp. But the people who will not profit from legalization of pot in Australia are the big commercial growers. Most big growers are organized crime and the corrupt element of the police." Commercial pot growers contribute nothing to movements to legalize it. The Nimbin Mardi Grass is funded and staged by a ragtag collective of activists.

Katelaris looks and acts the part of a yuppie, which essentially he is, being a medical doctor by profession. It's funny to wander through Mardi Grass with him. He's besieged by ferals bumming change. "The Australian media will come here, they won't show up for any of the seminars, they'll find the weirdest-pierced hippie, take his picture, and that'll be Mardi Grass," he says, sighing. He's been inspired to say this because a top-notch candidate for weirdest-pierced hippie has just walked by: a dread-locked feral with each earlobe stretched grotesquely to accommodate a black film canister.

✳

For Mardi Grass the price of pot doubles, and triples, as local dealers make their yearly killing. Wandering waitresses hawk cookies and space cakes: five dollars for tourists, two dollars for locals. To my untrained eye it seems that sleepy little Nimbin had transmogrified into Tribal Central for freaky ferals. But to certain more discerning Australians subtle differences divide the genuine ferals from the posers. I assume everyone in dreads and rough wool sweaters and tie-dyed hemp skirts is living the hippie life, but I get reeducated at the dance club in the community hall. As dancers give their bodies over to the sensual ambient dub beats, I mention to Jab and his girlfriend, Dorothy, how much I admire a certain striking woman's crown of tremendously elaborate cascading dreadlocks. Dorothy assures me the woman is a Sydney upper-crust yuppie who has laid down anywhere up to 2,000 bucks at one of the trendiest urban hair salons to get that "just crawled outta the tepee an' pulled these golden dreads togetha" look to take to Mardi Grass. Funny how much money some people are willing to spend for a look that's meant to say they don't care what they look like.

Ferals and posers alike are conspicuously absent at the seed swap on Sunday afternoon in Peace Park, an event for people in jeans and Bluntstone boots, with honest dirt under their fingernails. Sellers display their strains in little piles of ten-seed zip-lock Baggies, a card taped in front of each pile supplying consumer information. For example:

White Skunk Seed
height: 2 m
yield: 3–600 grams
time to maturity: 3 months or better
fragrance: don't plant too close to road
other comments: aim to maturity around christmas

The strains divide into three categories. First, seedbank seeds, where the parental strain is entirely known. Second, the next generation of seedbank seeds, where consistency is not guaranteed. Third, the "Lucky Dip," where one or more parental strains are not known. Australian varieties for sale are few and far between.

"Jimna. That would be an Australian mix," one seed breeder tells me. It's the only local strain on the table. "It's not really genetically traceable now, though. Just this is good, that was good, let's cross 'em. I have some other sativas I'm not selling today. People want those because they're established, they've had two hundred years in Australia and they're used to the soil and climate. You bring in these new strains—"

He's interrupted by a customer. "I want a short-termer. And I've got Kush, enough to swap. What do you got?"

"Lots of things. And I wouldn't mind Kush. A nice, spreading plant." And so it goes. Genetics are spread and shared by humankind's apparently insatiable desire for improvement. I ask around after Gypsy George's Sumatran Tripping Grass, but no one has seen it for years.

✳

During Mardi Grass, Nimbin's two-man detachment of the New South Wales police makes only one arrest for marijuana possession. Hearing that, a HempBar customer says, "He must have been pushing a wheelbarrow of it down the street."

"Maybe it was that guy with the twenty-inch bud sticking out like a feather from his cap," Cannabis Dave suggests.

A local grower takes me for a little drive. He parks the car out of sight of the road and we climb over a farmer's fence, then walk to where a curving line of trees marks a lowland stream carving its way through hay fields. Hidden at the bottom of a steep ten-foot bank, in a sunny gap between the water-loving, willowlike trees, a single, perfect, flowering female cannabis plant awaits. One solitary plant, where my grower friend six months ago planted ten seedlings.

"Cows knocked down five, a couple never grew, a couple were male—this is my only survivor," he says. He means at this particular spot, this secluded plot on a neighbor's farm. No worries, mate—he has plenty more successful patches elsewhere. Splashing through the stream in rubber boots, we reach the prize, appraise it, and gave thanks for this small miracle. "The growing experts would say it's too early to pick it, I should wait until all the big leaves turn yellow and fall off, but it looks good, no mold, looks healthy to me," he says.

One solid tug at the base and the whole four-foot plant, roots and all, comes free, to be carried, its long conelike buds making it look like a five-pronged pitchfork, briskly back to our vehicle and laid out behind us in the backseat.

"A little gift from nature. Might get three ounces of bud off of it. Six hundred dollars. Considering I never once had to water her—the stream took care of that—it's easy money."

✳

On the Saturday of Mardi Grass Gary takes me down to a temporary workshop near the river, where Graeme Dunstan and a handful of volunteers work to produce the banners and giant puppets that will be carried in Sunday's Cannabis Law Reform rally and parade. The Nimbin organizational style is very loose and flexible, as befitting a bunch of stoners. When the parade reaches Peace Park for the rally, Graeme is scheduled to be the final speaker; that much has been ascertained. He and his helpers take a break and we smoke a joint around a table that is in fact a gleaming stainless-steel drum from a discarded washing machine (they make durable, attractive, *found* patio furniture). Gary suggests Graeme end the rally with a call for a group hug, and Graeme, powerful little fireplug of a man, shudders, then explodes. "I don't want to be hugged, I want to be *heard!*"

We're all silent a moment. "Right, then. No group hug on Sunday," Gary says. "How do you want to end the rally, then?"

"I'm going to invoke the Eureka Stockade," Graeme says. "Link it to our Cannabist Internationale, to the Freedom Ride, to peacebus.com."

The Eureka Stockade was a turning point in the history of Australian democracy. In 1854, in reaction to British colonial brutality and corruption, 150 miners on the Ballarat goldfields built themselves a stockade, ran up their own flag, and declared independence. They were quickly, mercilessly slaughtered by British troops. To this day the martyrs to the cause of freedom who gave their lives at Eureka are evoked by Australians of the extreme left and right.

✳

The next day dawns cold and wet, but in the afternoon the rains hold off long enough to let the parade pass, although the green field called Peace Park has turned to muddy slop in places. Estimates of the crowd vary from four to seven thousand people. Closer to four, I'd say. A series of speakers make the usual rousing metaphorical calls to arms.

"Go home, pull out a joint, and show it to your mom, show it to your boss, show it to the cops, say, 'This is marijuana, I smoke it and I'm normal!'"

An aboriginal elder: "Smoking yarndi is much better than drinking for our kids. They get into much less trouble."

Key Mardi Grass organizer Michael Balderstone: "Let's tell our elected officials what we want. We should be able to grow at home!" A big cheer from the crowd. "We should be able to grow for medicine!" Another rousing cheer. "We should get rid of the black market in pot!" No cheer. Are there too many growers and dealers in the crowd for whom the inflated black market makes pot profitable? Balderstone continues on undaunted. "How do we do it? In coffeeshops like they do in Amsterdam! It separates the pot from the powders."

Then it's Graeme Dunstan's turn. Dressed in a T-shirt that replicates the blue and white Southern Cross pattern of the flag of the Eureka Stockade, he begins softly: "I want you to look into your heart, and go to those sad and frightened places we all have, and think of the prisoners of the drug war, locked away in inhumane jails, far from their friends and family . . . " By the end he is bellowing: "Our government has been subverted by the United States and their hysterical drug laws. We are now a penal colony of the United States! Remember Eureka. That's where Australia begins. That's where we said no to tyranny. It's time to say no to this new tyranny! THE WAR ON DRUGS IS NOT OVER UNTIL THE PRISONERS ARE RELEASED!"

There is applause, of course, but the crowd is not galvanized. The weekend hippies are already thinking about packing up and heading back to their urban lives. The doof out at the Star Earth Tribe's land went on all night last night (Judy is thrilled with the large turnout), and many of the younger crowd, having used speed or ecstasy to stay up until morning, have skipped the marijuana rally and crashed. For those awake and alert, Peace Park must now be hurriedly reconverted to an obstacle course for the finals of the Growers Ironperson competition of the weekend's Hemp Olympix, which involves among other things lugging a hundred-pound sack of fertilizer over hay bales and crawling on hands and knees in a leech-infested tunnel through a low, prickly, ground-cover jungle plant called lantana. "Here's another hydro boy who thinks he can carry a bag of fert! Good on ya!" shouts the announcer as the sun breaks out, and a shirtless young Australian pot grower awaits the starter's signal. Graeme's quiet moment of reflection for the prisoners of the war on cannabis is forgotten in the excitement of cheering the lad on.

As I walk back up toward town, the Cannabus passes by, a big old hippie bus with huge sloppy rainbows and an Eden of pot plants painted on the sides. Jab is at the wheel, and yells for me to climb aboard, without stopping, merely slowing the bus to a walking pace. I clamber in his driver's side door, somehow snaking up and over him to fall into the back as he steers his way through the thinning crowd.

"Where are we going?"

"The first-ever Cannabist Internationale," elfin little Jab shouts gleefully. "You are about to be part of history!"

So I've been kidnapped. Off we go over gravel roads and potholed country tracks into the rain forest of the Nmbnjee Free State, a 300-acre property collectively owned by thirty shareholders, about twenty of whom have built houses and cleared small fields against the ever-encroaching forest. Nmbnjee is an Eden, where paddymelons—cute little pint-sized cousins of the kangaroos and wallabies—play in the gardens, wild turkeys wander in the woods, and—okay, it's not Eden after all—leeches crawl up your shoes and down your socks and suck the blood from your ankles and toes. You've gotta be on guard against those little suckers, the best defense being a cigarette lighter to burn them off your shoe before they reach your sock. Without flame they are unkillable, unsquishable; you can mash them into the floorboards with a heavy boot, then watch amazed as they reconstitute themselves into slimy little inchworms, rearing up on one blobby end while wriggling the other around looking for some succulent piece of ankle to latch on to. And they are everywhere in the dank common house in the center of Nmbnjee, where the historic first-ever Cannabist Internationale unfolds somewhat as the universe does— without logic, without order, but as it should.

The Cannabist Internationale is Graeme, Paris, and Gary's baby, a webcast global linkup of cannabis reform activists and a plenary session for the Australian Cannabis Law Reform Movement's plan to take the Cannabus and any other running vehicle whose owner they can persuade, inspire, or cajole to join them on the road for a tour of New South Wales jails, blasting a message of hope to the victims of the war on cannabis imprisoned inside— like the trumpets of Joshua outside the walls of Jericho, as Graeme puts it. At times his eyes grow as wild and fiery as an Old Testament prophet's.

Earlier in the week, Gary mused about who might commit to the Internationale: "As the crowds arrive for Mardi Grass over the next couple of days, you'll see how many people actually care about cannabis law reform in this country," he'd said. "There won't be twenty of us. But that's more than Lenin and Trotsky had at their meetings. At the Communist Internationale in 1901 there were thirty people. By 1905 they almost won Russia, and in 1917 they did win it. They were trying to change a country—we're only trying to change *one law.*"

Gary and Paris have been inspired of late by reading Trotsky's autobiography. "He was a permanent revolutionary," Paris tells me. "A tireless pamphleteer, getting the word out."

"I was talking to Andrew Katelaris about it," says Gary. "How we were planning on invoking the spirit of Gandhi and Trotsky as our role models. He was saying, 'Gandhi with a gun?' And I said no, "'No, Trotsky with a dove.'"

And so is born the slogan of the first Cannabist Internationale: "Not Gandhi with a gun, Trotsky with a dove."

As Graeme frets about the need to give the meeting some meaningful structure, nothing seems to be getting done the first night except the smoking of huge quantities of marijuana. From his unkempt garden Gary harvests some of his "Struggle Bud." That's his pet name for plants left untended to fend for themselves. Three small, pungent cones have managed to flower, and are duly placed on the vent on the back of his computer monitor, the only source of warm air. In the subtropical climate of Nimbin, there is no problem growing cannabis plants, but drying them before mold can take hold is another matter. With the decline of dairying, this part of the country has seen the rain forest creep back down the hills to clog the meadows, and seen weather patterns change in a single generation. A typical summer used to be dry and sunny. Lately it's more likely to be dismal and showery.

The rain pelts down all night, and next morning everything is soaked. "I bet there's an air of doom and gloom in Nimbin town today," Gary says. "People spent a long night in a wet tent. They'll be looking in their pockets and realizing they're out of buds and out of money. The junkies will be saying they didn't make as much money as last year dealing pot to out-of-towners, and one lucky fuckwit will be bragging, 'I sold *ounces* and *ounces*.'"

The rain clouds break and the forest rings with the bizarre call-and-response song of the whip bird, so named because it sounds like a whip cracking. People start arriving from town, and eventually the delegates of the first Cannabist Internationale reach twenty in number, not counting a few checking in from cyberspace. As mist swirls out of the forest, Graeme tells a tale from the Eureka Stockade about the dog of a fallen revolutionary who followed the cart that carried his master's corpse all the way to the graveyard. The brave little terrier howled, inconsolably, for days afterward on the grave. "Before Eureka, Australia was a penal colony," he says. "And now, with the War on Drugs, we're in danger of becoming one again. This is the most Australian thing we can do—make a stand."

Everyone who has come has a chance to speak. There's Nigel Free Marijuana, who like Cannabis Dave has legally changed his name, and who has suffered for his activism. He tells of being anally raped on two occasions by the Queensland police. An older Queenslander, a longtime activist, speaks bitterly of the "franchising of drugs" in that state, "done by the police with impunity in return for ignoring the graft and corruption of politicians." A very quiet young girl from a small town in Victoria state complains, "Pot's gone missing where I live. You can't find it anymore. The only thing left for kids is heroin, and it's killing people." Although Gypsy George had been right about Nimbin having a junkie problem, at least in Nimbin pot is an option. In most other Australian towns heroin is much easier to come by. By police estimates there are three hundred thousand heroin addicts in Australia, and to keep that many people hooked takes a well-entrenched supply network.

The Cannabist Internationale has a modest agenda: to make plans for the Freedom Ride, a two-month tour of a hippie convoy, intended to shake the walls of every New South Wales jail. Jab puts forward a resolution. "Be it agreed, we need petrol." The Cannabus cannot run on righteousness alone. "And media," he adds. "We're the circus—people just need to know we're coming. We're poised on the edge of a big adventure, poised on the edge of a break-through for freedom!" Then it seems as if his enthusiasm is already beginning to wane, and he says softly, more to himself than the rest of us, "Forever fucking poised."

✳

In Melbourne I bought a book called *Marijuana: A Grower's Lot*. The book is written in Australian. Here's a sample: "If you've planted out in Spring (say October) then their sex won't show up till February when you'll be cursing because half of your plants will be male and you'll have to pull the cunts out." Here's another: "The main reason to grow marijuana is to make money. The next reason is to enjoy smoking it. And the next reason is to get satis-faction from the thought that you are fucking the system." And another: "When the spirit overtakes you then you will fucking know about it. Before I went to gaol I had never experienced it and I didn't believe all this spirit, religious, and psychic stuff. But, fuck me, I sure did experience it in gaol and I've been experiencing it ever since. It is good and helps you lead a more meaningful life."

The author of this book is named Kog. He is a farmer, a lover of old Triumph motorcycles, and lives with his wife and four kids on top of a hill an hour west of Nimbin. I visited him there. He picked me up in Kyogle, a cattle town that looks straight out of 1950s America. It feels like the anti-Nimbin. On the way we passed the Kyogle Lawn Bowlers at play, all dressed in white against their bowling green, looking just like the white cranes that everywhere stand in fields beside the cattle.

Beautiful bright green parrots flew wild in the thickets below Kog's hilltop farmhouse. There was something mystical about this place. In the distance you could see the National Forest, where long ago his father and grandfather pulled out giant red cedar using bullock teams. We sat outdoors on a damp afternoon and eventually lit a fire in the firepit. Nearby Kog had built a little shrine for his father and surrounded it with red cedar saplings. He offered me homemade beer in mugs he made in prison while serving time for growing marijuana. He had a bushy beard and wore an odd hat that looked like a magic mushroom cap, or a ten-gallon hat with the brim cut away.

"So Brian," he asked me, "is writing this book of yours the most important thing you've ever done in your life?"

In the beginning this book had almost seemed a lark, this golden gift from God and the American publishing industry. Go forth and discover, behold, inhale, *taste* the world and the very finest weed it can offer. Pure pleasure. But by the time Kog and I sat staring into this hilltop fire, I'd met so many people like him, whose love of marijuana had brought them persecution, and imprisonment, that I understood I owed these people something.

His wife, Mary-Anne, brought the kids home from school. Mary-Anne is a descendent of Peter Lalor, one of the martyrs of the Eureka Stockade. She went into the house to make supper while the kids talked to us around the fire. After supper Kog and I went out to his shed, where he kept his three old hard-ridden Triumph motorcycles. We drank more beer, from those big prison-made mugs that held a full liter. Then he pulled out a bag of his homegrown pot and we smoked some of that. It was very fine. Sitting in ragged old discarded easy chairs, staring at the oil-stained garage floor, we said nothing at all for about ten minutes. We both liked to smoke that way—feeling the high, not having to waste words. I felt hypersensitive to noise, hearing a tremendous sizzling sound in my ears that seemed to come in from the land outside and inhabit my mind. It was a hissing, as in the reeds by a riverbank in the dark of night. I have never had an out-of-body experience, but I felt in that moment that I knew what it would feel like. I felt something of a power beyond everyday life. I could feel my body become extremely frightened, and go rigid, even as my mind stayed unafraid. A very strange sensation.

Kog stood up and said, "Did you feel something, Brian?"

I said I had.

He took off his shirt. Tattooed on his torso he had a perfect, detailed replica of a biker's black leather vest, complete with badges and insignia. Front, back, and sides. Someday he will die and his buried corpse will lie rotting in the ground, and he will still be a biker. When the flesh dissolves there will still be bone and ink. I felt the rigidity that had been gripping my body race up into my skull and explode in release out the top of my head. It was the most amazing thing I have ever felt.

The strangest part was, next morning everything seemed completely ordinary again. The farm was just a farm. Kog was just a quiet farmer. He drove me back over to Nimbin, and in the hour it took we barely spoke.

6 : ENGLAND

On the train to Norwich two little boys, four and six, dressed in plastic miniversions of the chest armor and helmets of Roman centurions, chase each other up and down the aisle, slicing the air recklessly with their plastic swords. Their mother calls them back to their seats.

"I want to tell you something very interesting about Norwich," she says. "It's a very rich part of the world because they have a lot of sheep. And in Norwich they have more churches than pubs, rather than most places, which have more pubs than churches."

"How *many* pubs, Mum?" asks the four-year-old.

It's true about Norwich having more churches than pubs. On any given Sunday, however, most churches lure only a scattering of worshipers to break the tomblike gloom. The English, and Europeans in general, spent the last half of the twentieth century deciding that dogmatic traditional religion is irrelevant to their lives. But lately one tiny new denomination has sprouted in the City of Churches: the Universal Church of the Holy and Sacred Herb, known by the acronym UCHASH, which its members pronounce "You See Hash."

Jack and Tina are pillars of the Norwich UCHASH congregation. They're a couple in their fifties, and have the look and lifestyle of urban hillbillies. I could imagine them being very much at home in some ramshackle Appalachian cabin surrounded by rusting, abandoned cars, but unfortunately for them their ancestors stayed in Britain and made do, accommodating their urge to accumulate clutter to the compressed domain of cramped row houses. Jack is tall and gaunt, with a sharp-cut angular face that looks chiseled out of hardwood. Tina is short, round, doughy, friendly, and squinty-eyed through big lenses. They live in tiny houses crammed so full of junk there's no place left to sit. They are kindhearted people, happy enough with their own level of squalor. I felt anal about being uncomfortable with their cleanliness level.

Jack has been to court many times for cannabis offenses, and he always tells the magistrate that the plant is part of his cosmology and religion. His love of cannabis goes hand in hand with his love of God and Christ. For some years he was writing to the Anglican Bishop of Norwich, trying to get some discussion going about these religious beliefs. No answer. Finally he and some like-minded followers formed UCHASH, and announced in a press release that they would gather on a certain day at the Cloisters, a little green area on the grounds of Norwich Cathedral, where they would smoke a chillum, an act they consider their sacrament. They hoped that the Bishop would be cajoled by public interest in the matter to at least come out and talk to them.

What happened to Jack instead was eerily reminiscent of what his Lord and Savior went through two millennia ago. Thirteen people sat in a circle: Jack, ten followers, and two undercover policewomen. "I looked into the eyes of one of them," Jack remembers. "And I knew she would betray me just as Judas betrayed Christ." Outside the circle uniformed cops and some print and television reporters had gathered. A chillum loaded with tobacco and hashish was produced without anyone being sure where it came from. It was lit, and had started its passage around the circle when the two traitors made some small gesture, like sniffer dogs have been trained to do, as a signal for the soldiers of the state to move in, cut short the ritual act of religious defiance, and let begin the long process of determining proper punishment. Everyone was searched. Jack and one other person were arrested for possession of small amounts of hashish. The media ate it up. It was all over the local television news that night, and front page next morning.

From then on the Universal Church of the Holy and Sacred Herb became known to exist, in the sense that nothing exists until people acknowledge it does, and these days being on television qualifies as proof of existence. Members began to write down principles. One source of inspiration was a book called *Wisdom for the Healing of Nations,* by Dr. Henry Whiteside. Jack gave me a copy. The book is a Christian's attempt to defend the use of cannabis and naturally occurring plant hallucinogens, such as magic mushrooms and peyote, as valuable tools in the quest to fully understand God, Christ, and our role in the universe. Use of these plants and a great deal of meditation have enabled Whiteside to reach a mental condition where he feels imbued with something he calls the lovelight. "The lovelight is a continual source of joy and hope for the future. It gives an understanding of life and meaning to its tragedies. I can assure you that the overall experience of life is better as a religious one. This is a difficult concept to get over to previous wild-party loving friends who just see me as having become serious and boring."

I'm not a Christian myself, but I liked many parts of the book, especially this passage:

"If you want to change the world, you must change human consciousness, beginning with your own.

If you look into a mirror and see that you are ugly, what good does it do you to blame the mirror and smash it?

Why then do you blame sacred plants when they show you what's inside you isn't as it should be? Work on yourself—don't just throw away the mirror so you don't have to see how ugly you are."

Much of the book is hopeful in a way the godless cynic in me finds hard to swallow. Whiteside believes humankind will replace alcohol with cannabis, that our "diet of putrefying dead animal flesh" will give way to "pure organically grown, unrefined vegetable matter," and that these changes will allow us to "return to a state of consciousness we knew in Paradise."

Dream on, dreamer.

✳

Jack and Tina and I take a trip in their old Volvo, to the country-side around Norwich for some genealogical detective work. They're looking for St. Peter's Neatishead, a rural church in whose yard Jack's great-aunt lies buried. We eventually find a pretty stone church on a site that has been used for religious purposes at least since an abbey was founded there in 1020. You walk through a little avenue of lime trees, one each for thirteen local men killed in World War I, plus an extra fourteenth, either to keep it symmetrical or to avoid the unlucky number thirteen—no one knows for sure anymore.

The unlocked church smells musty inside. We sign the guestbook and Jack says, "This truly feels like a place of sanctuary." It's his dream to reclaim some idle, unused, neglected churches in the depopulated countryside and open them as shelters for vulnerable refugees, young and old, from the cities, get people back on the land for some healing.

On the drive back to town through fields of sugar beets and tall corn, I ask Jack how many members the Universal Church of the Holy and Sacred Herb has.

"That's hard to say. You don't have to be a Christian. We have some Muslims, a couple are pagans."

"If you believe in God and believe cannabis is a God-given plant, you're part of our church," says Tina. "Everyone believes in God on some level."

"Yeah, all God is is the word 'G-o-d,'" adds Jack. "It's what you believe God to be. God is wonderful, magnificent, creator, destroyer, father, mother. And under the influence of cannabis you have a base to begin with. 'This is something from God.' You then consider what God is from that."

The Church of the Holy and Sacred Herb finds comfort in the scriptures, particularly Genesis 1:11, wherein on day three of creation God said, Let the earth bring forth grass, the herb yielding seed, and saw that it was good. Therefore God gave humankind cannabis, and three days later, on day six, He said, I have given every green herb for meat, and behold, it was very good. Apart from this fairly literal interpretation of the biblical metaphor of creation, the church seems to have little other codifiable dogma. "In our church there's no regimentation, no dressing up," Jack says. "Unless you want to. There's none of the dogma—"

"—or the pomp and ceremony of organized churches," Tina finishes his sentence.

"So is there any consistent ceremony at all? What do you do when you get together?"

"Well, there is a ceremony of smoking a chillum, which we do in honor of the sadhu of India," Jack says. "They are the only religious organization that have a right to use it. From time immemorial they have been exempt from any prohibition. So in honor of them we create a circle, and the chillum is passed between the members and smoked in a certain way—usually touched to the forehead, but however you want to: to the forehead first, or to the mouth first—and the smoke from the cannabis is like a prayer, like incense is conceived as a prayer being sent up to heaven, with all that that symbolizes."

"For us to set fire to cannabis is an offering," says Tina.

*

Fungus Grows on Your Collected Dickens.

That's a line of graffiti not far from the flat where I stayed, near Elephant and Castle in South London. Elephant and Castle may sound like the name of a cozy British pub, but in fact it's a congested traffic circle, a clamorous roundabout of merging diesel trucks, fume-belching double-decker buses, and speeding tinny little cars, all converging beneath a bunch of postwar architectural disasters of steel and glass. Who knew that buildings intended to be huge and optimistically gleaming could end up looking so very shabby coated with soot fifty years later. In the middle is a sad old shopping mall with a Woolworth and some dreary 1950s Formica restaurants, nearly deserted. The crowds are outside, sparking some liveliness in a Caribbean-flavored market that's grown up like a shantytown against the gray mall walls, a labyrinth of stalls selling cheap Lycra and jeans, scored to a cacophony of rap, dancehall, and reggae on competing boom boxes. A little bit of Third World chaos washed up on England's sterile northern shore.

At the Museum of London, which by the way has a lovely herb garden in its courtyard (where it is noted, "In the Middle Ages and up until the early eighteenth century, the number of kitchen garden plants commonly grown [in England] varied between 50 and 100. Today it is between 25 and 40." So cannabis isn't the only helpful herb we've lost knowledge of), I bought some books, and the plastic bag they gave me quoted Samuel Johnson: *When a man is tired of London, he is tired of life.* I guess I was tired of life, because London depressed me immediately, what can I say? The odor of stale urine everywhere. When I complained about it, a woman in a bar told me that in her high-rise apartment building with a fabulous view looking north at Westminster, Big Ben, and all that, the ride up in the elevator is almost unbearable because so many yobs piss in it. The sidewalks around Oxford Circus are overlaid with litter from Burger King, McDonald's, and KFC, and no one seems to give a shit. Britain buys into this pathetic clingy celebration of its heritage of Empire and Importance, while burger wrappers and leftover fries get mashed into the sidewalks, drunks piss in the subways, and fungus grows on their collected Dickens.

✳

At one time London, like Amsterdam, was a city of canals, and some of these waterways survive, lined by footpaths winding along out of sight away from the choking streets. I was introduced to the canals by Chris Sanders, a cannabis activist who is one of the main organizers of the annual May Day Is Jay Day march in London. Chris met me at a food store called Tony's Hemp Corner near King's Cross and we walked from there to his flat in Camden Town alongside the tranquil canal, its sides lined in places by long, slim, low-to-the-water houseboats.

As we walked he told me about the latest May Day cannabis legalization march, which had started from Kennington Park, pulled fifteen thousand people into the streets, ended with a big party in Brockwell Park in Brixton, and garnered absolutely zero coverage in London's thirteen daily papers. Meanwhile a demonstration by two hundred anarchists around the same time made front-page news, and was the source of outraged analysis for weeks afterward, because the punks smashed a McDonald's window and made the floor all messy with ketchup and mustard. So this is The Gospel According to Modern Media: Peaceful protest by large numbers is boring. Violence by a handful is fascinating. Jack and Tina should have smashed some stained glass at Norwich Cathedral—their story would have gone national. I pity Christ when he comes back. A new Sermon on the Mount will be lucky to make page 48, unless Mary Magdalene comes back too and this time parades around topless. Maybe she could join the Spice Girls.

✳

I'd missed London's May Day march because I was in Australia for Nimbin's Mardi Grass. I scheduled my trip to England for another event, in early August: the annual Smokey Bear's Picnic in Portsmouth. My temporary roommate in London was Russell Cronin, a former cannabis activist I'd met on the Internet. Russell very graciously put me up and put up with me for days and weeks while I bitched about London and we got addicted to the television phenomenon *Big Brother* together. Russell and his girlfriend, Katie, and I took the train from Waterloo Station down to the south coast town of Portsmouth on a rainy Sunday in August.

We walked through the city of Portsmouth out to Southsea Common, a huge grassy plain along the bay, expecting to see

hundreds or even thousands of protesters. Instead we saw a handful of people outnumbered by fifty members of the Hampshire
Constabulary. The police all wore blue Victorian bobby helmets
and yellow Day-Glo raincoats; odd that they should be dressed
more colorfully than the pot proponents, who were mostly in drab
blacks or browns. The cops also seemed happier. "A nice bit of
double bubble for the Bill, herding potheads around," said one
observer. "Double bubble" means overtime pay just for standing
in the park on a Sunday afternoon, and "the Bill" (or "the Old Bill")
is what the English call the cops. The Bill was out in force.

A few of them actually had to work: they'd brought in a
sniffer dog from the London transit system, and an officer was
leading the canine through the scattered crowd, which slowly grew
in numbers but never amounted to more than two hundred drizzle-
dampened souls. Dutiful doggie (a Labrador cross) took short
sniffs of the pant legs of those standing, and of the backs and shoulders and knees and elbows of those sitting on the ground. By some
indecipherable gesture the canine would indicate to the handler
when it detected something illicit, the handler would say, "This
one," and four seriously professional cops would move in to escort
that unlucky person off the Common to a line of waiting police vans.

The Hampshire Constabulary had brought its own PR person, a middle-aged American woman who was telling members of
the press like me that the dog was so highly trained it could tell if
a person had ingested any illegal substance in the last forty-eight
hours, which was absurd, and I think she knew it. She had a press
release which said in part, "No application has been made by the
organizers to the Portsmouth City Council for use of the area this
year. Consequently, a police presence will be necessary again to
deal with any infringements of local bylaws and the criminal law."

No arrests were being made, it seemed, not even of one
grizzled, gray-haired old hippie who came back from the vans
crowing, "I've got loads of blow down my bollocks!" The year previous, dozens of possession charges had been laid. In England,
when you are charged with possession of cannabis for personal

use you can accept a caution the first time, which is like a simple fine. The caution system is meant to keep courts unclogged from all these time-consuming piddling little pot cases. Last year all the Smokey Bear attendees who were charged demanded their trial, tying up the Portsmouth courts with dozens of cases and straining the budget of the local justice system. The police apparently had been ordered not to charge people with possession this year.

No one was smoking marijuana openly, but some were smoking various herbal concoctions designed to cost the police even more money in forensic analysis. So it was an absurd pantomime: people were pretending to smoke dope and the police were pretending to arrest them. The constabulary also had a couple of officers videotaping the proceedings, and the organizers were ready for that: they were handing out leaflets headed, "Employ Big Brother to make a video of the Smokey Bear's Picnic!" Under the British Data Protection Act, anyone filmed by a police camera has a right to a copy of the tape. People were demanding the address to apply for their free copy.

A cluster of locals tried to start a sing-along of "Skin up, Pompii, Pompii, Skin Up . . . ," some variation of the song of the local Portsmouth football club. "Skin up" is how the English say "Roll a joint." Someone held a placard that read, "The Pigs Smoke It, Royalty Smoke It, Professionals Smoke It." The police made him cross out "Pigs," but he only did it with a single line, so that the word was still visible. So they made him tear up the sign. The only real arrest came when an officer wearing a toupee of a color not found in nature waded in to take part in the removal of yet another dog-indicated drug fiend. Someone said, "Is that a wig you're wearing? If it is I know where you can buy a decent one."

Another cop stepped forward and grabbed the smart-ass. This was the only moment of the day when things threatened to get ugly. The cop had him by the collar, eyeball to eyeball, and declared his intention to arrest and charge him under Section 5 of the Public Order Act. "It is an offense to cause alarm, distress or harassment to another person of sound mind" in England, according to someone in the crowd. That apparently covers making fun of a cop's tacky toupee.

But the charge, which the police defined later as "insulting words and behavior," was being laid by another officer, not the one with the nasty lid, who never said a word. The arresting cop "must be a mind reader, able to tell when his mate is 'alarmed or distressed,'" one of the event's organizers commented as the joker allowed himself to be peacefully led away. "It's ludicrous. Almost as ludicrous as last year, when they arrested someone for wearing a T-shirt with an obscene slogan: 'Fuck War.'"

Then the rains started to come down hard, and Russell, Katie, and I headed over to the little tourist boardwalk by the shore to find a pub. There were cotton candy and fish and chip stands, and rides for children, including a rocket ship called the American Simulator and some other time-waster called Virtual Reality. The big neon sign said, "It Will Blow Your Mind!"

"Isn't that illegal?" asked Russell.

*

"Foreward ever backward never!, Yes rude bwoy! This is the original cockney yardie telling you how to grow the best ganja, and all in the environment of your council flat, To make you know seh, 'A nuh nutting, any bad bwoy can do it, Anyway hold tight rude bwoy, Build up a bighead spliff and relax and settle cos we're going on a journey, A journey to agriculture, A journey from the seed to the root to the rizla,' So hold tight! Aaaal rude gal buckle up! Rude bwoy show dem seh you have the remedy!"

That's the foreword to a small book by Will Rogers called *Council Flat Paradise*. One evening Will took me to Brixton, where we walked past a rich white kid yelling into his cell phone, "It's fucking scary down here!" Will thought that was pretty pathetic, and he was also a little insulted by it. Then we walked past the big black crack dealers the kid found scary. They can tell pretty quickly who's a crackhead and who isn't, and they're not interested in the ones who aren't. I asked Will, "How come I see lots of black people in the streets and stores around Elephant and Castle, they seem to be like thirty, forty percent of the population, but I never see them in the pubs?"

He said, "When you see all the fine cars they drive, you know black people around here have a lot of money. One thing we don't do is waste it in a place like a pub." He was also down on coke and heroin as wastes of money. "Who would be stupid enough to want to become a junkie?" he asked.

"It's been glamorized for half a century now," I said. "William S. Burroughs, then Keith Richards and all the rock stars. Not to mention *Trainspotting.*"

"Keith Richards always had the money. Heroin is only a problem when you can't afford it," said Will.

✳

From *Council Flat Paradise:*

"It seems that this is such an appealing bush that many people are seeking to find out where it is and take it for themselves. The London police want it so much that they even use helicopters to 'buzz' nearly all council flats, looking to see if people are growing it in their frontrooms, bedrooms, balconies, bathrooms (etc) and then theres the neighbours who feel like doing a good turn to the police by telling them about your plants (dodgy!!) and of course theres the people who have spotted it by the shape or some other reason and are probably right now waiting for you to go out so that they can break into your home and steal all your plants. Yes we do have a lot of problems."

Under those conditions, my biggest problem would be paranoia.

We sat in a Brixton restaurant/bar, full of slickly dressed black people whose sense of what's chic made me feel like the Grunge yokel, but that's okay, that's pretty much who I am, so why fight it? Will talked about why he wrote his book: "People think it's all about dope, legalizing dope so people can get stoned, but it's not only about that. It's about to not let the government have that power over people's bodies. To have our own power over our own bodies, because they say you can't take drugs. It's a fight for freedom using ganja as a vehicle, and a nice vehicle it is as well; it's a good ride."

He's working on a new edition. Britain has come a long way in the decade since the first one was published. One of the reasons he wrote it was to stop people from smoking the leaves.

"They were that stupid?" I asked. But I knew the answer. I was that stupid in 1988, the only time I ever tried to grow my own pot. "People would be planting seeds they got from God knows where, and halfway through the summer they start picking them off and smoking those green leaves, wondering why it gives them a headache," said Will. "If you smoke the leaves the plant never matures, because those are the solar panels that power the buds."

✳

Cannabis in Britain at the dawn of the twenty-first century is all about skunk or soap bar. All high-quality fragrant cannabis buds are called Skunk, regardless of whether or not they are related to the Skunk strains developed in Holland, like Sensi Seed Bank's perennial best-seller Skunk Number One. Sue Arnold, a columnist for the newspaper *The Independent,* has an eye condition alleviated only by cannabis. Because she has an upper-crust accent, she is taken seriously, and is allowed on television to say things like, "I must have Skunk! Only Skunk will do!"

So good-quality locally grown weed—all of it called skunk—is available in England. That's the good news. The bad news is that most people don't know anyone who grows or even sells it, and end up buying Moroccan hashish that, upon arrival in England, is diluted with God knows what—cooking oil, animal tranquilizers, and other extremely unhealthy crap. It's called soap bar. Chris

Sanders and the coalition that organizes the May march issued a Public Health Warning under the heading, "Soap bar is a product of prohibition."

It stated that soap bar "contains many harmful substances and very little real cannabis. We advise all cannabis users to stop purchasing this substance for the sake of their health. We also call on the government to immediately lift the ban on growing cannabis so that those who wish to use it either for recreational or medical purposes may do so without risk to their health or freedom."

Chris is forty-five years old. A childhood spent suffering from a severe milk allergy that went undiagnosed has left him looking unhealthy, and the fact that he spends most of his life in front of a computer isn't helping either. He has never tried heroin in his life, but it is his curse to look like a junkie and have no interest in being one. To live on the West Side of London in a posh neighborhood (his son, at five, once saw Diana, Princess of Wales, crying by herself in the street) and look like a poor wretched junkie is to invite harassment by the police. In high-rent neighborhoods it's a cop's job to keep beggars and addicts moving along. Chris got so sick of being stopped and asked for identification that he went to the nearest police station with a poster for the notice board: a photo of himself above a note that said, "This is Chris Sanders of such and such street and phone number. He knows no criminals, engages in no criminal activity. Would you please quit stopping him on the street and asking to see identification?"

It actually worked, although lately a rookie or two has needed to be educated.

Why do British people put up with this crappy soap bar? Chris says, "The main reason they buy it is because it's cheap and widely available. It's also addictive—animal tranquilizer, that is. I know people who prefer soap to anything else—they must be addicts!"

In Norwich I had sampled some soap bar, but only a taste in the midst of better stuff, so although I couldn't form a clear impression of the psychotropic effect, I understood at least where the name came from. It actually comes in bars that look like brown bars of soap, but with an oily look, translucent almost, as if there's petroleum in the mix.

⚹

In March 2000 a report called "Drugs and The Law" from the Police Foundation, an independent think tank that included two police chiefs, recommended that cannabis be rescheduled in Britain from a Class B to a Class C drug. The report suggested that first-time cannabis offenders receive a formal warning and repeat offenders fines of up to 500 pounds. But it urged lenient treatment for people growing cannabis plants for personal use and said the law should be changed immediately to allow people to smoke the drug for medicinal purposes.

The reaction from Tony Blair's office: "The Prime Minister believes that whilst it is right that the greatest harm is done by hard drugs, it would send the worst possible signal if we were to soften our laws in the way being suggested."

Then in October, at a conference of Britain's major opposition party, the Conservatives, shadow home secretary Ann Widdecombe caught her party and the nation off-guard by pleading for tough new 100-pound-on-the-spot fines, carrying a criminal record, for users of drugs, including cannabis. There was an instant backlash, and Widdecombe became a laughingstock in the British dailies for wanting to criminalize a sixth of the population. Even the police union attacked her. In the fallout seven senior Tories admitted to cannabis use at university, and the leader of Britain's Liberal Democratic Party, Charles Kennedy, called for legalization of cannabis.

So even the Conservative power elites have had to fess up and admit they got high in college. I don't believe even the most hopelessly straight nerd could have attended university in England at any time between 1966 and the present and not been to at least one party where marijuana was smoked. British prime minister Tony Blair was apparently a political careerist who, even as a youngster at Oxford, and even while playing in a rock band called the Ugly Rumours, seems to have lived in terror of committing any "illicit" acts that might, decades later, turn into the kind of ugly rumors that could undermine his perceived fitness for leadership.

If even the police appear to be hip to the idea that legalization of cannabis would reduce crime, why aren't the politicians? It's been suggested by British commentators that the "nerd factor" does play a role: politics attracts a certain kind of person, generally one more cautious and worried about consequences and public image than the rest of us. In many ways this is good, as it protects against political recklessness, but in other cases it's bad, as it results in legislative paralysis and lack of courage.

✳

Tony's Hemp Corner on Caledonian Street near King's Cross Station is the unlikely, unheralded epicenter of cannabis as a beneficial resource, as food and medicine, in England. When Tony bought the health shop seven years ago, he weighed nineteen stone, a stone being the English equivalent of fourteen pounds. Nineteen stone is 266 pounds. "I got depressed about my weight, so I started drinking," he remembers. "And I kept getting fatter. Then a guy came into the shop and said try these hemp seeds, and he gave me a piece of really nice weed as well in a pipe, and then Free Rob Cannabis [a British cannabis activist who, like Dave in Australia, has legally changed his name] came in a few days later and gave me some more free weed and some seeds, and I started eating the seeds and smoking the weed and I felt much much better. I started to sleep properly and go to the toilet properly, and the seeds started clearing out my stomach, because that's what it does. I finally got rid of a candida condition I'd had ever since I'd taken lots of antibiotics because of a car accident. I went from being a meat eater to being a vegetarian, and I dropped from twenty and a half stone to sixteen stone in four months. I eventually lost ten stone in total, but I actually looked too skinny, so I've put on three stone."

He's now 182 pounds. "I eat about two pounds of seed a week, and half a pint of oil," he says. "I just had a meal of tomatoes, hemp oil, marijuana leaves, hemp seeds, spirolina, and avocado. Lovely. Really nice, the leaves are delicious and full of chlorophyll."

He now buys the seeds by the half-ton, or really by the ton, splitting it with Free Rob Cannabis, who runs a health food store in Glastonbury. He encourages his lunch customers to sprinkle hemp seeds on their buffet plates. "I sell bucketloads and so does Rob, because the seeds have twenty-five percent protein and essential fatty acids omega-three, -six, and -nine, which are the building blocks of our bodies and our brain . . . These plants look terrible." We've been chatting on the second-story balcony behind his shop and looking at an assortment of plants. Tony is a trial-and-error grower—mostly error. An error has been committed today by one of the shop assistants, who has watered the plants using buckets left caked in plaster by a workman renovating the second floor with new drywall. The soil in the buckets is white with thick, chalky, plastery drywall residue. "Hempsters," Tony spits in a tone reserved for useless fools, and then he mutters a soft lamentation on the travails of being the boss and not being able to find good help.

Tony calls himself a hempster. "The way we first thought about it, when the word first come up, was that these were people who were involved in hemp and would be straight up, honest, and proper, everybody would pay on time and everything would be cool because we are all involved in hemp, and we are hempsters. And it's bullshit—everybody knocks each other, nobody pays. It's the same as every other place, except we're more disorganized than most other people because we are all stoneheads; that makes it even more difficult," he says. He laughs. "I probably exaggerate when I say we're all knocking each other, but because there's not a lot of cash, the banks won't give you any credit; no one is up for hemp. It's all cash business and everybody is scratching for a pound, and there are a few people that are real basic assholes and you wouldn't deal with them any other way if it wasn't for hemp."

The police and the authorities are less of a problem. Through the store Tony supplies medical marijuana to those in need, and can also arrange ibogaine treatment for junkies looking to kick heroin. (Banned in America, ibogaine is an African root extract that takes you on a bizarre thirty-six-hour trip that's generally unpleasant, but cathartic.)

"The government actually physically came here for four hours," says Tony, "this woman from the Home Office, and we had a good chat about medical cannabis, and she said don't ever worry, you'll have no problems.

"And when I was arrested—you know, I was arrested here—I had nine ounces and two scales and fifty plants at home, and the policemen were really nice, the four of them. The sergeant, he broke a lump off the top and gave it back to me and said, 'You'll need that for later.' I told him I make cannabis tincture with brandy, and I also make some Moon Essence, and I make some Sun Essence, and I showed him the bottles, and said, 'Take them,' and he said, 'No, you keep them.' I said, 'Take them, it's evidence.' 'Doesn't matter.'

"They took me to the station and asked me all about herbs, the questioning was really easy. I went to court four times. I was in the dock like a criminal, and a lawyer said to the magistrate—this is a female magistrate—my lawyer said to her, 'This gentleman administered medical cannabis to a female multiple sclerosis sufferer, Madame.' And the judge says, 'Oh, did he? Right. Do you have any paperwork? If you don't bring it next time we'll throw it out of court.' So just like that they threw my case out of court. Then the copper came around a few weeks later and said, 'I will never nick you.' There is no way a sergeant decides to do that on his own; he'd get nailed to the wall. He's been told to do that and it's from the top, the very top.

"If anything there is a conspiracy among the police to NOT give me grief. You've got to treat the authorities with respect—if not they come down on you big time. We are bending the laws plus, so if you stick your finger up to them"—he holds up the reliable middle digit—"they come and smack you in the ass, and they've got a bigger stick than I've got. I haven't got any stick. All the local police come in here and buy food, and they all pay and they're all very nice. A couple of times they said can we walk around the building, and I said do whatever you want, the plants are upstairs. 'Oh, we won't go upstairs then.' That's what it's like. Partly because around the world policies are changing with cannabis, and we all like to think it's because of all the hard work we hempsters have done. But it ain't. It's because it suits the system now to use cannabis as medicine, and hemp for other things. I have a problem with someone ruining the planet, and the authorities are starting to have a problem with ruining it too. So they need alternatives."

✳

Tony gives me a tiny sip, a bottle cap's worth of Moon Essence, to be held and absorbed under my tongue. He makes it during the full moon and administers it mostly as a remedy to women with bad PMS, but it works its magic on men too. It shoots down my spine to my genitalia and ass, makes my legs jangly and jerky for a few minutes, and then a soothing peace spreads from my crotch out over my whole body. Plus my mind is floating free, and I couldn't be happier with the company I'm keeping. I want to hug them. It's remarkable stuff.

Tony sits in the August sun on the sill of an open second-story window, looking down at the chaos of humanity pulsing away from or toward King's Cross. Businessmen walk below with impatient gaits that indicate they'll be sprinting for the train by the time they reach the station. Hookers looking for business, crackheads looking for money, and plenty of normal folk, heads down, hurrying, late for something. Only a few groups of idle youth, out buying clothes or CDs, seem by their smiles to be taking any pleasure in the experience of walking. "Laws put in place by the rich because they were worried all their stockbrokers were on coke are the same laws now being used against a good plant," Tony says.

At the workman's table in this half-renovated room an assistant named Simon is calling the Home Office, trying to figure out how to get official approval to grow medical marijuana. "Regardless of whether it's a licensed medicine or not, it's the lesser evil," he's telling the bureaucrat at the other end of the line. "You go to prison and they're chasing the dragon in all the cells. 'Thank you, Home Office, for making me a heroin addict.'" That truly happened to Simon in prison. "Cannabis can be part of therapy to get people off heroin," he insists.

Tony says, "I come from it more from the seeds and health perspective than the smoking. Puffers need to know about that, or be reminded if they've forgotten."

Simon keeps making calls. Ultimately he hangs up and with great vexation says, "I've just been passed from pillar to post, nobody wants to take responsibility, nobody wants to change the status quo for fear of losing their job, or their mortgage, or whatever. The government switchboard put me through to the Medicines Control Agency, and someone named Richard sounded reasonably sympathetic and open-minded." His tone is getting increasingly ironic. "Richard suggested I speak to the Action Against Drugs Unit, so I pointed out to him that they were *against* drugs. He concurred . . ."

As I leave the store Tony is chewing Simon out for standing around near the front counter, flirting with a customer, yakking about his experiences as a submariner before the Royal Navy drummed him out for refusing to give up smoking cannabis. He was aboard a nuclear submarine during a near-meltdown emergency the public never heard a word of. "You can chitchat later," says Tony. Simon slinks off to his appointed tasks, and Tony turns to the customer. "That's the trouble with running a cannabis-based business," he says with exasperation. "The staff wants to be chitchatting all the time."

I'm reminded of something Chris Sanders said: English cannabis activists agree that their cause would be much further along if they didn't smoke so much of it.

✳

Cannabis use has stabilized in Britain, according to Matthew Atha of the Independent Drug Monitoring Unit, a private company that carries out serious long-term surveys of British drug users, keeping track of consumption, markets, prices, and valuations.

Atha points me to statistics on the effects of an arrest on a young person. Thirty percent of heroin users and 45 percent of crack users in Britain have been busted for other drugs before trying the new one. So is being busted deterrence or gateway? The gateway theory is that use of marijuana leads naturally to other, harder drugs. Does cannabis lead to heroin? Or is it being busted for cannabis that leads to heroin, as in the case of Simon, whom we heard at Tony's Hemp Corner, insisting to the bureaucrat at the other end of the phone that he'd learned to "chase the dragon" from a cell in Her Majesty's gaol system. "Once people have a criminal record they are much more likely to use heroin," says Atha. "So the policy of arresting young people is more likely to backfire than deter."

Atha's research shows that for a surprising number of British youth, speed and ecstasy use often precedes pot. "With non-smokers those chemical drugs don't have that smoking barrier to go through," Atha suggests. "In Liverpool in the 1980s, for forty percent of heroin users it was their first drug, even though heroin use is usually at first accompanied by vomiting." In British drinking culture, puking has a different meaning, so that vomiting associated with heroin can link up to this thought in the addled mind of a young, dumb user: "Oh, I'm throwing up, so I must be having a hell of a good time."

✳

Hanging upside down from a low rafter beam, slowly drying, is a nice big branch of an outdoor-grown cannabis plant, smaller branches spreading down from it like fingers, with maybe two dozen buds. If you stand on a chair you can stick your face in among these little beauties and breathe that sweet sticky resinous scent. It's what Pepe LePeu knew: Skunk is truly a fragrant perfume.

"If you can find a dry one, you can skin up," says Karen. I'm in her apartment, the former boiler room of an abandoned nursing home, and one of maybe twenty small apartments restored to a comfortable livability by a group of communitarians called the Exodus Collective. They live on the very outskirts of Luton, a big town within commuting distance of London. Jack in Norwich had told me, "The Exodus people are very spiritual, but they also know how to party." In London people had described the Exodus experiment as a kind of Rastafarian alternative communal society based on extremely high principles of equality. In other words, they share everything.

My first thought: not possible.

"We have a really simple philosophy which everyone can understand, which is to do good," says John, a huge, ruddy-cheeked former British Army career man. "To do good for the whole, and then everyone benefits individually. You have to believe that to live here. It's taking the competition out of life, rather than compete for jobs and money and material bits."

"Take the competition out of the situation and people behave in different ways, don't they?" asks Karen.

"More like a family," John agrees. "You don't compete with your family. You don't sit at the table and eat all the food when your sister down the end is starving."

✻

What I have to say about the Exodus Collective is likely going to sound very hokey. They seemed to me to be rare people, making a genuine, conscious effort to live as a self-regulating small-scale alternative community. They are dedicated to love and yet very tough, able in a town dominated by breweries to stand up without violence to a rigid, conservative, Freemason-dominated local police force. HAZ Manor is what they call the derelict nursing home they've squatted and are in the act of restoring (HAZ stands for Housing Action Zone, a variation on Brooklyn-based anarchist writer Hakim Bey's concept of a Temporary Autonomous Zone). It's a labyrinth of single-story brick units joined together. On the lawn they park three huge army trucks of the type that look like they could carry an ICBM in an old Moscow May Day parade. Onto these trucks they load a sound system with a gigantic stack of speakers capable of putting out between eighteen and twenty-one kilowatts of sound, and the generators to run them, and take them to vacant fields to hold illegal raves. No cover charge. Free dances for the community. They're trying to create community through music. The vibe at these events is this: pot and ecstasy are okay, but there is to be no dealing of anything except beer.

"The only way to prevent hard drug use is to make it unfashionable," says Stuart, another Exodus member who, like John, has wandered into Karen's looking for a cup of tea and company.

I ask where the Exodus name comes from. "We realized that collecting money and then putting it back in for the common good, that there was power in that," says Stuart. "We didn't realize what Exodus Movement of Jah People [a quote from the Bob Marley song "Exodus"] meant until we went from a hundred people that first night on Dunstable Down, and three speakers, to ten thousand people and thirty-two speakers in six months."

"And Bedfordshire police had never seen crime so low, because everybody was at the do," John says. "The crime rate just shut down. Exodus sent the crime rate down."

"You'd think that would make the police happy," I suggest.

"But because we was putting on our raves, all the people were coming out of the pubs at ten, to be at the convoy point at eleven," John points out. "This is Saturday night, the busiest pub hours of the week, ten to eleven Saturday night, so Whitebreads [a large brewery based in Luton] and all the pubs lost all their trade. The breweries started lobbying the police, and the government."

"We were mentioned in the House of Commons," Karen says. "'How are these people making their money, not charging for their events?' Implying we were drug dealers."

"The solution was to plant drugs on one of us and get the rest of us on conspiracy to sell," says Stuart. But the planting job was so clumsy and obvious that the charges were thrown out. Karen adds that in the past decade police have laid fifty-four charges against Exodus members, for infractions ranging from trespassing to noise bylaw violations to murder. This "deliberate policy of police harassment" has led to one conviction, carrying a fine of eighty pounds.

✳

They drove their three huge trucks, or lorries, as they call them, down to London to join in the big May Day parade. Stuart says, "That was the day the Old Bill learned we were massive but passive. 'One Love' was pumping through Brixton. It was brilliant. It was top, mate."

Locally they've been holding raves on land belonging to the Duke of Bedford, the largest landowner in Bedfordshire. The European Community pays the duke not to farm anything, as Europe produces more food than it needs already. The aristocrat was making money for doing nothing and wouldn't let anyone else in the community use the land. The police were only too happy to enforce this traditional British status quo.

Their numerous attempts to bust Exodus included a military-style invasion of a nearby farm the collective had bought, and another showdown on the night of a rave, when the convoy of lorries was encircled and seized by police. Forty people were arrested. The police station was soon surrounded by four thousand Exodus supporters and, according to Karen, one undercover cop with a baseball cap on backward, who moved through the thick of the crowd screaming, "Kill the Bill." The inciter eventually became an embarrassment to the police when the newspapers reported that he had been "arrested" several times that evening for trying to provoke a riot. "Every time they nabbed him, he was let out to try again," she says.

"We blocked the road off with our cars—it was standoff time. We sat down singing some Bob Marley songs," remembers another Exodus supporter who has come round for tea and to see how plans are progressing for the next Exodus festival, which they all call a Fezzie. "It was a peaceful protest, not inciting anything. Next thing we know they're coming out of the station with the shields, the helmets, and the truncheons."

Stuart sees it as just a dreary continuation of that long, grand British tradition of using the police as goons to keep landless people off the empty estates of the rich. "Heads on pikes and Freemasons torturing people." He sighs. "If that's our history let's get on with the future please."

For the Exodus folks the immediate future is a time of great hope. Lord Howland, the Duke of Bedford, had met with the Exodus leaders and taken a shine to them. In the summer of 2000 he gave Exodus permission to hold free community dances on his land. "Love and respect to Andrew Howland for freeing up this space without asking for a penny. We needed a 'landowner' who was brave enough to look over the fence and check for the difference between community and commercial," read part of the flyer given to those who came to the party.

✳

All sorts of people continue to drop by Karen's for a cup of tea, settling into one of the two long couches or many chairs in the big open room. Many are growing a plant or two in a spare closet or back garden, and the subject turns naturally to horticulture. One has a big bush along the fence in his housing estate, and has bent the stalk so many times to keep it out of sight of the neighbors that it "looks like a sea serpent now."

John says, "My mum grew me a plant for the first time this year. She spent forty years as a nurse. She's seen what drink does to people. She's seen me and my dad drunk. And she prefers to see me puffing."

This is early September. In a few weeks it'll be harvest time, and people will have more ganja than they know what to do with. In this communitarian environment it's sacrilege to sell it. "It's a good feeling, to just give weed away," says a drop-in named Robert.

"It's a great character giveaway at harvest," says Karen. "Some people get like that"—she wraps her arms as if guarding a big stash to her chest—"and others set it all free. Last harvest some looked like they gained energy from that."

"Your tempo to weed changes—you don't smoke as much," says Robert.

"I got sick of it last year," says Karen. "I never thought I'd feel that way, ever."

"How much did you have?"

"I don't know how much I had in weight. I never weighed it at all. I'm trying to get away from all that."

Stuart says, "Some people see a big bud and see two hundred pounds. Everything gets translated into money. It's a slow process to think of it as a God-given plant again." In the background the television on the fridge acts as a kind of periscope to Babylon, which is the word Rastafarians choose to describe the corrupted, money-obsessed, fallen-from-grace outer society around them. Stuart watches some half-minute confection of Disney images and says, "Disneyland is the height of Babylon in a commercial sense, but it's still amazing."

I ask him what role cannabis plays in the philosophy of the Exodus people. "Weed opens up that vessel to your conscience," he says. "It's the plant of peace, and yet it's banned." His own philosophy is an underlay of the love-based tenets of Christianity with some Bob Marley and Rastafarian love of cannabis spread like chocolate syrup on top of the sundae. "What's your spiritual belief, Brian?"

I tell him I'm still a seeker, but that I believe our lives have an important spiritual component and that there are times when I am high on marijuana that I feel closer to a oneness with some compassionate life-giving power.

"There's good things to be found in all religions," Stuart says. He particularly likes the Muslim idea that a good Muslim should know his forty closest neighbors.

✳

A schoolteacher drops by just to say hi. Some windows at a nearby school have been smashed. Someone threw empty bottles of Bacardi Breeze cooler through them. Everyone frets over the alienation of youth out there in Babylon. In here, in the clutter of cigarettes and ashtrays, teacups, and rolling papers on Karen's coffee table, the schoolteacher notices a copy of the August 2000 newsletter of the Bedfordshire Beekeepers Association.

"I woke up one morning and decided to learn how to keep bees," Karen says. "Within a fortnight I'd met five beekeepers, and I was having lovely teas and sampling varieties of honey. I'm thirty-one years old with dreadlocks, but as soon as you say you're interested in bees, they all want to help you. It's like puff, isn't it? A God-given thing."

"I love the bees because it's a perfect working community," says John.

"They dance to communicate, which is a really good thing," Karen adds.

"Like a rave. The bee does this dance called the wiggle dance, which communicates how far the pollen is, how much you need to eat to get there and back. They do this by dancing, while hanging on the vertical."

Why is the rave, and dancing, so central to Exodus? I ask.

"The dance is a minaret for the community," Karen says. "It's the only time in Luton you'll see Asians and Gypsies mixing together."

Luton is a mosaic of immigrants: Pakistanis, Afro-Caribbeans, Gypsies, and plenty of Irish. Getting them to party together is step one of the Exodus agenda.

Over two days we smoke most of the buds off that drying limb hanging at Karen's place. Some needs to be left, because the plant actually belongs to an Exodus member who has gone away for the holiday weekend. Most of the mainstays of the place are likewise absent, and the community is much less active than normal. But there's nearly always a joint burning and a lively discussion of how to shape the future. Exodus members plan to rehabilitate an unused factory in the heart of Marsh Park, the big public housing project in Luton, and convert it into a community center for a bleak burg where unemployment runs 30 percent. They have a vision of spreading the Exodus message to other depressed and stagnating towns in Britain. It's inspiring. For two nights I sleep in a little two-wheeled trailer out back, and leave the third morning with Stuart's motto in my mind: "Live clean and let your works be seen."

From the comfort of the HAZ Manor, the tiny autonomous zone, it's back to Luton, back to regular England, to areas under strict control of the State, the Crown, with its quirky hierarchy of Queen on top, then the Dukes of Bedford and all the other shires, and all their minions, and finally the great masses obsessed with soccer and girl groups and boy bands. In a shopping mall in the heart of Luton there's a children's beauty contest/ model hunt under way, hundreds of milling little prats and ponces in training. Outside, on a narrow street leading to the train station, two kids yell obscenities at an old man walking hunched over a cane on the far sidewalk. He stops to yell back, "Shut your FUCKING mouths!"

✳

London continues to irritate the hell out of me. On my last night in town Chris and I are walking near Oxford Circus, trying to discreetly smoke a joint on the street.

Chris is complaining about even having to be an activist: "This is all very boring and should have been sorted out twenty years ago. I resent having to work at this. But the reason it didn't work out is that people ghettoized it back then. It was, 'Oh, those crazy hippies.'"

I have the joint we're sharing in one hand, and in the other a bunch of grapes I've just bought, when some desperate and angry British dude steps out of an alleyway, grabs the wrist of my joint hand, and sticks his other hand in the grapes.

"Don't take them all!" I tell him.

We're eyeball to eyeball, and he's calling me a cunt and various other things, telling me he could lay me on the ground with one punch. It's surely true; I'm not a fighter. But he has nothing to gain by knocking me down in the bright light of busy Oxford Street, so he's trying to steer me into the alley.

Chris the pacifist moves to block his path, pleading softly with him to let go of me.

"Fuck off! You're Old School!" the guy yells at him.

I'm staying out of the alley. This sad bastard can't make too big a scene, so eventually he settles for a few grapes and lets us go on our way, muttering insults.

Chris and I wonder what the hell he meant by "Old School." Are we really that old? Being Old School is nothing you can control, I guess. Just to be old is to be labeled. We're forty-something, he was maybe thirty. Calling me a cunt over some grapes. If that weren't depressing enough for a final evening in London, my very last image of the place comes the next day on Victoria Station's vast concourse, in the unyielding din of trains, announcements, and scurrying, stressed commuters. Two custodians, each behind the steering wheel of vacuuming machines the size of forklifts, pull up nose to nose and scream insults at each other. In England, even the janitors suffer Road Rage.

7 : AMSTERDAM

At a country house along a canal twenty miles from Amsterdam, I'm baby-sitting a three-year-old boy named Henk. Out back along a side canal, like a little alley that gradually peters out to a dead end, soaking itself into the fields, young Henk, all curiosity, stands in the grass at the water's edge, stretching a hand toward a big hissing male swan that keeps his distance, positioning himself always between us and his mate and their two youngsters, who float placidly in place near the far shore. I envy Henk's innocent fearlessness. The big male swims too close for comfort, and looks too ready to go on the attack, so I edge closer to Henk, like a body-guard. The swan in turn interprets this gesture, which is just me protecting my young, as a threat against him and his, and flaps his big white wings menacingly at us. It's beautiful, a little scary, and Henk is only further entranced.

I've been thinking about thinking, about what Stuart at Exodus had said about cannabis being a vessel to the conscience. Conscience is having feelings that are opposed to your actions. Doing one thing, usually selfish and sometimes hurtful to another, and feeling you shouldn't have done it. Are we the only animal that regrets? And was recognition of that regret the first human recognition of consciousness? I'll have to check the dictionary, see if "conscience" meant "consciousness" at one time—

"Henk! Get away from Mister Swan!"

I'm finally in Holland, and I'm high. It feels at last like I'm on neutral territory in the worldwide war on marijuana, a place where a conscientious objector like me might breathe the smoke of peace.

But then I start to look more carefully at what's really going on in Holland.

✳

Amsterdam undeniably is a mecca for freaks and eccentrics from all over the world. "A hundred forty-five nationalities live here," a Dutch woman tells me. "More than New York!" The cabdrivers also speak better English than the ones in New York. The city is a surprising rainbow mix of races. In a local magazine a twenty-eight-year-old daughter of Moroccan immigrants, now an elected city councillor, complains she's getting old and can't go out on the town and party till morning like she used to. But there's nothing to stop her if she wants to. Amsterdam is Party Central, partly because the streets feel safe and sane at all hours of day or night.

Amsterdam is not Holland, though. If you get out to the smaller towns (so many of them crisscrossed with those pretty, orderly, essential canals) or to the countryside, you will find that the Dutch people are extremely conservative, and most of them aren't exactly thrilled to have quasilegal pot-smoking hangouts associated with their country. But they recognize it as the lesser evil. I struck up conversations with plenty of young Dutch people who had never even tried marijuana. Why not? A shrug, a shake of the head. Just not interested. A teenage Dutch girl told me, "Stoned boring people sitting in those coffee shops? That's not appealing."

Beer drinking is socially encouraged in Holland. One Dutchman told me, "If you go to work on Monday and say, 'I got so drunk this weekend I threw up,' you get a pat on the back, like, 'What a Man.' But say, 'I smoked a joint,' and you get stern looks and 'Hey, be careful, man. That's drugs.'" Taken as a whole the Dutch are way more conservative than Americans, maybe because they lack an attitude so many Americans have. Americans think it's their constitutional duty to pursue happiness, and if they're not happy they desperately chase after every new thrill. The Dutch accept boredom and unhappiness as periodic episodes in every person's life. They are even-keeled to the point of being dull.

Sasha, a Croatian immigrant who works at After the Harvest, a shop that sells among other things the Ice-o-lator do-it-yourself hash making system, told me one day, "Straight Dutch people are the straightest people in the world. Straighter than straight. It's like they've had a chip planted in their head. They're robotic." That might not be a bad thing. Robots are emotionless, objective. In most places on this planet the debate over drugs could do with less emotion and more objectivity.

As a society, the Dutch have managed to construct a state that is lenient toward drug users. It's just one of the many ways the citizens of the Netherlands have created a better country than the United States. Another is the police. An American expat, now settled in Amsterdam, told me, "The cops here are social scientists. They've gone to college and studied. Whereas in America, the cops are just thugs."

The American sociologist Craig Reinarman has written: "The Dutch have a long history of tolerance. Many of the Pilgrims who fled religious persecution in England were sheltered in the Netherlands before they came to America in the early 1600s. The Dutch were brutally conquered by the Nazis in World War II, so they know only too well what absolutist states can do to 'deviants' and to individual freedom. Down through the centuries the Dutch have developed a deeply democratic culture which has nurtured nonabsolutist approaches to many public problems. In the drug policy arena, they have bravely broadened the range of possibilities to examine, which is as useful for those who want to learn something as it is fearful for those who do not."

Another thought from Reinarman: "U.S. drug control ideology holds that there is no such thing as *use* of an illicit drug, only abuse. But drug use patterns in the Netherlands show that for the overwhelming majority of users, marijuana is just one more type of *genotsmiddelen* (foods, spices, and intoxicants which give plea-sure to the senses) that the Dutch have been importing and cul-turally domesticating for centuries."

New Mexico governor Gary Johnson, committing what amounts to political suicide in America by deciding to talk ob-jectively about the War on Drugs: "Holland is the only country in the world that has a rational drug policy. I had always heard that Holland, where marijuana is decriminalized and controlled, had out-of-control drug abuse and crime. But when I researched it, I learned that's untrue. It's propaganda. Holland has sixty percent of the drug use—both hard drugs and marijuana—the United States has. They have a quarter the crime rate, a quarter the ho-micide rate, a quarter the violent crime rate, and a tenth the in-carceration rate."

I spend my first few days in Amsterdam among the swans, kids, and countryside, recovering from England. In the evenings I watch Dutch TV, and can state with authority that the Dutch think it's hilariously funny when a clergyman farts.

For my first foray into Amsterdam I have a sidekick, Knute the Swede, who's staying at the country house too. He's in need of healing. "There's no hospital for a broken heart" is how our host expresses it. Knute was for many years a resident of the al-ternative community Christiana, in Denmark, where cannabis has long been tolerated by the authorities without the great in-ternational fanfare Holland attracts. In his fifties now, and still a true hippie and psycho-naut, he was part of the anarchistic Amsterdam scene of the 1960s. This is his first trip back in nearly thirty years.

He's in for a terrible disappointment. The sixties are defi-nitely over, even in Amsterdam.

Along the canal called Oudezijds Voorburgwal, near the Red Light district, where some of the best and some of the worst coffee shops are located, we pick one at random and saunter in to survey the menu. The place is dirty, divey, and generally unpleasant, and the only people smoking inside are wearing Hell's Angels colors from the Phoenix, Arizona, chapter. Knute chooses the most expensive hash on the menu, advertised as a hand-rubbed Manali, from Kashmir in northern India. Outside we settle ourselves into plastic patio chairs near the canal and get down to the business of rolling tobacco-hash spliffs.

I say, "You sprang for top of the line, eh?"

"I'm protecting you from worse things."

"Like what?"

"Like the Pakistani headache. Old LP records melted down and mixed with some kind of solvent and horse tranquilizer."

"Wait a minute, this ain't England, this is Amsterdam."

He rolls his eyes. "Let the buyer beware, my boy."

We share the first joint of the day, and this black hashish is okay, but hardly top of the line. First I need to cope with the stinky dark Van Alle tobacco that Knute favors for rolling hash joints. It smells like pipe tobacco to me, not something I want to be inhaling and holding in the lungs for any length of time. The Dutch love their tobacco strong, and any self-respecting Dutchman rolls his own. Those who don't are considered weak, corrupted by the American ethic that gratification must be instant and the consumer must be coddled. Consumer culture's spreading tentacles can be seen in bus shelter ads all over Amsterdam: Drum tobacco, Holland's best known for roll-your-own, has caved in and is marketing its new filter-tip cigarettes under the slogan "For Lazy Bastards." But I never see anyone smoking them.

During my stay in Holland more than one Dutchman will put this proposition to me: prerolled American cigarettes are dangerous because American tobacco is grown using radioactive chemical fertilizers. And more than one Dutchman will dismiss American smokers as ignorant sheep, knowing nothing about the tobacco they inhale except which end of the little white tube to light; but good Dutch tobacco, grown in Indonesia, Zimbabwe, or Brazil, bought in a pouch and rolled by the smoker, so that the substance to be ingested can be examined and judged fit, is safer, cleaner, more fragrant, and tastier. The Dutch generally think of themselves as superior to Americans, and this is just another little proof.

✳

You figure out quickly that among Amsterdam's three hundred or so coffee shops (there are twelve hundred in all of Holland), many of those near the city center cater to ignorant tourists, and sell crap at inflated prices. Dutch people claim that some of them even sell joints of that strong Dutch tobacco and pass it off as containing hashish. They also complain that many coffee shops sell pot that has not been flushed or cured properly. And it's true— sometimes you can't roll a spliff of pure pot in Amsterdam because the damn stuff won't stay lit unless you cut it with tobacco.

In Amsterdam you also figure out quickly that some coffee shops take the craft of marijuana growing seriously, and do their utmost to supply the best. But I have to say, even in the better coffee shops, like De Dampkring, or De Rokerij, I felt a sense of disappointment, a letdown. Finally a place where you can freely buy marijuana, and they're pushing it at you just like booze or tobacco. Is this what legalization would be like? Would pot become just another consumer product, marketed like any other line of goods in Babylon?

"When I was living here in the early seventies," Knute says, "hashish was the drug of artists, musicians, actors, thinkers. Now it's been commodified, made as bland and mainstream as beer."

This realization makes him very cranky. He refuses even to step foot into one coffee shop we pass on our pot-based equivalent of a pub crawl. It's part of the Bulldog chain, geared to British tourists who want soccer on the big screen. "They've completely obliterated the hippie ideal," Knute spits in disgust as a bouncer with "Bulldog Security" across his black polo shirt gives us a mean, move-along look.

A few minutes later I drag Knute into a tiny coffee shop called Grey Area that caters to techno twenty-somethings. The decor reminds him of a McDonald's. Techno twenty-somethings would feel that's homey, I guess. I take a stool at the counter and linger over the choices on the menu, not knowing what to buy. It's between the Silver Haze and the AK47.

To hurry my decision, the cue ball–headed kid behind the counter places a little tabletop sign at my elbow. "No Loitering." Jesus Christ, man. Have you never heard of the hippie ideal?

✳

Contrary to the belief of American policy makers and their political and economic dependents in American law enforcement, the Dutch didn't dream up their drug policy just to piss America off. America never entered into it. The Dutch debate was and is pragmatic, starting from the mature position that it's human nature for people to seek out highs and painkillers. The Dutch philosophy can be summed this way: There will always be drunks and junkies. Stigmatize them, but don't criminalize them.

This policy dates to 1976, when the Dutch parliament revised the country's Opium Act, creating a legal distinction between cannabis and other drugs. President Nixon's handpicked National Commission on Marijuana and Drug Abuse had recommended a similar distinction, and called for the decriminalization of marijuana in America in 1972: "Marihuana's relative potential for harm to the vast majority of individual users and its actual impact on society does not justify a social policy designed to seek out and firmly punish those who use it." Thus spake the sages. This advice was ignored in America, but the Dutch in the same era were coming to the same conclusions and incorporating them into policy. In Holland drugs deemed to have an unacceptable health risk (including amphetamines, cocaine, heroin, and LSD) were listed as schedule I, and cannabis products (hashish and marijuana) as schedule II. This approach came to be known as the "separation of the markets" for soft and hard drugs. By allowing people to buy and consume cannabis in small amounts, authorities believed, people would be less inclined to experiment with hard drugs. The idea was that if all drugs, hard and soft, are left equally illegal, the pushers will sell everything, and someone looking for the relatively benign buzz of cannabis will inevitably encounter dealers offering a special deal ("Try it, you'll like it!") on coke or heroin.

Possession of less than 30 grams of cannabis was deemed a misdemeanor and assigned a low priority for prosecution. Eventually possession of this amount was allowed in practice, although still an offense in law. Certain rules were set out for the coffee shops that were already selling marijuana: no sales larger than 30 grams, no advertising, no tolerance of any public nuisance, no sales to minors under eighteen, and no use or sales of hard drugs. In 1995 the maximum acceptable coffee shop purchase was reduced from 30 to 5 grams, but the total quantity of cannabis a coffee shop was allowed to have in stock on the premises was raised from 30 grams to 500.

Now if this sounds like the work of an enlightened and benevolent government, it ain't. In the beginning the coffee shops seized their rights and freedoms—they weren't offered them. The coffee shops were not legislated into existence—the legislation was merely an attempt to regulate what already existed. The coffee shops existed because of pioneers who pushed the envelope, people like Ben Dronkers, the founder of Sensi Seed Bank, who has been arrested more than eighty times so that you or I or any Dutch person can walk into a coffee shop and have a paranoia-free experience. This process is what the Dutch pot pioneers refer to as making the law by breaking the law.

✳

Ben Dronkers is waiting for me at his Sensi Museum Coffeeshop on Oudezijds Achterburgwal, just a few doors up from his Sensi

Seeds store and the attached Hash Marihuana Hemp Museum. He's fifty, fit and vital, jovial, well-dressed. The founder of Amsterdam's preeminent seed company, he's been in the marijuana business nearly thirty years.

But there's no resting on laurels. Life for Dronkers and all the other cannabis crusaders and capitalists in Holland is in fact getting tougher all the time. The Dutch authorities are clamping down on growers.

"At a certain moment the minister of justice said people were allowed twelve plants for personal use, then it was six, now it's four," Dronkers complains. "And they raised the punishment for commercial cultivation from two to four years. They're targeting commercial growers. Like if you have a watering system, rather than watering the plants by hand, that's a longer sentence. Nobody really notices these harsher penalties in Holland, because most marijuana smokers aren't bothered with politics; they smoke anyway. We've had a liberal tolerance policy here for three decades now—you can smoke a joint with a policeman on the street next to you—so when laws change for the growers the average Dutch consumer feels it doesn't affect him, because he can still go to the coffee shop and get it. But it's harder for us all the time to supply it. Now the authorities are saying anything grown indoors under lights or in greenhouses is forbidden."

That rule came into effect in January 1999, and was intended to close a loophole whereby growing seeds was legal, but growing herb to smoke was illegal. Commercial growers were all claiming to grow seeds. Now it's all illegal.

While Dutch authorities have made a few concessions to marijuana consumers over the years, when it comes to growers and suppliers, Dutch policy is as hypocritical as any other. Growers and coffee shop owners complain about the "front door legal, back door illegal" conundrum, whereby it's okay for you to come in the front door of a coffee shop and buy up to 5 grams, but it's almost impossible for the seller to bring enough stock in the back door to meet demand, unless he breaks the law. "It used to be people from small towns where there are no coffee shops would come to the city and buy five or ten bags and share costs with friends, but now it's one small bag per person per day," says Dronkers. "In Rotterdam the police really check that, and if you sell two or three bags to the same person, the coffee shop will close. So you're allowed as an individual to possess thirty grams, but you're only allowed to buy five grams at a time. It's crazy! Our minister of justice just announced they want to bust more people at the back door again."

Other Dutch marijuana businessmen have been making the same complaints to me. Roland, manager of the nearby Flying Dutchmen Seed Company, another of the well-established seed banks in Holland, told me, "So you're allowed five hundred grams in a shop. If you have five oh one, they take it all away and close you seven days. Next time it's a month, and after that they close the shop permanently. They really make it difficult for people."

Changes in the law threaten the very existence of seed companies like Flying Dutchmen and Sensi. "We probably will be forced out of Holland to grow our varieties," Dronkers says. "We've applied for a license and there's a possibility they'll give us a license, because there's so much evidence of medical usage. We have enough seeds in stock now for a couple of years, but after that we may have to grow abroad. It's going to be hard to keep the Sensi Seed Bank intact, to keep the genetic stock intact. People forget cannabis is really a gene bank. All the new varieties that have appeared in the last few years didn't just come out of the sky. It was a lot of work."

✳

The history of marijuana growing in Holland begins with the to-bacco shortages of the Second World War. Some Dutch people substituted hemp in their cigarettes, and likely some varieties produced a mild buzz. In the 1960s this weak *Nederweit*—Dutch weed—made a bit of a comeback as the counterculture kicked into gear, but most of the cannabis smoked in Holland through the 1960s and '70s was imported hashish from India, Nepal, Afghanistan, Lebanon, or Morocco.

As far as breeding and developing new strains of marijuana goes, Ben Dronkers says, "I'm definitely not the number one person, but I was one of the first, for sure. It was about 1974 that I really went into it. In those days I had a clothing boutique, and I traveled to India and Pakistan for nice chiffons with embroidered beadwork. I was in Pakistan for three months, and I went to the hills and mountains, where the farmers were growing good hash. In the Khyber Pass, I got tired of hash and said, 'Can't you give me some grass?' The grass had seed in it, and I thought, In Holland we know gardening, we know greenhouses. The first time I brought back seeds and grew them under lights, we had no idea, we built a tepee, and in the beginning we gave the plants twenty-four hours' light. We didn't know how long to leave the lights on."

At the same time in California and the Pacific Northwest, American growers were bringing home seeds from all over the world and growing them out, often indoors under lights, and through trial and error discovering how to identify and remove the males early, how to alter the light cycle to coax and nurture the girls to sprout those gorgeous, stinky, seedless, fully flowered female buds, the famous sensimilla. Seeds from everywhere were bred and crossbred—Oaxaca, Jamaica, Colombia, Afghanistan, Nepal, Thailand, South Africa.

Then Ronald Reagan became President, and the War on Drugs began in earnest. "We are making no excuses for drugs— hard, soft, or otherwise. Drugs are bad and we are going after them," Reagan declared on one of his weekly radio broadcasts. Some of the finest American growers read the writing on the wall, fled the gathering storm of repression, and made their way to Amsterdam. In the mid-eighties an anonymous American, now referred to as Skunk Sam or the Skunk Man, brought to Amsterdam the first wave of American marijuana genetics. He shared his knowledge and his seeds primarily with Ben Dronkers of Sensi Seeds and Eddie, owner of the Flying Dutchmen Seed Company, who remembers, "He was really into seeds, I mean like nobody else was at that time, maybe a few people on earth, and he took a whole lot of seeds here, different strains, and things really happened fast. The old Dutch outdoor grass was forgotten and everyone went with the new genetics. It was the Great Leap Forward."

Among the strains he brought over were the Colombian ancestor of the sativa Haze strains, and a few crosses of his own, among them an infamously stinky, 75 percent sativa, 25 percent indica, Colombian-Mexican-Afghan cross called Skunk Number One, which has been a mainstay of the Sensi Seed Bank catalogue ever since, and is sold by many other Dutch seed companies as well. In the catalogue for Homegrown Fantaseeds company, they warn, "Nice taste and smell, but [it will make you] sleepy if you smoke too much." In the Flying Dutchmen's catalogue it's called "The Pure." At Sensi Seed Bank, Skunk Number One is nearly the cheapest seed in the catalogue, at 35 fl ($15 American). Compare that to 260 florin ($104) for G13 x Hash Plant, a hybrid from the 1980s now in production again and renamed "Mr. Nice," in honor of the entertaining autobiographical book of that name by legendary hashish smuggler and Oxford graduate Howard Marks. The most expensive, at 275 florin ($110) is "Jack Herer," named for the author of the seminal pro-hemp tract *Hemp and the Marijuana Conspiracy: The Emperor Wears No Clothes* ("This variety produces so much resin that even the branches bristle with stalked glands").

In 1989 the Drug Enforcement Administration in America launched a huge coordinated assault called Operation Green Merchant, shutting down hydroponic gardening supply stores across the country, and making use of UPS delivery records of individual sales from companies advertising in marijuana magazines like *High Times* and *Sensimilla Tips,* jailing many of the best growers and destroying their lives and families, and driving more of the genetic development of new strains out of America to Amsterdam and Canada. Northern Lights, a heady sativa developed indoors in Washington State, became a staple in Amsterdam after winning the Cannabis Cup in 1990. As the Haze, Skunk, and Northern Lights genetics mixed with the predominantly indica Afghani and Hindu Kush genetics already found in Amsterdam, the genetics of marijuana became truly global. Amsterdam seed companies still scour the world for pockets of overlooked genetics to add to the mix.

But with recent changes in the law in Holland, all this is in danger of being driven back underground. There has been surprisingly little public reaction—young radicals aren't exactly filling the streets to protest. Eddie of the Flying Dutchmen says, "There's no real legalization movement here because the young people already believe that it's legal. You could legalize the back door tomorrow and nothing would change. For consumers it's just this word. 'Legal,' 'illegal.' The government taxation people treat me as if it's legal. My biggest problem is with the tax people—they tell me my profit margin is too low. Here in the city center the profit margin on a coffee shop they expect to be a hundred percent. But my shop is a small one, in a neighborhood without tourists."

Called Metro, the shop is almost antitourist in its simplicity. The walls are adorned with jerseys of Dutch football players, framed under glass, and the kind of big team photos you see in auto repair garages and barbershops. There's a small pool table. Zero pretentious decor. A low-volume shop for sure, just a good place for locals to have a coffee and a joint and read the papers on a rainy afternoon.

"My margin in that shop is only sixty percent, which the tax people don't believe," Eddie says. If laws were loosened to the point where cultivation and distribution were legal, then "the growers could relax and be more comfortable, knowing they weren't going to be prosecuted. And they would pay taxes, too."

✳

"Marijuana is a nontoxic substance. To make it toxic, you'd need a swimming pool–ful of THC, and even then you'd have to drown yourself in it," Ben Dronkers is telling me over a glass of hemp wine. "So what is dangerous? You can take twenty aspirins—that's the toxic level, twenty aspirins. Any more, you can die on it. And you can buy it in a drugstore! With cannabis I can swallow a swimming pool–ful and I cannot die on it!"

"But a lot of people believe it's amotivating," I say. "It makes you lazy. This is why they are against it, not because it will kill you."

"In the museum we have lots of rebuttals of that," he says. "In Holland we have this Dr. Gunning, who told all these funny stories. I should have breasts now. I should be impotent, I should have no brain cells left, I should be incapable of sitting here talking to you, I should be having psychosis! All these things, and after thirty years of smoking, none of them has occurred. I'm horny like hell, my sex life is always too short, I've got six children, my hearing's good. My sight, too, especially if I see a nice-looking woman. What else can I tell you? I'm healthy. I eat hemp oil. It's amazing, you know—you should eat hemp oil, it's so good for you."

He has a company called Hempflax, and for seven years has been paying farmers handsomely to plant hemp, attempting to revive the hemp industry in Europe and develop such products as edible oils, paper, cloth, and building materials that are lighter and stronger than concrete. Hoof oil for horses is one definite product that beats all competitors, but that's a pretty tiny niche market. The costs of hemp farming are still high, partly because special machinery needs to be developed and manufactured for harvesting. Dronkers has made millions in marijuana, and lost it all again in hemp, but he considers it a worthy cause.

"You can say hemp oil is good for your health, but another good thing would be to stop smoking tobacco," I say.

It's always Americans who come over and nag, nag, nag about tobacco, he says. America. "You know what the biggest union in America is? The prison guards' union. In Texas they decide who's going to be the governor." He tells me about a "beautiful documentary" he saw on television, where a Dutch crew went to America to look at the drug war. "Oh man, it was so dismantling! A squad of police deciding who to bust by who's got the most money, because with American forfeiture laws the police get to keep all the property of whoever they charge. They don't even necessarily have to convict them! So this television crew followed the cops around for months, and at first it was like that TV show *Cops*—you know, very macho and tough. And then, slowly, slowly, the television crew started to turn it to the Dutch approach, starting asking the Dutch questions. Like, 'You got any family involved in drugs? Did you bust any of them? Do you support them?' It was beautiful.

"Then they come to the prisons. They're on the stock exchanges in America, and if you're going to buy stock in a prison it's like buying stock in a hotel. 'What do you want, full or empty?' Of course a stockholder will want the prison full! They'll be putting people in jail for tobacco in ten years because the prisons will start to empty again—they've already busted everyone they can for marijuana.

"The drug war should be finished, everything should be legalized. All that money wasted, all those people in prison. Who else can we put in prison? Someone who steals a bike? We don't do that in Holland. You know, in Holland you can steal a bike and they're not going to put you in prison. Of course you should be punished. In Holland we all think you should be punished, you know, but we all think also as soon as you go to the police station for an hour you should go out again. That's what we all think, all of us!"

I must look skeptical.

"No, really, try it!"

"Wouldn't they fine you, at least?"

"No. Give you a lecture. What the fuck you do, you crazy foreigner? Sit here an hour and think about it."

*

Yesterday I was sitting on a park bench when a panhandler, seeming slightly deranged, but not in a threatening sense—maybe "disarranged" is a better word—asked me for change. In Dutch. When I didn't respond he switched to English and said, "Excuse me, but have you ever seen normal people in your life?"

"Yeah."

"Oh. How was it?"

He told me this was Dutch humor. We shared the bench and a smoke, because he wanted me to sample some of a lighter Dutch blend of rolling tobacco, called JJ, with a brightly colored antiquated painting of an African tribesman on the pouch.

Why are you begging? I asked him.

He told me a long tale of woe about how a friend of his had been date-raped, but for whatever reason didn't report it to the police. So he took justice into his own hands. The next time he saw the alleged rapist, he tried to punch him out. The rapist, unfortunately a very large, tough man, laid him out on the cobblestone street with one punch and walked away laughing. My new friend pulled himself to his feet, picked up the nearest object at hand— an empty beer bottle from the gutter—snuck up from behind, and broke it over the rapist's head. Down he went, and my panhandler friend started compulsively kicking him in the head. He felt no remorse for what he had done. But he'd gone to jail for it, and now he was fresh out and unemployed.

Dutch jails, he said, were a holiday. Three meals a day, twenty-four-hour television in your room, and an hour a day in the library. "Third World people I met in there, they told me it's the easiest their life has ever been," he said.

✳

All of which leads me to say to Ben Dronkers, "I met a guy who did time in a Dutch jail, and he told me it wasn't that bad. Almost like a hotel, except you can't leave."

"No, it's horrible," said Dronkers. "Some of those prisons are still horrible. Don't take any risks to end up in prison, because prison is very bad. It destroys a lot of people."

"You said you've been arrested more than eighty times. What was your longest sentence?"

"Six weeks. It was a funny situation. It was for something that was really not mine, I had nothing to do with it. Caught in the middle." Some marijuana smugglers were driving through Rotterdam with a bag of imported grass the size of a hay bale in the trunk of their car. They weren't sure if they were being followed by the police or not, and didn't want to go to their rendezvous without being certain. They passed Dronkers' Rotterdam coffee shop, and thought, Well, if we stop and take it in there, and nothing happens, we're okay. So they brought a bale of pot into the shop, and the police came marching in behind them.

"Later the police knew it was a joke, that I was innocent," Dronkers says. "They heard it—they usually hear the truth eventually. The police themselves told me this time, because they busted the real guys later on, and they heard the real story."

"Did they apologize?"

"No no. They laughed at me. Bastards."

He's lost in thought for a minute.

"Believe it or not, I respect the police a lot. I can tell you names like Mr. Visser—he was the first narcotics officer in Holland, a very nice man, very much a gentleman and a sharp policeman, by the old book.

"I understand these people believe in what they did, but the people who put people in Auschwitz thought they were doing the right thing too," he says. "How can you put kids in prison? Three months after my first joint, I was in prison. At eighteen! But I've learned to respect the police, because I used to hate them—they beat me, they locked me up, they put me in a straitjacket, I hated them for sure, but I understand they don't know better. I'm lucky I can put it aside. Probably I was a pain in the ass to them." He sighs a heavy, tired sigh and stares into the candle on the table. "It's not nice, because I'm still a pain in the ass, and I don't want to be a pain in the ass anymore. I want what I do to be accepted."

That's no nearer to happening than it ever was. Canna-business is a never-ending struggle, even in Holland. For example, this coffee shop we sit in. The local government has revoked its license because they are trying to reduce the number of coffee shops in Amsterdam. And they are refusing to grant a permit to allow expansion of the Hash Marihuana Hemp Museum up the street. Two more court battles that suck Dronkers' energy and resources.

✳

Amsterdam grows on you. I love the old bicycles parked in neat rows everywhere. I still remember how touched I felt at the sight of a mother and her ten-year-old son riding by, straight-backed and proud on rickety one-speed bikes, the boy with a dozen roses placed carefully in the little carrier behind his seat. I loved hearing cyclists singing songs as they pedaled along—one night I heard "I'm Only Sleeping," that same favorite Beatles song I'd sung to Bhawani in Nepal. I tested my marijuana mettle by negotiating that great semicircular maze of intersecting canals, bike paths, tram tracks, sidewalks, and cobblestone streets filled with citizens moving through busy lives, wending my way to great galleries like the Van Gogh or the Rijksmuseum.

Buying and smoking good pot in the coffee shops of Amsterdam, you can get high in comfort, stumble into the street, and ask a cop for directions. I said "Excuse me" to get the attention of a cop one time, and he smiled back and said, "You are excused." I knew at that moment I reeked of weed, and I knew what an American activist had meant when he told me that sometimes in Amsterdam he felt like hugging the police.

✳

The Greenhouse Heat Coffeeshop has the ambience of a cozy pub, where young people, like the well-groomed Italian couples giggling at the next table, socialize by candlelight. Some clients, aging lost souls, seem to be killing time, like the world-weary Irishman at my table. We roll and share spliff after spliff, smoking compulsively, with no expectation of getting higher.

"Do you think cannabis induces sloth?"

"*Slothe?* Yes. Is Leonard Cohen still alive?"

"Oh yeah. He's a monk, or something."

There are long periods where we say little. The joint is passed, a silent sacrament touched to the lips.

"Tell me why I should buy your book."

"Haven't written it yet. Could be a disaster."

I buy the Nepalese Temple Ball, 25 guilders a gram, and we smoke it all up with some of his.

"In Ireland we used to smoke hash that would knock you on your ass for three hours. Do these kids today ever get that?" he wonders.

Was it stronger in the old days?

At the Hash Marihuana Hemp Museum, Eagle Bill argues that today's marijuana is much stronger, even dangerously potent. Eagle Bill is one of the many American refugees from America's War on Drugs who have found sanctuary in Amsterdam.

"I have used and abused cannabis for thirty-eight years, of which thirty-six years I didn't know what it was like *not* to be high," he tells me one afternoon. He's preparing a hit for me on his vaporizer, a three-gallon glass jar with a pipe stem and a bowl on top in which he turns fresh cannabis into vapor using an electric paint stripper as a heat source. The paint stripper's heat causes the THC resin to turn gaseous without igniting, so that the big jar fills with a slightly moist, sweet, aromatic gas that you can inhale without having to worry about all the nasty tars associated with smoking.

"I would go to bed with a joint, wake up in the morning, and finish the joint from last night before I drank my morning coffee, okay? But I was very lucky—I was living in America and we were growing sativa. If I'd been in Holland, I'd have just vegetated, because the pot is so strong. You know what's really wrong with pot? It's too damn strong. They've been free here to breed the THC way up. It really is so strong you could waste your life. You're looking at a person who for the first year I lived here in Amsterdam, 1993, I was overweight, out of shape, I was just stoned all the time staring at the television. Because I was finally free to do it, I was wasting my life. What a waste. Now out of a seven-day week, three or four days I'm not high."

In England drug researcher Matthew Atha had scoffed at this idea that marijuana has become way more potent. "You'll find the material grown indoors hydroponically varies between 5 and 15 percent THC," he told me. "Occasionally you'll get it as high as twenty or twenty-two percent. What people tend to forget is that while people in the sixties were smoking mostly poor-quality ditchweed effectively, lesser amounts of truly good-quality material was available, and always has been. From the early seventies people were getting Jamaican bush at 17 percent. The argument that today's pot is just so much stronger than anything before is just nonsense. It's quite incorrect to say we have these new superstrains."

But it is true that there is a lot more of the good stuff around. Eagle Bill smoked a lot of ditchweed in his day. Now that he's older and wiser he's smoking less, vaporizing more. He swivels the giant jar so that the glass pipe stem aims at my mouth. I take a big draw. "That's going to hit your consciousness in about ninety seconds," he says. And it does. Smoking any plant is going to put a lot of tars in your lungs, so I like the idea of the vaporizor. But I don't enjoy it. It feels too moist, like inhaling humid air.

✻

De Dampkring Coffeeshop is a goofy little golden psychedelic cave of a place on Handboogstraat. It's got stalactites hanging down from the ceiling, and the walls are all lumpy like some hobbit roadhouse where a troll might roll through the front door with a wheelbarrow of magic mushrooms. It's the favorite hangout of a grower named Soma, an expat American with Rasta dreadlocks down to his ankles, which he usually sweeps up and wraps around his head in a great gray woolly turban of hair, just like Milky Baba in Nepal. Soma offers me some of his Dutch Moonshine, a water hash he produces that's on the menu at Dampkring. It bubbles happily in the bowl of the glass pipe as he ignites it. Very powerful hashish. I've come to ask questions, but I'm instantly too high to play journalist, although I manage to scribble a few notes.

"Plants demand responsibility from you. If you're off, those things go down fast. For a long time I thought I was just the bodyguard, but now I realize it's symbiotic," he tells me, looking over the top of his glasses. "I'm feeding them carbon dioxide, they're feeding me oxygen."

He pulls an arrowhead-shaped rock from his pocket and hands it to me. It's heavy in my palm. "This is ninety percent iron, ten percent nickel, in a combination not found on earth," he whispers. "It's from an asteroid that hit Siberia."

*

Soma has a room where he keeps about seventy mother plants representing forty-two varieties. If you ignore the bright lights and the white-as-white walls, the room is beautiful, like a garden, because the plants are not in rows, but snuggled together, and each plant is different in age, size, and shape from its neighbor, so that the overall effect is the diverse, organic feel of a naturally occurring forest. Even the shape and color of the leaves vary greatly from plant to plant, the long thin pale green leaves evincing sativas, the fat dark ones indicas.

"I was in another grow room today, and they were complaining about aphids," I warn him as we enter. Aphids are one of a battery of pesky insects that growers have to watch for. "Should I be worried I'm going to bring aphids in here?"

"No, because I spray neem oil on my plants, and nothing like that stands a chance with neem oil," he says. Neem oil comes from the neem tree of India, and is a natural bug repellent. It also gives the plants a strange glossy finish, a shine like what you get when you spray car tires with Armor All. While we talk he starts spraying the plants with what looks like water.

"Is there neem oil in that?"

"No, this is vitamin B and kelp seaweed."

"How often do they get that?"

"Maybe once a week."

Each plant has a label to identify the strain stuck into the soil at its base, but Soma says he doesn't need to read the labels anymore. "In this room I can recognize each plant just by its leaf shape, its body language, or body type, and then, whether it's healthy or sick," he says.

"How do you know?"

"The only way to get to know is to spend time with them. Like you and me, we just met, and the only way we are going to get to know each other better is to spend time together. Get to know each other's face.

"The thing with cannabis is, it hasn't been allowed for people to get to know it for the last seventy years. A lot of valuable knowledge has been lost, but it's starting to get relearned."

"That knowledge was mostly for hemp, outdoors," I suggest. "Now it's being grown today in a new way, for a new purpose."

"No, it was grown outdoors for these purposes, at certain climates and elevations, for centuries. Now it's being worked with in this way, indoors, because the illegality of it around the world has forced it indoors, into these artificial conditions. In the process that's created all these minilaboratories to study it, without people even thinking of them as that. But they are mini–botanical laboratories in which to study all the stains."

I mention something Jorge Cervantes, the grow-book author, once told me, that indoor growing spurred great advances in developing new varieties, because instead of one or two harvests a year, an indoor grower could have as many as five, which means five generations' worth of experimentation.

"That's right," says Soma. "I've been working with some strains now for over five years, and I'm only really starting now to understand them, because like a person, plants aren't that simple."

Today he is making a tray of sixty clones, with the help of an assistant, a taciturn Welshman. At a workbench outside the mother room Soma's cutting the large lower leaves off each selected plant in turn, and the Welshman is planting the cuttings in individual soil containers, pushing a little plastic label identifying the strain into the soil beside them.

"This is one of the amazing things plants can do—grow a whole new plant from a cutting," says Soma. "You cut the plant in just the right spot, with a scalpel to get a really clean edge, then dip it in this root hormone powder that's a fungicide also. It stimulates the roots to grow, and it also keeps mold from growing in that wound. The reason I cut all these extra leaves off"—each clone has a single cluster of leaves from which he shears two thirds off— "is because with the plant having no root system like this, the less weight they have to hold up the better."

"You should have a gardening show on TV," I say.

"If it were legal and free I wouldn't mind doing that, because I love watching even the regular gardening shows—it's all similar techniques," he says. "These days plants are my role models. They have such an earth-friendly existence. They are so patient, and they sustain so much of the life on this planet just by their mere existence. Us humans, we destroy so much just by our mere existence. I'm trying to get more like a plant, actually. Because as humans I don't think we've been doing so hot. I think we'd be much better if we were more like plants."

He clips about a half dozen cuttings from the lowest branches of each mother before replacing the plant in the mother room and bringing back another. "This one is called Peacemaker; it won the Cannabis Cup one year. Not my favorite but quite a nice strain. The ones I don't like I got rid of a while ago."

"You're really cutting it back."

"Yeah, I like to make bigger clones, because they get a head start."

"How old is this plant?"

"Two and a half months."

I ask him if clones of clones of clones eventually start to lose their health and vigor, as many pot people have told me, among them Marc Emery in Canada and Will Rogers in England.

"It's not true."

"People believe it. They told me sincerely."

"I know, but I don't find it to be true. This strain I've had going for four and a half years—it hasn't lost one bit of energy. I mean I make new mothers all the time, from clones, some of the clones I'm making right now could end up being a mother—probably will. But with this strain, in four and a half years, if anything, since I've gotten to know it better, it's got better."

❊

A few years ago the Dutch police busted Soma for cultivation.

"In the time that's gone by, magical things have happened," he says. He went to trial with a medical defense, that he was supplying three prescriptions to patients who legitimately needed cannabis. "I got found guilty, but with an explanation. My fine was suspended, and I was put on two years' probation. They told me I could never grow during the two years or I'd have to pay the five-thousand-guilder fine. But I couldn't stop. Because there is in

Dutch law this principle of a higher force. If there is a higher good to what you're doing they can work with that."

"So the state has to recognize a higher good?"

"Yeah. And in this case there is. My own health depends on this. I have to be doing this for my health, because if I were dependent on getting quality like this from a coffee shop, I'm not going to get it. I've already checked it out and it just doesn't happen. I have to do this myself, or I'd have to train somebody to do it with my exact method so that I'm not going to get poisoned while I'm getting medicated, because other people are putting pesticides on it, or all these chemical fertilizers, or the systemic poisons people use in the soils so that bugs can't live on it. You can't tell me that stuff is good for me, if bugs die from it."

"This one looks kind of sickly," I say when he brings out the next mother plant.

"It is. I'm killing it."

"You're going to kill it? Right now?"

"Yeah. It's getting old. I've already taken a lot of clones off it. I'm going to take the last few cuttings off it and just cut it down, because I need the room. You can see how crowded it is in there."

"Do you have any conscience about killing them?"

"No. It's fine with them. It's like they know everything I'm taking off is furthering them through offspring. They know that in a silent way."

❊

Compared with grow rooms I've seen in England and Canada, the Dutch commercial grow room I visit is precisely organized and immaculately clean. Five hundred two-foot-tall plants under twenty 600-watt lights. Half of them an Edelweiss-Silver Haze cross, the rest Orange Bud. An extremely stinky crop.

"You know what we say here?" says the grower. "'A good cunt stinks. It stinks so bad it makes the cock throw up.' It's the same with weed. The more stink the better." On the outside of the building, where the air is vented, there's not the faintest trace of a scent. The Dutch have developed great air-filtering systems.

If the police were to bust this kind of setup, the penalty would be 140 hours of community service and a 5,000-guilder fine.

"That's the tax you pay," he says. "I see it like bootlegging in America, almost like a game. Everyone wants to smoke it, but where's the money? You still have to hide that from the government."

"There's a culture here now," says his partner. "It's been here thirty years. Second generation. People have grown up in it. It could never be suppressed now."

We sit at their kitchen table and roll joints of the Orange Bud mixed with that super-strong Van Alle tobacco, which one of the growers claims caused him to be thrown out of a disco in France—the French were certain he was smoking hashish. The Dutch have little goodwill toward the French, who when it comes to drug war hysteria are second in Europe only to Sweden. Knute the Swede had earlier been very worried about flying back to Stockholm from Amsterdam, because Swedish customs officers can order you to take a urine test, and if cannabis is found in your system that's considered possession. I always thought of Swedes as liberal folk. They're always being portrayed here in North America as an overtaxed welfare state half a step from pure social-ism. But when it comes to cannabis, they're nearly nazis.

✳

Up the street from the Hash Marihuana Hemp Museum is the Can-nabis College, which is overseen by Eddie and Roland of the Fly-ing Dutchmen Seed Company. The Cannabis College (*For the Cannabis Knowledge,* as the T-shirts say) is devoted in part to spread-ing the word about organic growing techniques. It has a healthy, five-plant garden on display in the basement, including a Swazi Safari that's had the stalks bent down to keep the branches from growing up into the low ceiling. Five plants is the maximum local police will allow them to grow. "There's still a tolerance policy of five plants for personal use," says Roland. "But for commercial growers, now they make appointments with the electricity companies, and the electricity company is going to tell the Justice Department who's using too much power. That's a new policy here. Ridiculous."

"It's all part of the way Prohibition creates more criminal activity," he says. "To avoid detection you might start to bypass the electrical meters, and then you're not just a grower, you're a thief."

✳

After the Harvest is a little store on a quiet street in a residential neighborhood far from the tourist zone. There are rows of little green peyote buds, each a living cactus the size of a chocolate, in small soil pots in the display window. The store specializes in the next generation of natural hallucinogens: peyote, San Pedro cacti, ayahuasca, various mushrooms. It also sells equipment for making hashish. Inside the two staff members are making what they jokingly call "thirty-meter hash"—that is, hashish that gets consumed before it ever gets more than thirty meters from the bucket where it's made. They're using the Ice-o-lator, a simple method for making hash from the discarded leaves, and shake from the manicure of commercial or personal bud. The Ice-o-lator is essentially nothing more complicated than placing in a bucket a bag with a fine mesh screen for a bottom, adding water and plenty of ice, then adding your shake or trimmings. The THC-rich trichomes will filter through the bag to the bottom while you stir the lot like a witch's cauldron. Blond-haired Ben is doing just that as I come in the shop.

"I usually stir each batch for half an hour," he says. "I like to, as a meditation."

I don't think so. He gets bored with it quickly, and sets about showing me the dried remains of yesterday's screening, sitting on a cloth screen stretched taut over a ring of wood like a tambourine, and then we pop a bit in a pipe and smoke it. It's pure and clean, hashish as it should be. Very quickly work is abandoned and we sit around a table cluttered with ashtrays, dirty teacups, newspapers, and other odds and ends, drinking herbal tea and discussing life in Amsterdam.

The store's other employee, Sasha, from Croatia, runs the inch-high flame of a lighter back and forth across the white-paper body of a cigarette, turning the paper brown, or maybe gray with soot, but not igniting it. Then he puts the cigarette to his lips and starts blowing hard, as if it were a peashooter or a trumpet. What for? He claims, somewhat dubiously, that heating the tobacco and then blowing on it somehow gets rid of the nicotine.

"But I thought nicotine was the whole point of tobacco."

"No no. Nicotine is a depressant and cannabis is a stimulant, so I don't like to mix the two."

I'm skeptical. "I always thought nicotine was a stimulant; from what I've read marijuana defies easy medical classification as a stimulant or depressant, displaying qualities of both at the same time," I say, paraphrasing pot author Joan Bello. A bit later I'm doubly skeptical, when Sasha opens himself a vodka cooler.

"Now alcohol is *definitely* a depressant."

"Yeah, but it's only four percent."

The store's owner, Mila Jansen, arrives. She's been smoking pot since 1965, except for a seven-year break when she went heavily macrobiotic. All that smoking has given her a very deep, froggy voice. When I spoke to her on the phone the first time, I thought she was a man. In 1995 she began marketing the Pollinator, a drumlike dry-sifting precursor to the Ice-o-lator. She still sells some of those to larger commercial operations, but the Ice-o-lator has really captured the imagination of do-it-yourself small growers.

"Making your own hash from your own plants is always going to be the best," she says. "I'm getting all these fan letters from customers. One American wrote me that it's the greatest thing since apple pie. Is apple pie considered a great thing in America?"

I assure her it is. We look at some of the pressed water hash under a microscope, and it's loaded with crystals that look tremendously globular when magnified. "Bubbles" or "glands" better describe them.

Mila spent fourteen years living in India and still misses it, especially since her grandson is there. She gestures through the shop window across the street to rows of identical apartment windows glumly withstanding a cold rain.

"He could be trapped three floors up in the city, or he could be living on the beach in Goa, with chickens and piglets running around," she says. "So he's in the right place."

She remembers returning from India to resettle in Europe with her kids years ago. The plane landed in London in a blizzard, and in the next few days she had a chance to gauge the English reaction to snow and ice. Stress and bitching. "This goddamned storm has made me late for work!" When she finally made it over to Amsterdam the canals had been cleared in places for skating, spontaneous stalls had been set up to sell hot chocolate and pea soup, and old and young couples were strolling arm in arm watching snowflakes fall on silent streets. "I think I'll live in Holland," she decided.

One day it turns crisp and cool, and I go ice skating at the Sporthal Jaap Eden, an Olympic-sized outdoor oval only a short tram ride from the city center. They rent those long-bladed speed skates there, and it's the first time I ever wore a pair. You can get a great speed up in the straightaways, but in the curves crossing the legs one over the other requires a completely different shifting of weight than with normal skates. I'm feeling like my hip might dislocate if I'm not careful.

Skating is like swimming—outdoors in the fresh air is so much better than indoors. A pack of about forty Dutchmen—mostly men, anyway, a few women—all of them in aerodynamic suits, glide by me super-fast, as if they're about to take flight around the inner edge of the oval, riding in each other's slipstreams. With the wind at my back I'm skating probably as fast as I've ever skated, but because all these supersonic Dutchmen are sailing past, it doesn't feel fast enough.

I stop along the bleachers on the far side of the oval, where young people have stepped off the ice to discreetly light up cigarettes and reefers. These are the dawdlers, out in the fresh air more for socializing than for fitness, and getting a little bit higher than the get-high-on-life crowd. It seems as though those super-fit, super-straight hard-skating endorphin fanatics racing past are willing to make allowances for deviants sparking up and sharing doobs on the sidelines. Live and let live. Even stoners are free to come out and skate.

And I'm thinking, this is why I love Holland.

8 : SWITZERLAND AND SPAIN

Every time some national government sloughs off the prickly question of what should be done about marijuana, and appoints an independent body to study the matter, the voice of reason prevails. It happened most recently in Switzerland in 1999, when the Swiss Federation Commission for Drug Issues released its report. You can find the whole document, in English, in PDF form on the Internet, and parts of it are quite amusing, as when the commissioners, comparing pot laws in various countries, can't help indulging in the traditional European sport of America-bashing: "Richard Nixon's plan to eradicate cannabis is widely considered to be a good example of how repressive measures can backfire. . . . Once more, the United States has produced astonishing yet interesting regulations for cannabis . . . For instance, the death penalty for serious drug crimes would be more at home in an integralistic state like Iran than in a modern pluralistic society."

For Switzerland the commissioners unanimously recommended "a model which not only removes the prohibition of consumption and possession but also makes it possible for cannabis to be purchased lawfully." They called for an age limit (18), a minimum price, and an advertising ban. "For self-supply purposes, it should be lawful to grow a specified number of plants. Commercial production should be closely regulated," they noted. "Furthermore it would be necessary to impose a requirement of proof of residence in order to avert a 'drugs tourism' phenomenon."

Proof of residence just to smoke something? It may not sound fair, but it's a common enough policy. Did you know non-residents cannot legally buy tobacco in California, nor beer at Fenway Park in Boston?

✳

I guess I'm the kind of "drugs tourist" the writers of that Swiss government report worry about, because I arrived in Bern, the capital of Switzerland, on an overnight train from Amsterdam this very morning, and by afternoon I'm already on the street looking to score some marijuana. I've heard it's quasilegal, and tolerated. A Swiss grower I met in my travels told me, "Growing the plant is legal, because the plant is God-given. But smoking the plant is illegal." That would account for some strange Swiss Internet sites I examined back at home, like the Cannabis Store, which offered scented pillows—potpourris for your clothes drawers, to kill odors—containing five grams of sweet-smelling flowers of a well-known marijuana strain.

In any case Bern is small—only three hundred thousand people—and pristine clean. In how many capital cities of the world is it safe to swim in the river? Along with hundreds of others, on a sunny autumn afternoon I swam in the Arno, the swift mountain river that snakes through the city. You jump in upstream, the current hustles you relentlessly along, and three hundred meters later you angle to shore. Don't miss it—there's a hydrodam around the next bend.

In the middle of town there is a medieval clock tower with moving figures that were added in 1530 and have been appearing every hour ever since. Now maybe in 1530 it was a thrill to see a couple of tiny figures slowly transiting an eight-foot arc on a little shelf way up the side of a building, but I was raised on Disney, and I need spectacle. Busloads of Japanese tourists seem to feel the same way. We stand on the cobblestone street and crane our necks, expecting more, but there is no more. It's a big letdown for all of us. Here we are now, entertain us. At best it's a lesson in how far technology has come since 1530.

There's a gray-haired lady in the crowd, dressed like a flight attendant. She's a city employee, a tourist helper, there to guide lost schmucks like me. I approach her, all indirect and circumspect: "Do you know where I could buy *hemp* products around here? Like clothing and stuff?"

She thinks a minute. "Hmmm. Hemp clothing . . . No . . ." Then she brightens. "But we have three stores where you can buy *grass*!"

✳

Growland is one of the stores she recommended. It's just around the corner. There's a big display of California Orange and K-2 clones for sale, growing right in the window. One of the employees, who calls himself Monkey, and who indeed looks a bit like a monkey, tells me there was recently a referendum in Switzerland calling for the legalization of all drugs, but the idea was defeated because of fears it would cause a flood of junkies to invade from Germany and France. The dreaded drug tourists again. Down in the basement he sells me some grass, which I dutifully take to a lookout in the park beside the nearby cathedral. Far below the Arno is spilling over the dam, and I do my best to get high by smoking that newly purchased pot. But I just cannot get high. It has virtually no scent, and won't stay lit, either. A disaster.

Later in the afternoon two young neo-hippies with long blond crusty dreadlocks, carrying swathes of fresh-cut, six-foot-tall cannabis plants over their shoulders, ride by on bicycles. I stop them.

"Can you really carry it around like that without worry?"

"Sure, as long as we don't smoke it. Or let anyone see us smoke it."

I want to tag along, and try in a passive-aggressive way to cadge an invite, but they're on bikes and I'm likely too unhip-looking to be their new pal so fast. Dreadlocks like theirs can be a uniform to make people cliquey.

✳

In 1993 a woman named Shirin Patterson figured out that Switzerland had no laws on the books whatsoever regarding the cultivation of cannabis. Hemp, marijuana, it didn't matter—cannabis was legal to grow. Patterson launched a twelve-acre hemp farm called Cannabioland, started producing hemp products, and allowed people to come out and pick their own—ahem—hemp. I keep dialing Cannabioland (phone booths in Switzerland all have a computer keyboard attached, so you can send e-mail and search a computerized phone book for any number in the entire country), but there is never an answer, so I set off on a Sunday morning to visit in person, unannounced.

I take a train, a bus, then wander on foot for hours down country lanes to the sound of wooden cowbells clanking around the necks of very contented-looking beasts. It's so quiet sometimes I can hear the clanking of lunchtime dishes in farmhouses. Then a faint noise grows louder—the *doof doof doof-doof-doofdoof* dregs of the morning after (afternoon after, actually) of a rave being put on by the "Ride Inspiration People," whoever they are, a bunch of bushy-haired boys and tanned hippie girls trampling the grass in a wooded hollow. All very strange, and I'm not even high.

Nearby I meet some Kosovar refugees out for a walk, and then a tourist girl from Australia who gives me a ride on her bicycle, me sitting on the back rack while she half stands on the pedals, her ass cheeks jiggling about six inches from my nose. I'm almost glad I'm not high. It would be *too* weird.

At last I find Cannabioland, where row upon row of cannabis plants grow green and leafy in a sloping fenceless field next to a paved road, overseen by a big guard tower at the top of the slope, like some prop from a POW movie. There's no one around, which is eerie. At the farmhouse the farmer won't talk to me. All he'll say is the farm is closed "because of trouble with the law."

*

Later I stop in to see Monkey again at Growland and he tells me Cannabioland is under the jurisdiction of the police from the town of Fribourg, and those cops are not as pot-tolerant as the Bern police. He suggests if I want to see a major cannabis operation, I should go to a certain little town not far from Zurich.

First thing off the train in Zurich I ask at tourist information in the station where to buy marijuana. The woman behind the desk happily pulls out a free city map and circles the streets I should seek. Three options. "Here is the store called Biotop. You can buy grass in there, and on the street outside there will be people wanting to sell you hashish. Then over here, this is the sleazy part of town, with bars of exotic dancers. There is also a shop here. And then there is one more over here, near your hotel."

"Jeez, are you really allowed to give this information out freely? In my country they wouldn't allow civil servants like you to tell tourists where to buy weed."

She shrugs. "It's going to be legal in a few years anyway."

Biotop is selling foot-long branches with clusters of bud still on the stem and most of the leaves trimmed off. These cost between 110 to 140 Swiss francs. It burns poorly, but the high is fairly effective.

"We can't talk to journalists because of problems with the law," the salesman says. Problems with the law. The exact phrase they'd used at Cannabioland.

In the evening I see plenty of people smoking in the streets. One of them tells me he has eight plants growing on his balcony. "Humungous plants!" says his girlfriend. I saw the occasional plant growing on apartment balconies in Bern, and there are even more in Zurich. It seems a strange phenomenon, to see pot displayed so openly in a country with a reputation for being so highly regimented and conformist, with its compulsory military service and antinoise laws that make it an offense to shower in an apartment building after eleven at night.

I buy some hash on a Zurich street, low-grade Moroccan, and smoke a bunch before going to sleep. I proceed to have horrible dreams, but it might have something to do with the weather. Through my window come the sounds of wind, rain, and a crying baby.

The next morning I take the train out to that little town with the big grow operation that Monkey had recommended. It's a huge complex of greenhouses that supplies about a dozen retail outlets with marijuana, including Growland in Bern and Biotop in Zurich. They have a few massive bushy twelve-foot plants which make great subjects for photos, big happy green monsters against a backdrop of white walls and the steeple of a sturdy church. In a big sunny room beside the cafeteria (lunch was meatballs, rice, and purple cabbage salad) fifty employees busily manicure bud (anyone caught smoking it at work is fired) brought in from another (secret) location where it is dried.

The man in charge, Beni, has an extremely depressed, hangdog aspect as he gives me a tour of the place. In the largest greenhouse, full of Skunk 44 and White Widow clones still in the vegetative phase, he tells me that four months ago a Swiss judge handed down a ruling that all cannabis with a THC level higher than 0.3 percent could not be called hemp, but was marijuana, and therefore illegal. So for the first time in Switzerland the courts have divided cannabis into "hemp" and "marijuana."

"The Swiss government is waiting for the moment to decide on a new law for drugs," he says. "No one knows how that will go. It could go good, but there is intense pressure from France and Germany to stay tough on drugs. You could come back a year from now and there will be nothing here."

✳

Lugano is in the southernmost part of Switzerland, near the Italian border. In Lugano everyone looks, acts, speaks, and dresses like Northern Italians—that is, with elegance and style—but they are Swiss in their sense of punctuality and tidiness. It's a ritzy vacation town. There are several shops where you can buy marijuana, which comes in sealed little plastic pouches. "*Sacchetto Profumato*" is what it says on them. Perfumed sachets. A potpourri, or closet freshener. The instructions are in Italian, German, and French: "With a sharp needle prick around a dozen holes and place the sachet in your drawer. As an aroma for the bath: take two grams and stir in the water. Warning: this product cannot be exported or sold to minors."

In the first shop I enter the woman pulls up a little display board from behind the counter. "I think this is what you look for, no?"

Yes. There are five varieties stapled to it, three indoor, two outdoor. I select an outdoor, organic, Durban Poison. That boastful South African woman I met in Phnom Penh had called it "the best!"

"Is this legal?" I ask.

According to her it's legal for her to sell it to me, but it's not legal for me to open it. That's the point where it becomes illegal. "Crazy," she says.

There used to be a dozen stores like this, but most of the others were closed by the police for selling ecstasy or harder drugs. She's been open three years without problems. At another store, more of a grow shop, they dispense with the "perfumed sachet" bit and just sell you the little plastic bag, although it is sealed tight. I buy some Anapurna, which when I open the bag turns out to be quite wet. A day left in the air in my hotel room is necessary to dry it so I can smoke it.

Lugano is blessed with a Mediterranean microclimate. I never thought I'd see palm trees in Switzerland. There's a beautiful park along the shoreline, where I sit cross-legged on the grass, enjoying that organic Durban Poison, which is the best high of my European vacation so far, or maybe I am again influenced by the beauty of the surroundings and the mellow, relaxed pace of the afternoon strollers in the park. Into the joints I mix tobacco from a "Barclay Smooth and Light XS mit der Extra Smooth Filter," which is made by British American Tobacco Switzerland, under agreement with the Brown and Williamson Tobacco Corporation, Louisville, Kentucky.

A young mother walks by, dressed elegantly, Italian style. She's being poked in the bum with a stick by her four-year-old son.

"No."

"Si."

"No!"

"Si!"

"Prego . . ."

I close my eyes and listen to the wheels of bicycles and baby carriages crinkle the cinder path. Church bells and laughter.

Someone is drumming in the distance. A duet of young Lugano neo-hippie drums. Later I'll wander over to watch and listen. In a park bench nearby someone has carved *"Parco del Drogati."* A kid comes up and asks to borrow my lighter. He's too young to be smoking. Maybe fourteen, so I'm reluctant. He explains himself. He wants it to burn a picture of his girlfriend. "Let me see, let me see." He shows me. A nice uncomplicated-looking girl. And she's gone and broken his heart. The chemicals in the photographic paper prevent it from bursting into flame, so he holds a corner with his fingernails as it melts slowly, like plastic.

✳

Another overnight train, this time from Switzerland to Spain. In Barcelona I pay a visit to the offices of *Cáñamo,* which with a circulation of 40,000 is the leading Spanish cannabis magazine, Spain's equivalent to America's *High Times.* While I wait to speak to the editor in chief, I can hear a British guy pitching a product, a complete little indoor growing kit for the home, to one of the magazine's subeditors. "This one is particularly useful in Holland, where they have a limit of four plants per person," he's claiming. "It's been tested extensively in Australia."

The Spanish editor is encouraging about the future, but explains that for the moment the market for such a thing is very small. Although there are an estimated three million cannabis smokers in Spain, he says, "Five years ago there were only maybe a dozen people growing their own, now there are a few thousand, but mostly for personal use, not commercial. It's coming. People are learning. But most Spanish smokers are still buying Moroccan hashish on the street, and have never even tried marijuana."

❋

Cañamo's editor, Gaspar, tells me that every year the quality of Moroccan hashish declines. "The theory is that the Moroccans are not preoccupied enough with seed."

He outlines the various grades of Moroccan hashish: top grade is sold to Holland and Germany, mostly to "very old and reliable customers." Second grade goes to the major smugglers, who pack it out by the ton. Third grade is what you see mostly in Spain. Even with this lower-quality product, there is great variation. One type of hashish available on the street is called *ficha*. A *ficha* is a gambling chip; the hash is hard and dry. *Petrolero* is oily, as the name suggests. Dark and malleable, it is often cut with henna. Then there is *chocolate*, "the worst." *Cañamo* had recently run a feature on these dodgy substances, featuring a cover shot of some *chocolate* coiled like a lengthy turd, with the cover line: *Le mierda que te fumas.* The shit that you smoke.

Cañamo proselytizes what Gaspar calls "autocultivation." The magazine is crammed with shots of Spanish gardens, most of them outdoor, personal affairs of a few, often huge, plants. In 1998 *Cañamo*'s grow editor made a splash at the Cannabis Cup in Amsterdam with a seminar slide show of more than a hundred Spanish outdoor marijuana gardens.

Spanish legal tradition is nonintrusive. It gives great respect to an individual's right to privacy, which makes the state reluctant to prosecute people who are growing a few plants for personal consumption. In 1996 a marijuana legalization organization called ARSEC launched a major court battle to test the limits of state tolerance. A very public marijuana cooperative of nearly two hundred members was formed. If individual growing was tacitly acceptable, would group cultivation for group consumption be tolerated too? That year a lower court ruled cooperative grows, or any noncommercial growing of pot, presented no threat to public safety. The year 1997 was one of euphoric harvests for the newly formed pot co-ops that sprouted. Then in November the Spanish Supreme Court overturned the lower court ruling and declared that any and all cannabis cultivation posed an "abstract danger" to society. Again in 1998 the Supreme Court ruled against cannabis freedom, overruling an appeals court judge who had refused to fine a woman for possession of sixty grams of hashish.

This sudden chill has slowed the legalization movement in Spain. ARSEC, with four thousand members, soldiers on. The acronym stands for Asociación Ramón Santos de estudios sobre el cannabis; the Ramón Santos Association for the Study of Cannabis. Ramón Santos was a brilliant lawyer, now dead, who won many cannabis cases and was a lover of the plant. When I visit ARSEC in its cramped offices above a comic book store in Barcelona's Placa sant Josep Oriol, the director, Jaume Torrens, complains that while punitive laws for cultivation are still in place (fines of 50,000 to a million pesos for possession; prison terms of six months to four years for cultivation, even for personal consumption) and judges are giving tougher sentences, the average Spanish pot consumer seems to think the battle for legalization has been won.

Certainly Spain seems pretty free and easy to me when it comes to marijuana. In certain neighborhoods of Barcelona you see plants growing openly on plenty of balconies; as in Switzerland, they're plainly visible from the street. When I stop in at a local grow shop the owner disparages the quality of these urban outdoor plants. He says they don't flower well because the amount of city light at night interferes with their natural pattern of flowering as the days shorten in the fall.

At the same grow shop, two growers urge me to get out into the countryside around town. "Everywhere you look, you will see three-meter plants waving in the wind." I'm sure there's a certain amount of Iberian bravado in that claim. But acceptance of cannabis seems pretty entrenched in Barcelona. Late one evening, in one of the bars in Barcelona where cannabis can be smoked freely, an old-timer rolls up a spliff of homegrown Spanish Skunk sprinkled with some Tanzanian hashish, and announces, "I feel there is only one problem left to solve with cannabis in my country: which variety is best!"

9 : MOROCCO

Morocco is part of the Arab world.

My only previous experience with Arab culture was twenty years ago. Backpacking around Europe, I met a woman named Irene on a nude beach in Greece. We started traveling together and decided to go to Israel, via Jordan. We flew from Athens to Amman, Jordan's capital. I don't remember seeing a living tree in that whole city. If there are any, they're caked in dust. We arrived late at night with no hotel lined up, and wandered around in shared taxis looking for a place, which was difficult because we had no guidebook and none of the streets had names anyway. Eventually a taxi driver ditched us in front of a hostel that hadn't been open for two years, and we sat down on the curb feeling dazed and confused.

A passing white van full of United States Marines came to our rescue. They were stationed in Jordan to guard the American Embassy. They all lived together in a party house, where they enjoyed drinking beer and bourbon in the evenings. On mornings off they would arm themselves with BB guns and climb a staircase to the roof, where they opened fire on unsuspecting locals waiting at a nearby bus stop. The roof was flat with a low three-foot wall around the perimeter, so they could fire a shot, then duck quickly for cover as their innocent Arab target flinched in pain from a direct hit. While the victim swiveled around frantically looking for a culprit, the guilty ones, grown men giggling on their knees, kept themselves hidden a mere thirty yards away.

After a couple of days of Yankee hospitality Irene and I tried to get a taxi to the famous ancient carved-in-pink-rock city of Petra. In the midst of a taxi pool of black Mercedes, two drivers broke into a fight over us that ended with one of them chasing the other down the street, kicking him in the ass as he ran. It's the only time I've ever seen that cartoon gesture carried out in real life, and it was made all the more surreal by the way they hoisted their ankle-length white cotton robes while they sprinted. There was something delicate about it, spritely, like Julie Andrews kicking the von Trapp kids across Austria.

*

Morocco, like Jordan, suffers no shortage of odd moments of cartoonish violence. I've never seen children in the streets wrestle with such ferocity. In Fez I remember a ten-year-old kid standing over his battered opponent, squeezing his head in a vise grip between the knees, yanking on the hair, then letting go, and just *gloating*. The loser fell limp and passive, lying there with a terrified, submissive, surrendering look in his long-lashed child eyes. And grown-ups just walked by oblivious.

Adults fought too. In Fez one evening before the streets cleared—and they cleared early, by ten o'clock—I joined a crowd encircling two men in the midst of a heated argument. With exaggerated gestures both of them stripped off their shirts and handed them to friends, as a prelude to what I expected to be a fistfight. They stood eyeball to eyeball, hands at their sides, bumping chests and spitting insults for the longest time. When the actual fighting started, no punches were thrown. There appeared to be strict rules: you try to cup a palm under your opponent's chin and then shove his head back to knock him off balance. Very difficult. No one succeeded, and eventually a giant of a man stepped between them to end the stalemate and scold them both.

*

"Countless first-time visitors to Morocco, fleeced or hassled by 'guides' the minute they get off bus or ferry, leave before they have become accustomed to the initial shock of the street culture."

You'll find some variation of this warning in every guide-book to Tangier. The ferry ride from Algeciras in Spain, past Gibraltar and across the strait to Tangier is a two-hour trip from Europe to Africa, and from Europe to Arabia. I'm barely through the gates of the port of Tangier before Ali latches on to me. He's maybe thirty, a compact, pug-faced, pitifully desperate hustler. I'm fresh meat off the boat. I'm wearing my little pack on my back, *Lonely Planet* in hand, thumb stuck in the middle to mark the page of an unreadable city center map. I must be his ideal of a foreign sap.

My sudden new best friend insists in emphatic English (pretty good, considering it's his fourth language) that my guide-book is useless: "Morocco has a new King, you must know! Mohammed VI is our King! This is a new era, a new reign, a new life, new everything. Everything is changed. Most hotels have changed their names in honor of the new King!" It's laughable, but since I have no clue which direction I need to go, and the guy is aggressively, doggedly persistent in wanting to "help" me find a hotel, I succumb to phase one of the hustle. As I head up a major street that seems to lead toward the hilltop city, Ali falls in step at my shoulder. Five steps behind us lurks another hustler, possibly his sidekick. Ali is almost handsome, but this guy has only one tooth in his head, bottom middle, and it wobbles when he talks like a tea-stained bowling pin. They discuss me in Arabic without looking at each other.

"Who's he?" I ask Ali.

"I don't know."

"Why is he coming with us?"

"Maybe he needs to go this way."

Squinting in the midday heat, I make out some backpacker tourist types waving and calling to me from the sidewalk tables of a café across the road, urging me to come over, presumably so they can warn me, save me, the *Lonely Planet* Lamb being led to his fleecing. I just wave back, getting into my role as the dumb yokel. Ali cranks his patter up to speed, and a crackling patter it is, brimming with nonstop declarations of veracity and trustworthiness. The man never shuts up.

"My grandfather always told me, 'Ali, if there is one lesson to carry through life, the most important is always tell the truth! Don't you ever lie! And I never do. I never lie, Brian! I tell you a man's honesty, his word, is all a man has in the end. Is that not so? Yes, my friend, to never lie is so difficult and yet so important, so vital to a life—"

"Uh, hey Ali, where can I find this place?" I'm pointing to a name in my guidebook. It says you can still rent, and cheaply, the very hotel room where William Burroughs wrote *Naked Lunch*. He'd come to Tangier in the 1950s because it was the home of self-exiled American writer Paul Bowles, author of *The Sheltering Sky,* an amazing novel about fucked-up American seekers wandering off into the desert. I say the hotel's name, and Ali cries out: "No no no! That place is for faggots. It's where tourists take boys. And you're not a faggot, I can tell that about you, you are no faggot, Brian!"

He might be bullshitting, in fact he almost certainly is bullshitting, but he's right about my not being gay, and he has succeeded in putting me off the place.

So we pass on the Burroughs shrine. No loss. I'm a bit down on myself anyway for having that impulse to stay where Burroughs stayed, for trying to be all writerly, which in this case would be nothing but some pretentious bullshit on my part. I never managed to actually read *Naked Lunch*. Years back I gave it my best shot a couple of times, but it wasn't long before I'd think, Fuck this, it's a good thing his daddy left him a fat trust fund because this crap wasn't written to pay the bills. A waste of his time and mine. I suspected he wrote it just to pretend he had something to do between bouts of boy-taking tourism.

But I must tell you, a few weeks later when I got back to Western Civilization I read somewhere that *Naked Lunch* was written on a hashish high, so I gave it one more try. This time I kept glazing over, snapping out of it, and skipping ahead to the next "routine." I found it impossible to read linearly, and not that interesting to read period. But you have to respect Burroughs, or so people keep telling me. He listened to his dark side and turned it into twisted humor, back before sick and twisted was cool. In fact, almost single-handedly he made sick and twisted cool. So in a way he was a great pioneer, but on the flip side he has Marilyn Manson to answer for, it's his fault sick and twisted became just another marketable gimmick.

I got more out of reading a collection of Burroughs' letters, which show a different side of him, especially the ones to Allen Ginsberg. For once Burroughs wants to be liked, wants to be charming. A letter from Peru got me interested in Yage: "It is like nothing else. This is not the chemical lift of C, the sexless, horribly sane stasis of junk, the vegetable nightmare of peyote, or the humorous silliness of weed. This is insane overwhelming rape of the senses. . . . This is the most complete negation possible of respectability." (I eventually figured out Yage is the same thing as ayahuasca, the drug some religious Rasta types I met in Amsterdam were experimenting with.) Burroughs' letters from Tangier describe the city in a freer time. To Neal Cassidy: "This town would please you. Weed absolutely legal, and you can smoke it anywhere." To Allen Ginsberg: "Their lousy weed tears your throat like it's cut with horse shit." And his opinion of Arabs: "What's all this old Moslem culture shit? One thing I have learned. I know what Arabs do all day and night. They sit around smoking cut weed and playing some silly card game. And don't ever fall for this inscrutable oriental shit like Bowles puts down (that shameless faker). They are just a gabby, gossipy, simple-minded, lazy crew of citizens."

They aren't.

Nearing fifty years later, as far as weed goes, you can't smoke it anywhere in public anymore. And the descendents of the crew of citizens Burroughs so loathed seem pretty damned purposeful and busy. Nearly everyone I met behaved well toward me, helpful with directions to a stranger, glad to see a tourist. I'd happily go back to Morocco, now that I've learned a few Arabic phrases to disperse the hustlers. Not that they always work. In Fez one day, I got irritated by one persistent harasser who kept running through the list of nationalities I might be (*Deutsch? Francais? Espanol? English?*), so I started to singsong the Arabic for "No thanks" back at him, "No no no thank you, *La la la shukran,*" to the tune of Boney M's classic 1970s ode to "Russia's greatest sex machine," "Rah Rah Rasputin."

"La la la!" he shouted. "Negation! To express negation like that you must be English!"

You had to admire these guys. My friend Lorenzo, whom I met in Chefchaouen and traveled with to Fez, recited to me a Spanish expression he thought applied. *Ser más listo que el hambre,* which he translated into English for me as: "Hunger makes you more clever."

✳

In any case, fifteen minutes after my arrival in Tangier Ali and I have stopped in front of a little hotel that seems perfect. It's on the upper part of a steep slope down to the old railyards and the beach. Two whores are hanging out the front window calling to me, "*Bonjour, Monsieur.*"

Later when I'm at the front desk one of them comes wandering downstairs in her slip, complaining in French that her Wednesday afternoon regular is causing her mental torture. He's boring, dull as dishwater, and takes forever to leave. He's still up in the room—getting dressed, she hopes, but possibly wanting more. She figures the longer she stays away, the more likely he is to get dressed. "He wants me to keep him company. I can't stand his company!" she moans.

She waits for us to say something, but I never know what to say to prostitutes. On the one hand I want to be nonjudgmental, even supportive. Sex workers are horribly exploited, usually come from abusive backgrounds, need our sympathy, and all that. On the other hand, some little puritan voice in my brain is wanting to ask her, "Do you *really* let anyone fuck you for money?"

The young guy at the front desk doesn't have anything to say to her either, he just shrugs at her and gives me a glance suggesting that the complaints of whores are not worth comment. He's busy anyway, putting my passport and credit cards into the hotel safe by simply lifting the metal plate off the front of it and stuffing them in the hole in the wall behind. The safe door isn't even on hinges, let alone locked.

"Can't you lock it?" I ask.

"I don't know the combination" is his answer.

That sums up the casual air of the place. My room has cockroaches the size of Hot Wheels, genetically programmed to skitter under the bed and stay there whenever I'm home.

For twelve bucks a night, what do you expect? For a room with roughly the same view of the harbor, docks, and huge sandy beach that Burroughs would have had from his room a few streets over. And I like the sign in the upstairs hallway: "*Le silence de chacun assure le repos de tous.*" The silence of each assures restfulness for all.

Half an hour after checking in, I'm back outside, striding up the hill toward the Ville Nouvelle. I stop to look back at the lovely view of the harbor, the beach, and the blue sea, and notice that a lot of roofing tiles have tumbled off the hotel. I also notice Ali at my shoulder again, wanting to take me to the Medina and show me the sights. His one-toothed buddy hovers ten steps behind.

"I don't need a guide," I tell him.

"Not for money, no money, just as friends," he insists. Later I'll find out that "unofficial" guides are illegal in Morocco. If I'd known that, it might have been easier to get rid of him.

His partner says, in French, "Better to have one mosquito with you to keep the hundred others away."

Ali tells him to shut up.

"I want a Coke," I say. Ali takes me to a cafe where every-one sits around low tables on padded ottomans, drinking mint tea and watching boxing on TV. It's the Sydney Olympics. A Mo-roccan is boxing, but everyone watches with apparent indiffer-ence. They don't seem to feel any of that nationalistic fervor crap that we in the hype-heaping West slather all over the Games. I remember Dave Cannabis in Australia calling the approaching Olympics "The Running and Jumping Junkies Show" because of all the performance-enhancing drugs athletes take. I prefer the Arab attitude to athletics, which isn't indifference, exactly. They like to watch, but even when Moroccans are involved they don't seem to worry about who's winning. Later this week I'll read a newspaper article that says the Muslim definition of a hero is someone who saves a child from a burning building, not a trained and practiced athlete. Heroism isn't making a calculated decision to devote oneself to sport. It's a braver, more selfless act than that.

As we watch the televised sluggers circle each other, Ali leans against my shoulder, going on again about how his grandfa-ther said to never ever, ever—

"Lie. Yeah, I know, you told me," I say. I pull out a pack of Noble cigarettes, a Spanish brand, and Ali suddenly perks up.

"You smoke? You smoke!" His solid, strong-looking teeth flash in a big tea-stained grin, as if at last his ship has come in. "You like to smoke hashish? Moroccan hashish? Finest hashish in the world? You must! People are come from all over the world to try our finest hashish!"

Hashish takes over as the exclusive topic of his patter until our Cokes are drunk and our cigarettes smoked, the Moroccan boxer has lost his first and only Olympic bout, someone turns the TV channel to an old black-and-white Spanish movie, and we are out on the street again. Ali scrounges a rolling paper from a guy on the sidewalk who leans all day on a whitewashed windowsill selling Marlboros singly or by the pack. Our toothless sidekick produces a pea-sized ball of blond hash, which Ali tears in two and hands to me to smell, one little half-pea for each nostril.

On a crowded sidewalk in my first hours in Tangier I really don't feel like lingering over it and making a public spectacle of myself. Despite Morocco's reputation as the hashish breadbasket of Europe, it's still illegal to possess or consume under Moroccan law. Ali tears the strip of glue off his rolling paper and flicks it to the ground. "Here in Morocco we never, ever smoke the glue," he says solemnly.

"It's poison," says his sidekick.

"What's your name, anyway?" I ask.

"Ahmad."

Ali takes back the hash and asks for a cigarette. He strips out the tobacco, breaks the powdery hash into it in the palm of one hand, lays the paper upon it, then closes and flips his palms, Spanish style. The pile atop the paper he quickly rolls into a workmanlike filterless joint.

We smoke it while we walk, me getting the lion's share. It's hard to isolate the effect, the high, what with the grit, the heat, the pace, the noise, the *newness* of every sight and sound on these Tangier streets. Muslim women waddle along, their plump bodies encased in baggy *jellabas,* those hooded neck-to-ankle pullover robes. Men and women alike stare aggressively at me, the tofuskinned blue-eyed Infidel sucking on his suspicious cigarette, striding to keep up with Ali's breakneck sidewalk pace and emphatic banter about the large number of wonderful Quebecois who come to Morocco for holidays and return to Canada with a souvenir of at least half a kilo of the world's finest hashish tucked away in their baggage. "Half a kilo, or even a kilo, Brian! Very easy to hide in a suitcase for the flight home!"

On the busy sidewalk he nearly runs over a matronly woman in a white head scarf and conservative gray *jellaba.* Only her round jovial face is exposed. They know each other, and stand talking a while, very close, noses almost touching, having a lively exchange in Arabic. They part and we continue on our way.

Ali says, "That lady keeps a house. She suggested I bring you by there later. She has girls there." If Ali makes a big payday out of me, I know where he'll be.

Later I'll read in an old guidebook to Morocco: "It should be understood that sex in Morocco has never been anything shameful. It is enjoyable and everybody knows it and it is only the Westerners who have debased the selling of it by their inhibitions."

Ali is supposed to be leading me to an e-mail shop, but I get the feeling we're walking in circles. If he is trying to confuse and disorient me, he is succeeding. He keeps up the sales pitch about the half-kilo and I keep insisting I don't want any. His stuff is crap, I've decided. Ahmad crosses the street at a run, dodging the mix of tiny taxis and white SUVs. I watch him talk to some guys loitering along a corrugated tin fence that protects a vacant lot, while Ali hurries me along. Ahmad comes sprinting to catch back up with new merchandise: a hunk of hash half the size of my thumb.

Ali steers me into an alley, breaks open the hash for me to smell. It crumbles in his hands. It smells very dusty, like old straw. He wants 800 dirham; that's the name of the local currency. The exchange rate has not yet settled in my brain. Is that eight bucks or eighty? Eighty, I think. It's more than what you'd pay in Amsterdam or America for that. And it looks like crap. And I'd rather not be carrying hashish around before I have my bearings, after little more than an hour in this strange new city. I'm not buying.

"You must buy. He's already paid for it."

"I don't want it."

"Then you owe us four hundred dirham for that hashish you smoked."

"What? There is no way—"

"Four hundred! You fucking pay! Give us fucking money for our hashish you smoked."

They have me where they want me: outnumbered and lost on day one in Tangier. Legitimate, decent, non–hustler type people glide by, on their way to or from jobs or cafés or shops, and look upon me with stone faces, a flicker of curiosity or amusement in the eyes. None of them are going to help me out.

I get Ali down to three hundred dirham, and hand over the bills.

"Good. Now you must pay for my guide service."

"What? You kept telling me you didn't want money for that—"

"I HAD TO SAY THAT OR YOU WOULDN'T HAVE LET ME FOLLOW YOU!!!"

"I thought you said you never lied. Your grandfather—"

"Give the fucking money. Two hundred!"

"You said you never lied and now you're telling me you HAD TO LIE?"

Ahmad has suddenly turned tail. He's hurrying away without a backward glance. Ali looks over my shoulder down the street and, inexplicably, twists off a hunk from his little handheld stash and presses it into my palm. It's all powdery and breaking into little bits.

"Here, take it, take it!"

"I don't want it!"

"No, you take it!"

"I don't—all right. All right." And just like that I have a lump of hash the size of a chocolate in my hand. I'm pressing it between my sweaty fingers, trying to keep it from crumbling to nothing. I look up and Ali is striding away quickly, but not fast enough to gain on Ahmad. I can't figure out what's happened until I pull a 180 and three policemen are looking me over through the windshield of a paddy wagon, or at least a big cube van, white with orange Day-Glo stripes. They're the reason Ali and Ahmad have turned tail and fled the scene, and the hunk of hash in my palm is, I guess, intended to prevent me from complaining to the cops that I've been harassed.

I step to the side and the van moves forward. Should it slow to a stop, I'm preparing to flick the contents of my palm as unobtrusively as possible through the chain-link fence behind me. But the van keeps moving, and so do I.

✳

Back at the hotel I need to vent. I'm bitching to the desk clerk in my fractured French about being forced to pay for guide services I never agreed to. "He was trying to sell me bad hashish I didn't even want—"

His eyes light up. "You want hashish?"

The nervous sweat of my hand has helped that powdery hunk of hash from Ali congeal nicely into a little ball. When I smoke it in my room, I get high, but there's a paranoia with it, which I put down to circumstances, not the product, although the product can't be perfect since part of it is my own nervous sweat. I am such a wimp. I remember how I felt so smug that I could handle the police and petty officialdom in Cambodia when I lost my passport, but this is different. The prospect of a Moroccan jail scares me shitless. When those police looked at me with their hard eyes through that windshield, I knew that if they came after me I'd crumble into little pieces like the powdery hash I held in my palm.

✳

The progress of this famous plant has been something like the progress of truth: suspected at first, although very palatable to those who had courage to taste it; resisted as it encroached; abused as its popularity seemed to spread; and establishing its triumph at last, in cheering the whole land from the palace to the cottage, only by the slow and resistless efforts of time and its own virtues.

The foregoing sentiments aren't about cannabis. They were composed in 1790 by Isaac D'Israeli, and describe the manner in which the habit of tea drinking spread in Britain. I came across them in Morocco in an article called "Mint Tea," by Abderrahmane Lakhsassi.

"The tea ceremony has become deeply engrained in the fabric of people's lives in Morocco," Lakhsassi writes. "Ask anyone in the street when Moroccans started drinking tea, and he will say naively and without hesitation, 'from time immemorial.' In fact tea only became known to most people at the end of the last [nineteenth] century." Tea as a widespread consumer product was introduced to Morocco by the British in the 1850s, when access to their usual markets in the Baltic was interrupted by the Crimean War. Excess Chinese green tea in the British-controlled global trade flooded into Tangier.

The British built the first great capitalist empire largely on the global trade of such drugs and drug foods as sugar, coffee, tea, alcohol, tobacco, and opium. "Without drugs and drug economies, capitalism could never have come into being," argues the Australian economist Carl A. Trocki in a recent book, *Opium, Empire, and the Global Political Economy.* "These new consumer markets and the apparatus which served them were not built on wheat, nor wool, nor widgets; not even cotton comes close. They were built on commodities that no one had ever really consumed before, and which, in general, were totally unnecessary. They were truly nothing more than smoke and water. Their great attraction was their ability to create an addiction for themselves, or at least an habituation." Smoke and water? What are Marlboro and Coca-Cola, the two most visible pillars of American global domination today?

"Coca-Cola!" Sometimes Moroccan kids would shout it at the sight of me, which is sure to warm the hearts of Coke shareholders, but gave me the creeps. Ten years from now they'll be shouting "Hostess Twinkies!" if all goes according to the grand American plan.

✳

In any case, what Moroccans say about tea, they also say about cannabis. Ask anyone in Morocco and they will tell you that since time immemorial they have smoked kif, their name for the green flower tops, which they traditionally chop into a fine powder and smoke in a little long-stemmed pipe called a *sebsi*. A Moroccan told me, "About kif, it's part of the earth. You burn the field in the fall and plant it in the spring. It comes from nature. It's been like this from the beginning. Since before there was a thing called Morocco."

But while cannabis may have been used since Shiva discovered it near the beginning of time, and while certainly its use in the Arab world predates Islam, historically cannabis was eaten. This method still survives in Morocco in a traditional pastelike dish called *majoun,* which can be used in cooking or simply placed between cheek and gum. In one of his letters from Tangier Burroughs described his novel in progress as "long majoun parentheses." I had no luck finding *majoun* in Morocco, partly because I kept forgetting to ask. But most cannabis consumed in Morocco is now smoked, although the habit of smoking cannabis or hashish didn't begin until after the introduction of tobacco from the New World created nations of nicotine addicts in the Old. (Opium poppies are native to Switzerland, and began their spread across the globe between 3000 and 2500 B.C., but that's another story.)

Until the 1960s almost all the cannabis smoked in Morocco was kif, the finely chopped flowers. Most farmers had a small garden of tall plants near their house. When the sixties counter-cultural revolution kicked in and the hippies began arriving, the sudden boom in demand for cannabis turned kif growing from a hobby, or a diversion, into an industry. "Increased demand changed the entire focus of Moroccan production and consumption, from kif smoking to the previously unknown practice of hashish smoking," writes Robert Connell Clarke in his large and lavishly illustrated book *Hashish!* which is pretty much the last word on the subject. In Morocco, out went the tall, willowy, well-tended kif plants, in came mass planting of lower-quality seeds, mass harvests, and mass production of hashish. Declines in Western markets of the amounts and quality of hashish available from other source countries, especially Lebanon and Afghanistan, have gradually given Moroccan hashish, almost by default, the largest share of the European and world market.

✳

In Tangier in the late afternoons I kept going to a cafe I could never remember the Arabic name for. I called it the Famous Cafe (as in "You know—the famous café!"). It was famous because Bowles and Burroughs used to frequent the place. It was only a short walk from the Medina, and it had a great view of the straits. You could see Europe across the cold blue water, and Europe felt even closer after dark when the lights twinkled across from the far shore.

The first time I went there was with an American woman I met in the narrow streets of the Medina. In the square below the museum I was distracted by a local berating a couple of skinny Scandinavian tourists: "You come here and no buy nothing! No smoke hash, nothing! Better stay in your own country. Why you come here if you no smoke hash?" They slunk away like scolded schoolboys, and it was then I noticed that a woman had sat down beside me. Her name was Melissa. We went to see Malcolm Forbes' mansion. Though the house was closed to the public, the caretaker was so bored he let us in anyway. Forbes is dead now, but there's a big poster of him in the waiting room looking extremely butch in leather on a motorbike. Another American drawn to Tangier by those sexy young Arab men. There's also a photo of son Steve with four former Presidents, and they've all signed it. Carter, Reagan, Bush Senior, and Ford. They're all smiles, and Steve looks nerdy as ever front and center.

After that we ended up at the Famous Café, and Melissa started telling me how she had tried marijuana only twice; the first time she'd felt nothing, and the second she'd gone on some neurotic-sounding nightmarish paranoia trip that she claimed lasted all the way into the next day, and it scared her off ever trying it again. I was skeptical, but what can you say? Can't deny someone her own experiences.

I went back to the café by myself often after that, and made some Arab friends. Jamil, Ibrahim, and Mohammed were three best friends in their twenties. They were the flip side to the Tangier hustle. Cool characters happy to share their kif and hash with me at no charge. Ibrahim had a *sebsi,* one of those little long-stemmed pipes. He would fill the tiny bowl to the top by dipping it in a little bag of kif. Apparently the word "kif" derives from the Arabic *kayf,* meaning "pleasure," and it was a pleasure to share a pipe this way. Generally one to three people could get a hit from a single bowl, depending on how hard they inhaled. When the bowlful is all burnt the pipe is lowered to the side below the table. You blow until the little ball of ash plops out and flutters to the floor. Sometimes after dark you can see it glowing like a little firefly as it descends.

That's the traditional way of smoking kif. But it seemed most of the young Moroccans in the place were smoking hashish, not kif. They roll it with tobacco, usually from a Marlboro cigarette. They save the filter, carefully remove the inner wool-like wadding from the tube, discard half this wadding, then roll the other half up and shove it back into the hollow filter tube. I have no idea why. "Because it's better" is the only answer I ever got.

In Barcelona a Frenchman I met who had spent time in Morocco insisted it had to do with Muslim concepts of cleanliness. "They don't like to put anything dirty in their mouths, and they trust very few things to be clean. But one thing they do trust to be highly germ-free and sanitary is a Marlboro cigarette." Possible, I guess. Anyway, they use this revamped filter in a joint of two rolling papers. Like Ali the hustler, they hated the glue. They always wetted, tore off, and discarded the glued edge of the paper.

One day I ask Jamil if the police ever come to harass smokers at the café.

"Artists and thinkers used to come here to talk art and philosophy," he says. "Now it's changing. More and more it's young people who come just to kill time, talk nonsense, get in fights over who owes who money. So now the police *have* to come. But they leave those alone who are sitting quietly and just smoking." He demonstrates for me how he hides a joint if he sees a cop coming—he hunches his shoulders down and tucks his hands under his armpits as if he is cold. Not that he has to pretend to be cold today. It's freezing. As the twilight fades and the lights of Europe spark on the far shore, nasty gusts of wind blow in off the water.

"Tell him about the one and only time the cops took us in," he says to Ibrahim.

Ibrahim protests his English isn't up to it, so Jamil continues. "They took us to the station and asked us our occupations. I said 'artist.'

"'What kind of artist?'" He mimics a stern cop's voice.

"'Singer.'

"'And you?' the police asks Mohammed.

"'Artist.'

"'What kind of artist?'

"'Singer.'

"Then the police turns to Ibrahim. 'And you, I suppose you are a singer too?'

"'Yes. Singer of reggae.'

"'Singer of foolishness!' the police shouts. He says, 'Now you're making fun of me.'"

But he let them go.

✳

Although he was born and raised in Tangier, Jamil told me, "I am not Moroccan. I'm a Tangerien. A Tangelino. I'm a good Arab, a Muslim, I want to go east before I die, to Mecca, to see the big box there. But Morocco? What is that? I only know Tangier. This is an international city. That is the history of this place."

From 1923 to 1956 Tangier was a loosely regulated international zone overseen by the agents of France, Spain, Italy, Portugal, Sweden, Holland, Belgium, Britain, and the U.S. Morocco got it back after gaining independence from France. But the free spirit of Burroughs' Interzone lives on. The last King, Hassan II, who ruled from 1961 to 1999, never once made an official visit to the city in his entire reign. In Tangier and throughout the nearby Rif region, the mountains of Morocco's northeast, the King was never forgiven for overseeing crackdowns in the 1950s, when the new state was trying to establish control.

Psychologically Tangier and the Rif have remained rebel territory. There were major riots in Tangier in 1996 when the government moved against the hashish trade. This trade had begun in earnest only in the late 1960s, and up until the 1980s was still largely an industry dominated by small mom-and-pop operations. But in the finest traditions of capitalism, there was eventually consolidation as big fish ate small. By the mid-nineties two kingpins were arrested and convicted in what were essentially show trials.

A longtime observer of Moroccan politics suggested to me that the show trials served two purposes. First, it gave Europe the impression that Morocco was serious about doing something to curb the production of drugs. (America doesn't make too much noise about Moroccan hashish, in part because so little of it finds its way to the States, in part because Morocco, of all the Arab states, has traditionally been soft on Israel.) Second, it allowed Moroccan officials to take a large chunk of the hashish trade and give it to people more sympathetic to the government. The convictions sparked rioting in poorer neighborhoods in Tangier. People felt the government was threatening the only way they had to make money.

"This isn't just a matter of local yokels making bucks off the tourists," the observer said. "This is a huge industry that has tentacles into security forces and the highest levels of government. It's a challenge to the state. What is a state? It's the ability to control people."

The new King, Mohammed VI, has made gestures of peace to the disaffected north. First he fired his father's feared and sadistic interior minister and invited home some exiled dissidents. Then he started pouring money into high-profile infrastructure projects in Tangier. Most important, he's turned a blind eye to the hashish business. Not surprisingly, he is more popular in the north than his father ever was. Maybe at last Morocco is led by a realist. Hashish earns Morocco three billion dollars a year, is the prime source of hard currency, and is estimated to account for between a third and half of the country's total foreign earnings. Why fight it?

✳

But the new King's regime isn't all sweetness and light for the young men who like to smoke hash at the Famous Café. At street level, the state has been imposing a new public presence and power. Like Rudi Giuliani in New York, Mohammed VI is on a campaign to get the deadbeats off the streets. Drunks and idle young kif smokers are in danger of prison sentences. The hustlers are looking over their shoulders. Any Moroccan in the company of a foreign woman without a damn good reason risks three months in jail. (Melissa wasn't bothered by hustlers at all, while every day they swarmed to me like bees to honey, or humans to money.)

"Jail!" Jamil said. "What is that going to teach us? Why don't they send us to school?"

I took a taxi out to Tangier's jail. I'd read somewhere that there were supposed to be four hundred foreigners in Moroccan jails for drug offenses. I thought I might be able to talk to some. I'd done it in Nepal just by showing up at one of the jails in Kathmandu and asking; there they'd brought a prisoner out for me immediately.

But Morocco is tougher than Nepal for the foreigner without an appointment. The warden told me I'd have to get written permission from the ministry in Rabat, the capital. So all I got to see of the prison that day was the first interior courtyard, which held the warden's office and the crowded meeting rooms where prisoners and their loved ones sat on cheap plastic patio chairs. I noticed, against the dull gray walls and the khaki uniforms of the guards, a young Arab woman in psychedelic red and yellow pants, looking like a tropical bird in a cage.

Later I met her outside while we were both waiting for a cab back to town. We shared one. She was from Morocco's eastern neighbor, Algeria; her family had recently fled the civil war in that country and settled in Tangier. On Sunday her brother, all of nineteen, had been picked up by the police for drinking in public. According to her he'd drunk only a couple of beers, but made the mistake of admitting that to the police. The consumption of alcohol is a worse sin for Muslims in Morocco than smoking kif or hashish. The police took him in. On Monday he was tried, convicted by a judge, and given a six-month prison sentence. Only on Tuesday did the family receive a telephone call notifying them. Now it was Thursday, and she had been for the first time to see her little brother.

"He's crying all the time," she said, barely holding back the tears herself. "The conditions are terrible, the food is full of insects. I'm going to have to bring him food, but I can't afford to pay like I did today. Twenty dirham. Every guard, every door—everything is twenty dirham."

✳

The roughly two hundred thousand acres of cannabis grown in the Rif Mountains of Morocco supplies nearly all the hashish Europe needs: about two thousand tons. Eighty percent of the cannabis consumed in France is Moroccan hashish. Most of it is not quality stuff. What the English call soap bar and the Spanish call chocolate, the French, with a more cynical sense of metaphor, call Chernobyl. But it's not the Moroccans' fault if the French and English and Spanish smoke shit. The Moroccans are farmers selling a crop, and what's added later is out of their hands. The European Union has made some halfhearted attempts to persuade farmers in the Rif to raise goats and stop growing cannabis. But the system as it stands suits everyone: the farmers grow a valuable crop, and hashish is not really a high-priority crime problem in most European nations. And having it grown abroad has advantages for Europe: the trade is kept under observation and regulated by border searches, and European politicians get to blame the problem on foreigners.

Chefchaouen is a beautiful little tourist town nestled in the hills on the edge of the kif-growing part of the Rif Mountains. On the bus ride from Tangier the landscape looks like how I imagine northern Mexico to be: dry, craggy, flint-gray hills reaching for a blue sky; kids playing soccer on a little patch cleared of rocks; cacti; donkeys standing in the sliver of shade along the walls of whitewashed shacks; peasants wearing strange sombrero-like hats. On the bus Lorenzo and Juan, both twenty-one, two young Spaniards on a hashish-smoking adventure inspired by an article in *Cañamo,* look a bit shell-shocked. They've been hustled in Tangier. Now they're on their guard.

Stepping off that bus we are all three a bit wary, but Chefchaouen turns out to be as laid-back and cool as Tangier was crazed. A puffy-faced local named Dadhu is watching for likely-looking stoner types as we unpile, and he picks out the two lads from Spain. I tag along. We're led to a hotel where cannabis can be freely smoked in the rooms and the rooftop. We can buy kif and hashish of good quality from Dadhu at a reasonable price.

Everything is settled quite effortlessly, and we're then free to wander the steep narrow streets that climb and descend between windowless walls painted pale blue. It feels like walking in the cracks of glaciers, and is strangely cooling in the hot climate. This hillside town was founded in the fifteenth century by Moors fleeing Spain. It has an Andalusian feel, like the Spanish town of Granada, and a lovely little Casbah right out of an old French Foreign Legion movie. In one of the rooms inside the fort walls you can see the neck shackle used in 1926 to imprison a great local revolutionary, Abdel Krim, who had managed to drive out the Spanish only to see a French army come in and kick his oppressed colonial ass.

I shouldn't say we're completely free to wander. Dadhu the hash supplier designates himself our official guide, dragging us to various carpet, clothes, and trinket shops. He likes to take me around separately from the Spanish boys. Divide and conquer. Before we hit the carpet shop we pause for a mint tea in a little alcove tearoom, and he rolls me up a huge spliff, getting me nice and high in order to heighten my impressionability, so that my eyes will be dazzled by those intricate, brightly colored Berber carpets and kilims, the blanketlike rugs of the nomads' tents. Get me high, and watch me buy.

The Spanish boys, more careful with their money, have brought trade goods to barter. Good old alcohol, in the form of two bottles of Johnny Walker Red. Booze is impossible to obtain legally in Chefchaouen, so naturally it's worth a lot. Dadhu likes to drink, and the boys negotiate some kind of deal with him to buy souvenirs in which he acts as middleman and gets to keep a bottle for himself.

Dadhu invites us in the evening to a café near our hotel, to share his good fortune and his booze. The rest of the clientele are locals, seated on benches at long, ten-seat tables, sipping mint tea, smoking kif quite openly, and watching the Olympics. Dadhu and a buddy of his retire to a small table in a back corner, keeping the Scotch bottle out of sight, refilling their glasses under the table. They're pouring shots and throwing them back in one gulp—not exactly savoring their Scotch. I try to show them how to do that, to linger over the olfactory pleasure, to take small sips and let them spread across the tongue, but Dadhu pulls my glass from under my nose and whispers, "No, no. You have to *hide* it!" Some of the younger Arabs, fascinated by this violation of locale mores, study Dadhu and his pal keenly for signs of the dreaded, forbidden, ungodly drunkenness. The older Arabs ignore us, drawing unself-consciously on their kif pipes and spectating the track and field on TV.

It's funny how one drug is accepted and the other demonized. Prohibition turned upside down.

Dadhu sets me up with a guy named Medhi who grows kif on a farm in the hills near Chefchaouen. The three of us meet and agree that, for a price, I get a tour of the farm, a demonstration of hash making, a nice chunk of hash, and some kif. Medhi will explain everything, Dadhu assures me.

But it turns out Medhi's English is pathetic. Me and Medhi pile into some guy's van for the trip up to the farm. Before we have even left town, Medhi gets out and starts walking. I'm told to stay in the van. We drive on without him. A hundred yards later we come around a bend and hit an intersection, with a cop directing traffic in the center.

This cop is serious—he's peering deliberately and thoroughly into the windows of each vehicle as it passes. In the backseat I'm trying to keep my head low and to be fairly discreet, but through the open front passenger window the cop gets a perfect view in at me for a few seconds, and we lock eyes. His go wide. What's that blue-eyed infidel doing heading out into hashish country?

Two hundred yards past the intersection, at the top of a hill, we stop and wait for Medhi to catch up. The driver wants me to stay in the van, out of sight. Five locals, squeezed tight together on a roadside bench made for four, watch and discuss me. Here comes Medhi, jogging up the road to rejoin us.

I'm feeling paranoid. Medhi got out and walked back there in order to avoid being seen with me as we passed the cop. This cloak-and-dagger stuff has me thinking again: a Moroccan jail would destroy me.

Half an hour later the van has climbed a rutted path as high as it can and we get out and start trudging up the steep incline.

Earlier I'd thought Medhi looked pretty rough for a man his age. He's only forty, but his face is lined and weather-beaten, like an old cowboy's, as if he sleeps outdoors a lot. His teeth have never seen a dentist and kif, tobacco, and sweet Moroccan tea haven't been kind to them. But now I'm beginning to understand that face and teeth aside, the man is healthy, robust even. Strong like bull. He's hardly winded by the run up the hill. I'm the one begging to stop so I can catch my breath. He's the one hardly panting, and getting impatient with me.

"Take time," he says, but then by gestures he makes it clear that there isn't time. It's evening, and the light will be fading soon. "You're in good shape," I compliment him. "You've got great legs and lungs."

He says it's because he often walks tens of miles bringing hashish out of the hills to market. He carries thirty kilos in a backpack along the mountaintops from here to the town of Tétouan, fifty miles away. "Sometimes Tangier," another thirty miles beyond that.

I look up toward the craggy peaks. Why on the mountain paths?

"Police," he says, pointing down to the highway.

We climb the hill and take in a stunning view back down toward an increasingly shadowy Chefchaouen. We stand on a flat-bottomed bowl of land, maybe two acres, planted in corn about a foot high. "Here is where I grow my kif," says Medhi. He harvests in July, or this year early in August. It was a very good crop this year. Then he plants corn, to harvest in late autumn. "Then in spring, we grow kif again."

"Do you ever let the land lie fallow? Plant nothing for a year?"

"No. The soil is getting tired," he says. "But no."

Inside a nearby barn three men are watching a television caked on top with pigeon shit—bird shit of some kind, anyway. "What is that?"

"Television."

"No, I mean what's that all over it?"

Medhi just shrugs.

I can hear fluttering in the rafters but never see the birds. The whole place is dusty and smells like a barn. It is a barn, but it smells like an *abandoned* barn, with that moldy odor of decay.

The plants are stacked in small sheaves, upright, to dry. All the flowers have been pollinated and have gone to seed. Moroccans make no effort to weed out the males and grow sensimilla. It's too tough to do that when you've got acres under cultivation and you'd have to painstakingly go through the field plant by plant. But letting the females go to seed means the THC output is much lower.

To begin we put a black nylon screen over a plastic washtub, securing it with an old bicycle inner tube. Then some kif—seedy, leafy, twiggy, dusty kif—is produced from a big sack. Medhi cups his hands like a bowl to pull kif out of the sack and places the contents on the screen. Three bowlfuls are spread about an inch thick over the surface. The entire crop appears to be made up of what Gary in Australia would have called Struggle Bud: neglected plants, left to fend for themselves in a harsh land. Medhi picks out a couple of likely-looking buds and gives them to one of the others, who starts manicuring them, chopping the best bits into powder with a big curve-bladed knife that has handles on both ends. This will be my kif.

Meanwhile the cannabis on the tub screen has been covered with a piece of heavier canvas, also secured tight to the tub with elastic tubing. It looks like a big lumpy drum. Now Medhi starts wailing on it with two sticks, one in each hand. I relieve him at times. *Whap whap, whap whap,* we knock the crystallized resins off the plant so that, because they are smaller than the other parts of the plants and (hopefully) smaller than dust particles, they fall through the mesh and collect on the bottom of the basin. By the time we are through whapping a couple of helpings of kif the basin bottom is covered in dust. This dust is hashish. Simple as that.

Medhi writes in it with his fingertip: "007." Bond, James Bond. An internationally recognized symbol. Could have been worse—he could have drawn the Golden Arches. The point is, you can write in the resin as if it were sand. For resin it's very unresinous. Medhi sweeps it all into a little bit of plastic torn from a bag. Twists it tight and starts kneading and compacting it until it's golf ball–sized. It's mine. So is a slightly bigger bag of kif. The show's over, and it's time to hurry back down before it gets dark.

✳

Evenings pass easily; I spend them smoking kif and hashish with Lorenzo and Juan on the roof of our hotel. They're jealous that I got to go up into the hills to see hashish made. That was their dream for this trip: to see for themselves how their favorite substance is manufactured. When I describe what I've seen, they're disappointed. They seem to think it should be a lot more mysterious than that. Beating powder off dried plants? Is that all hashish is?

I tell them what Gaspar had told me in Barcelona about the declining quality of Moroccan hashish. You want superb herb, go to Amsterdam or Vancouver, or grow your own, with good seeds, dedication, and a green thumb, I lecture them. I tell them about smoking great Moroccan hash with a grower in Holland who had traded some of his own best for it. "Look at the glistening crystals of pollen," he had said as he shaved a bit off the golden-brown bar with a sharp knife. In Morocco I never do get to see glistening crystals like that. But we're at the low end of the food chain. Tourists, not big-timers.

"Even if you could find really good stuff here, the paranoia wouldn't let you enjoy it as much anyway," Lorenzo says.

The two Spaniards speak Catalan between themselves, having grown up together on Mallorca, the Mediterranean tourist island that gets invaded every winter by cheap-charter tourists from northern Europe, primarily Britain. Growing up on Mallorca sounds like every boy's fantasy coming-of-age story. Lorenzo slept with more than a hundred tourist girls in the three years after he turned sixteen. "The southeast beaches are for the Germans, with their red bellies and beer-drinking songs," he says, imitating the clinking of a giant stein. "The Italian beach is like an eternal picnic—people playing guitars, eating good food, drinking wine. Very civilized. You will never see the Italians fighting. Or the Germans either, no matter how much they drink. But the English! The English, my friend, they are something else. What word would you use to describe the English tourists?" he asks Juan.

"Cattle," Juan says.

"The English women get drunk enough so they can fuck, while the blokes get drunk enough so they can fight," says Lorenzo.

From a bus window in northern Morocco, you will see orchards of cork trees, the bark stripped and piled in neat squares ten feet high. You will see shantytowns with roofs of tin held in place by old tires and discarded toilets. And you will see many buildings that appear to be permanently half-finished. They are. They're essentially money-laundering projects. They never get finished, because every year there's new money from the hashish business that needs to be run through them.

On a bus in northern Morocco you will see Berber women with tribal patterns crudely tattooed on their faces; their men look severe enough without tattoos. You will feel far from your own culture and civilization, until one of these people starts digging into a pocket or purse because his cell phone is going off. And you will have to laugh when the cell phone ring is the opening bars of the theme from *The Simpsons*.

Sooner or later when you hang around with Arabs you're going to be drawn into a conversation about religion. Back in Tangier I share mint tea and kif again with Jamil and company. Jamil looks across the waters toward Europe and asks me why people there fear Islam. It's his opinion that fear of Islam is the reason the Spanish and French limit the numbers of Arabs who can settle in their countries. "Why fear God? Why fear the truth?" he wonders.

I tell him I don't have any god and don't feel I need one.

"What makes you get out of bed in the morning?" he demands.

"What do you mean?"

"What makes you get out of bed in the morning, face the day?"

I don't have an answer. Because I'm not sleepy anymore? Because I have to pee? It's just time to get up, and usually I'm looking forward to it.

"We Muslims get out of bed because our God insists. He expects it. First thing when I wake up, I must go to the mosque and pray." He says in order to know God you must talk to Him regularly in the form of prayer. Five times a day is what He wants.

I say I feel that as long as I live a good and proper life, do harm to no one, exploit no one, any good and gracious God that might exist will for certain let me into heaven when I die, so I'm not worried.

"Of course we must all live a proper life," says Jamil. "I'm not interested in drinking alcohol. I'm not interested in fucking girls. I want to have a wife and a kid and come home to them every night, kiss them, ask them, 'How was your day?'" He makes a gesture of stroking the hair and cradling the chin of a child. "Eat a meal together as a family, and all go to bed early. I must sleep early, because at five o'clock the muezzin will call, and I must go and talk to my God. Brian, you must meet your God every day!"

He tells me the very first thing Arabs say to a baby when it comes out of the womb, the very first words the newborn child hears, are "Allah u Akbar." God is great. I'm thinking, If God is so great, how come the godless guy, me, gets born into the easy life in the land of plenty, and the good followers of Allah are born into suffering and misery on the desolate northern shores of Africa? But of course I don't say that. I respect their faith. They are good men.

Much later I'll still carry around, near that place in mind and body where guilty feelings are stored, a kind of pity for these young men, able to see the lights of Europe twinkle across the Strait of Gibraltar in the Andalusia of their ancestors, but prevented by politics and borders from making the crossing.

"You will be there tomorrow," says Jamil. "It's as if you have wings."

The way he says it, he sounds happy for me. None of the three ever betray jealousy at my good fortune, although Jamil curses his own earthbound enchainment.

✳

Later in my hotel I'm lying in bed with that spinny bombardment of thoughts and ideas you get sometimes when you're high, the semitranscendent state where ordinary thoughts and words grow fraught with deeper meaning. In the morning most of them return to their ordinary state, just like the mind. Ideally some ideas still resonate as true and beautiful.

This night it's *Every generation needs healing.* That phrase seems so wise and profound that I want to write it down, but in my stoned state it's the small tasks that confound, and I can't find a pen. After much fumbling around I find the pen and set myself to writing it down, but now I'm having my doubts about whether it's profound: 'Every generation needs healing? EVERY GENERATION NEEDS HEALING??! That is so patently fucking obvious!'

I write it down anyway.

✳

The next day I catch the ferry back to Spain and make a series of train connections from Algeciras to Granada so I can party with Lorenzo. In Granada, the old Andalusian architectural shapes, those Moorish arches, still predominate in the narrow streets of the old town. It's like Morocco with money, and without Allah. Granada is a town of four hundred thousand, a fifth of them university students. Party Central. Masses of beautiful carefree young people wandering from bar to bar eating tapas and drinking beer and wine—and smoking big hash and tobacco spliffs, on the streets and in some of the bars, with more freedom and comfort than is possible to even imagine in the country that produces all that hash-ish, Morocco, the poor cousin 150 miles to the south. Morocco, where the losers in the fight for Andalusia were banished so many centuries ago.

On my way to Granada, fresh out of Morocco by mere hours, I have to switch trains in a little town called Antiquerra. While I wait in the station café, seven young Spanish women come in and take up a table. They order wine or coffee, and something sets them off, and they all start to giggle and laugh, and the laughter fills the cafe, and turns heads for a moment, rising and falling like birdsong.

That's what I missed in Morocco. I'd forgotten the sound of women laughing.

10 : THE KOOTENAYS AND THE COAST

One evening a few years back I sat on the porch of the double-wide trailer that's home to Brian Taylor, who was then the mayor of Grand Forks, British Columbia, population 4,300. We shared a drink and a toke, admired his hillside view east across the Sunshine Valley, and together tried to make some sense of his complicated life. For starters he'd just been dumped by his girlfriend, and was now officially a miserable fifty-one-year-old bachelor. He was sharing the trailer with his twenty-two-year-old daughter, Theresa, who wandered out to the porch as we sipped our rye and listened to her father moan about his lost lady love, by all accounts a beautiful woman young enough to be his daughter.

"How come you never date hippie women?" his actual daughter finally asked. There are plenty of hippie women in that part of the world—the valleys of the Kootenay, Selkirk, and Purcell Mountains, collectively known as the Kootenays.

"Hippie women don't shave," Taylor answered, and turning to me said, "I like a woman who wears makeup and high heels. I had a girlfriend once who wore high heels when she gardened. High heels and those little white socks with lace on 'em. It was the sexiest thing I've ever seen."

Taylor's small nose, big cheekbones, and square jaw gave him a Jack Palance look. Behind his trailer he had a barn he called the Grand Forks Yacht Club, despite the fact that it sat on a hillside miles from water. It was Taylor's homemade party space, complete with stage, dance floor, and room for a hundred. He kept a horse, a "heavy colored" Morgan named Rocking Comet. Some evenings when the mood struck, he would wander out to the Yacht Club, strap on a guitar, switch on the P.A., and do severe injustice to the songs of John Prine, until Comet came in from outside to stand by the railing around the dance floor and blink at him. That's one way the mayor liked to unwind. Another was to roll up a big reefer. It takes a certain kind of woman to tolerate that in a middle-aged man.

"She said she left mostly because of pot. If I thought that were true I'd quit," he insisted. "But there's no doubt in my mind that she left for very complex reasons she didn't understand."

✳

One weekend in the mid 1990s Taylor drove a couple of hours east to Salmo, B.C., to attend something called a Hemp Fest. There he met Jack Herer, the American author of *Hemp and the Marijuana Conspiracy: The Emperor Wears No Clothes,* a book that argues hemp was an historically important cultivated crop that only lost its supremacy to cotton with the invention of the cotton gin. In the 1930s an equivalent machine for hemp, called a decorticator, was perfected, causing *Popular Mechanics* magazine to predict in 1938 that hemp would be America's first billion-dollar crop. "Hemp is the standard fiber of the world," the article gushed. "It is used to produce more than 5,000 textile products, ranging from rope to fine laces, and the woody 'hurds' contain more than 75 per cent cellulose, produce more than 25,000 products, ranging from dynamite to Cellophane."

Before that article hit the newsstands, the American Congress had passed the Marijuana Tax Act, which imposed tariffs stiff enough to make hemp cultivation unprofitable. In *The Emperor* Herer makes the severely undersubstantiated claim that the Marijuana Tax Act was engineered behind the scenes by the Du Pont Chemical Corporation, at that time busy establishing petrochemical-based fabrics like nylon, and not eager for competition from any new wonder crop. The more likely primary motivation for stifling hemp was that it was indistinguishable from marijuana, and law enforcement agencies, whose budgets had been fattened in the 1920s to fight the War on Booze, needed a marijuana scare, a new peril, a new demon, to keep their jobs.

Prohibition of alcohol had created more problems than it solved, and had been repealed. What were all those booze-suppressing cops to do? Go back to civilian life? Harry Anslinger, former director of the anti-Prohibition branch of the FBI who later became head of the newly created Federal Bureau of Narcotics (which was renamed the Drug Enforcement Administration, or DEA, during the Nixon administration), is the villain of the piece, lying to Congress, creating the "Reefer Madness" myth, and inventing lurid racist stories—which were eagerly sensationalized and spread through the newspapers of the Hearst chain—of marijuana-crazed Mexicans and African-Americans getting white girls high and sexually exploiting them.

According to Herer, the banning of hemp farming (lifted by necessity during World War II, then reimposed) through the Marijuana Tax Act was a victory of hydrocarbons over carbohydrates, of the petrochemical industry over more environmentally friendly sources for plastic and fuel, a turn in human development that produced grave consequences for the health of the planet. Herer's book became the foundation text for the pro-hemp movement that has transformed the politics of cannabis in North America in the past decade. Herer gave pot activists a whole new language to bring to the debate on marijuana laws, namely a defense of cannabis on agricultural, economic, environmental, and medical grounds. When Brian Taylor met Herer at the Hemp Fest he bought into Herer's argument that not only is hemp good for the planet, but that the road to legalizing pot passes through hemp fields.

✳

Combining civil disobedience, political theater, and a green thumb, in 1995 Brian Taylor committed the criminal offense of planting two pounds of cannabis sativa seeds on his seven-acre plot up the hill behind the Yacht Club. Just so no one would miss the point, he planted his crop so as to spell out the word "HEMP" in letters fifty feet long. Anyone driving west from town could see them. Although the seeds were low-THC hemp smuggled in from Amsterdam, as the plants grew Taylor regularly phoned the local Royal Canadian Mounted Police detachment to inquire when officers would be dropping by to charge him with marijuana cultivation, as the law required. In response to police indifference, he persuaded the publisher of a local one-sheet newspaper called *The Informer* to come out and take pictures of the plants, which never grew much beyond two feet because the valley's abundant deer kept nibbling at them. *The Informer* superimposed a photo of Taylor in front of the plants to make them look twelve feet tall. The paper came out at nine on a Wednesday morning. By nine-thirty the cops were at Taylor's door.

They laid charges of cultivation and possession of marijuana. The impending trial almost two years later first brought me to Grand Forks, but at the last minute charges were stayed, because Canadian law had changed. Hemp cultivation was now legal, although still strictly regulated, and an arbitrary line had been drawn between hemp and pot: any cannabis with flowers containing less than 0.03 percent THC was now hemp. Any more THC than that, and you had marijuana.

The charges may also have been stayed in part because Brian Taylor had managed to get himself elected mayor of Grand Forks on a pro-hemp platform. His election rhetoric had conjured up a vision of the town as Canada's Hemp City, a center for research and development of new strains of his favorite plant. Taylor was as surprised as anyone when he won. Media outside the valley began to take note, and Taylor's pot habit became very public knowledge when a Vancouver weekly described him as "a veteran (and outspoken) pot smoker." Taylor had not expected it, but decided that since he'd been officially "outed" as a pothead, there was no going back in the closet. On a popular Vancouver talk radio show heard throughout the province, he was asked directly, "Do you smoke pot?"

"Yes."

"Finally, an honest politician," the host said.

✳

Honesty can get a Canadian in trouble with Uncle Sam. Unlike most British Columbia valleys, the Sunshine runs east-west, and so spreads under a full day's sunlight like a broad smile, the bottom lip just brushing the American border. One afternoon in the summer of 1998, as Taylor zipped across to tiny Danville, Washington, for his weekly run to buy cheap Yankee milk and cheese, he was asked by the American customs officer if he had ever smoked marijuana. He declined to answer and was denied entry. The reason for refusal was not merely his having publicly admitted to smoking in the past; now there were suddenly accusations of his having trafficked in marijuana. The evidence: media records of Taylor's growing those fifty-foot HEMP letters up his hill, even though charges had been dropped by Canadian prosecutors.

"The Americans put this dossier together on me that just amazed my lawyer," Taylor says. It included transcripts of most of his radio and television interviews. "They obviously wanted to make an example of me."

In November 1998 he was granted a hearing before an immigration judge in Seattle to decide his admissibility to America. "They wouldn't let me across the border to argue my own court case," he remembers. "I ended up having to pretend I was a businessman at five in the morning with my suit on and sneak across in a rent-a-car at the border north of Seattle. Then at the hearing the judge threw all the charges against me out, but at the last minute said, 'I have to ask you this. Do you still smoke marijuana? If you tell me it's only occasional I can let you back into the country, but if you tell me it's more than that I have to ban you.' I told him, 'I smoke it every day when I have it, Your Honor.' And he still granted me permission to enter."

He's luckier than some Canadians. American customs officials have the right to ban foreigners from entering the United
States for five years, arbitrarily, on grounds of moral turpitude,
which can include admitting having tried marijuana, even once,
at some time in their life. More than four hundred Canadians have
been banned in this way.

In 1998 hemp was grown legally on a few sites around Grand
Forks. The largest plot was ten acres up the North Fork Road. The
farmer, growing this new crop for the first time, attempted to harvest it using a combine machine of the kind intended for grain.
But the twelve-foot hemp stalks were so thick and woody the combine jammed up and caught fire. It took days to get the cellulose-
rich fiber out of the gears and pulleys. The farmer brought in a
silage cutter and mowed the field down. But now the crop was on
the ground, where it got rained on for a few days, so that it had to
be flipped over and allowed to dry, then fed from the silage cutter
into the combine, which jammed up again. To make a long story
short, they never did get the crop off the field and ended up plow-
ing it under, seeds and all. And naturally, these hardy Russian
cannabis seeds sprouted and came up the next summer. "You
should take a trip up to that field and check it out," Brian Taylor told
me. "One of the hemp varieties, Finn 14, just blasts up from nothing in three weeks and produces a big cone of seeds, like the Mighty
Mites on the marijuana side. Summerland Donkey Cock," he said
fondly, recalling an infamous strain from the sunny Okanagan
Valley, seventy miles west.

✳

I head up to the hemp field the next morning, to a place fifteen
miles from the United States border. On one side of the narrow
valley the hills drop suddenly to the river, on the other side to the
road. In between there's room for a ten-acre field of tall grass. If
you look closely you might notice some other plants poking up in
the fallow mix, tall weeds like mullein, which was smoked by the

native Indians of this area as a detoxifier, and cannabis, which is smoked by plenty of the white people who have supplanted them. This particular cannabis is Zolotanosha 11, a Russian strain of hemp with a dual purpose, for seed and fiber. On the back edge of the field Pavel Demitoff sits out of sight of the road in a little area of trampled-down tall grass. With him are a hemp activist named Ron, his three-year-old daughter, Kerry, and Mark, a nineteen-year-old hippie who keeps interrupting to insist that he is a Universal Light Being and that if we meditate together he can take me to a higher place.

"We've picked the taller hemp plants, the ten-footers that were real visible from the road," says Demitoff. He pulls some seed from a swathe of six-foot plants. "Have you tasted the difference between dead seed and viable seed? This is viable. The government wants us to eat dead stuff."

He's spent the night in the field because he's expecting a Canadian government bureaucrat to come out and take samples of this crop for THC content. Why wouldn't he just spend the night in town and drive out in the morning? Well, he's got no driver's license, because he has no ID. "The government can have this and that's all," he says, holding up a thumbprint. "They promised my people when we arrived we wouldn't have to sign anything, and I'm holding them to it."

He is a descendent of the Doukhobors, Russian communalist pacifists (the name means Spirit Wrestlers) who settled five thousand strong in the Kootenays in the first decade of this century, having fled torture in czarist jails for refusing to join the Russian Army. Tolstoy donated all income from his last novel, *Resurrection,* to help finance the movement of Doukhobors to Canada. He felt they lived closest to his own utopian vision of Russia as a communal paradise of nonviolent, truly Christian peasants. Tolstoyans also supplied the Doukhobors with a handbook for learning English that included such useful phrases as "All governments are based on violence" and "Oppose private property."

When the Depression hit in the 1930s, the Doukhobors' farmland, owned communally, was not protected by the government from foreclosure the way individually deeded farms were. In 1939 they lost most of their land and buildings in the valley. There were suddenly a lot of Doukhobors on the streets of Grand Forks with nothing to do and no place to live. Some found work and private lodgings and started down the road to assimilation. As for the others, a rancher named Gilpin donated some land for them up in the valley ten miles east, across the river from the highway. The community came to be called Gilpin, and for decades was a ragged chain of squatters' shacks. The buildings looked temporary because they were. Some Doukhobors who lived there, a splinter group of radical arsonists and bombers called the Sons of Freedom, would periodically burn down their own houses as a denunciation of material wealth. They weren't completely crazy: usually they removed the doors, windows, and furniture first.

If you drive out to Gilpin today, you'll notice a hand-written welcome sign that reads "God's land can't be bought or sold, leased or taxed. Peace will reign only when the land is free." Born and raised there, Pavel Demitoff is a living remnant of Tolstoy's utopian yearnings.

The welcome sign on Highway 3 into town says Grand Forks is "Famous for Borscht and Sunshine," but borscht doesn't begin to describe the Doukhobors' legacy. For nearly seventy years, until the 1970s, Doukhobors made up the majority in the valley. Now their influence is waning. On Spencer's Hill, just down the lane from Brian Taylor's place, is the house of their leader, which Doukhobors still call the *Sirotskii Dom,* or "orphanage" in Russian, for traditionally this house also served as a refuge for community members, as well as being the storehouse and dispenser of communally produced wealth. Now it's just a modern, normal-looking house, rebuilt after it was torched by the Sons of Freedom in 1978. When I met Doukhobor leader J. J. Verigin Sr. there, he seemed resigned to his people's decline.

"If you lose your language, then your customs and traditions follow," he said wearily. "Our parents have succumbed to the practice of communicating in the home in English. Not that we don't want to integrate; with integration everyone contributes the best they have. But we are deathly afraid of assimilation."

It may already be too late. The language is dying. But the Doukhobor legacy lives on in the form of community support for freethinkers and radical ideas—like Brian Taylor's push to make Grand Forks Canada's Hemp City.

Hemp was not a hard sell to the Doukhobors. J. J. Verigin can recall hemp oil's being used for cooking in his youth. "We're very much interested in hemp, and know its good qualities," he said. Another Doukhobor told me she could remember that in her childhood her grandparents grew hemp in the middle of their cornfield, to hide it from the authorities. She recalls her mother "giving shit to my grandmother" for it. Now grandma's ways might be vindicated.

J. J. Verigin's son Barry told me, "You shouldn't try to legislate human appetite. This plant is part of our tradition. In Russia they used to burn the leaves in the *bania*—their bathhouses—and obviously they didn't think they were getting high, it was relaxing in the bath." In one of the earliest recorded references to cannabis, the Greek historian Herodotus (484–430 B.C.) commented that the nomadic Scythians carried out similar smoke rituals with hemp, in the same part of the world, the Ukrainian steppes, that the Doukhobors once called home.

✳

Pavel is an old grower. "In 1979 I went bush," he tells me. "I surrounded myself with ten horses and fourteen dogs and just grew the best marijuana." Then one night years later his cabin burned to the ground. "I woke up and my hair was on fire. I survived, but it made be think. The natives told me I had too many blankets. It's just as easy for me to go back to the bush and make lots of

money. But I promised Brian Taylor I'd work with him and promised not to grow it. I used to teach people how to grow it. It's a really
easy thing to do. I think I'm the best outdoor grower on the planet.
But I want to grow it legally now. For medicine. I don't want to grow
it for hippies to get high, although I do believe recreation is an
important part of good health. But I want to grow it for people on
AIDS wards, and cancer wards."

He picks at the seeds of a huge hemp bud. "Human be-
ings almost lost the ability to grow this plant. It's silly. I believe
there is good medicine in all parts of the plant. The roots, the
calyx, the bracts—different medicines for different people." With
Brian Taylor's help he has formed a company called Brown Bear
Medicinals, and the two of them are trying to win a contract from
the Canadian government, which has recently announced it would
spend $7.5 million to do clinical trials of medical marijuana. Who
better to grow it for them but a man with decades of experience?
As the application makes its way through a tangled and timid bu-
reaucracy, Demitoff is not sitting still. He has Brown Bear marketing a tea made from the prefloral leaves of the crop in this hemp
field. "Hempty," he calls it. "I thought it was a permit violation to
use the leaves, but Health Canada told me the prefloral leaves are
not illegal, so we can use them," he says. He's already filling Internet orders from as far away as Guam. "I'm getting all kinds of testi-
monials. One woman told me she's sleeping well for the first time
in decades, and ordered another five ounces."

David Malmo-Levine, a twenty-nine-year-old pot activist who
is living off and on at the mayor's trailer while putting together a
court challenge to marijuana laws that will eventually take him to
the Supreme Court of Canada (see Chapter 13), tells me Hempty
is the perfect beverage for urbanites forced by the marketplace to
smoke profit-maximizing, chemically fertilized indoor marijuana.
"Indoor pot like that doesn't have the full range of cannabinoids,
especially CBDs," he says. CBD, or cannabidiol, is one of sixty
canabinoids found in cannabis. "This CBD tea doesn't get you
high, but it is relaxing, mellowing. It's a nice complement to that

super-potent hydroponic weed, where you get the massive THC blowout, where you get so much euphoria it's almost paranoia. Combine that with CBD tea and you get closer to what a good outdoor organic pot buzz gives you: euphoria with relaxation. A nice day-to-day stress management system."

✳

Many Kootenay pot lovers insist the finest pot is grown outdoors and organically. Through tree-clad mountains that at night look like the shadows of giant, sleeping bears, I make the ninety-minute drive from Grand Forks to Nelson, the administrative hub of the Kootenays, with a population of 12,000. There, Dustin "Sunflower" Cantwell runs the Holy Smoke Culture Shop, a basement head shop tucked in an alley just behind Baker Street, Nelson's main thoroughfare. Cantwell tells me, "Organic is better, because whatever environment the plant grows up in will be in the bud. So for a bud that grows up under a thousand-watt light, all its experience of living is *Bzzzzzzzzz.*" He makes an electric drone noise. "But the organic plant grown up on the mountain, blown with the mountain winds, urinated on by a deer, pecked at by a bear, lightning strikes, rain—that's going to be your experience when you're smoking. So even if you're not getting the thousand-watt buzz, you'll get the spirit of the area, not some artificial environment. Plus chemicals that are used in indoor growing *must* interfere with cannabinoid production. The Compassion Club patients here like outdoor better because all of the various cannabinoids are in the buds. In the indoor you might not get all the range that help your head, or your cramps, or your lower back."

He asks if I want to go to the waterfall, a little parklet tucked behind the location of Nelson's Saturday farmers' market. This being a weekday, the stalls are empty, but he points out where the drumming circle forms, at a distance from the little stage where a pickup country folk band plays on market days. Whereas Grand Forks appears on the surface to be a typically conservative Western small town, Nelson is one of the funkiest towns on the planet. When I ask a cop one day what he thinks of all the hippies hanging out on Baker Street, he out–politically corrects me: "Alternative lifestylers, don't you mean?"

The town is the nexus for the Kootenay party people, the grower-snowboarder crowd, and there are a lot of them. "You cash in the fall crop and buy season's passes for the ski hills," one small grower told me after offering a sample of his own KGB—Kootenay Green Bud. He grows about four pounds of indoor to sell and one pound of outdoor to smoke himself each year. One of the downtown bars was advertising a band called Phattie Phattie and the Roaches the week I was there. I asked the waitress if they were local. "With that name they should be," she said.

Cantwell discovered Nelson eight years ago. He's a working-class kid who, Tobias Wolff style, talked himself into Lakefield, an exclusive Canadian prep school where Britain's Prince Andrew was sent in his youth. When he was finished with high school in 1991, he spent a year hitchhiking around B.C.

"I just knew this was the place that was the best," he says, eyes lighting up in a baby face that's swathed in thick brown hair and a full backwoods beard. We're sitting at a picnic table within earshot of the falls. "There's a conscious community here, people who are aware of the world and take into account how they live in relation to it. Growing good food. There's a good arts scene. The mountains, the lakes. Good cannabis. That was definitely a deciding factor. Holy fuck, look at those blackberries!"

He leaps up from the table and strides excitedly to a cluster of wild berries ripening on thick, thorny vines. We pick a few and taste-test them. They're tongue-curdlingly tart. "They need a frost," he says.

Then we wander out of this little valley and back to the Holy Smoke, where the sign on the door says, "FRIENDS WELCOME, COPS STAY OUT!" It's nearly 4:20, and there's a big cluster of magnificently dreadlocked stoners in back, starting in early on the daily ritual. One's just come from accidentally rolling in poison ivy.

"Don't panic, it's organic," someone advises.

The afflicted one says, "Yeah, it's true. When I relaxed the itch went away."

Another guy is looking over a photocopy of a series of stickmen drawn to teach the movements to the Phish song "Meat Stick." He tells me, "We're going to get enough people together to break the record."

Through the cloud of marijuana smoke a shirtless guy named JahFree says, "Record for what? The most people doing the stupidest thing?"

Asked to describe Nelson, JahFree says, "Overall, there ain't no crime here. People bring their kids up right. There are no B-and-Es."

The others supply superlatives for their town, until a nineteen-year-old-girl in a dark mood starts bitching about what she calls "hippie elitism." The town has three generations of hippies now, and the older ones look down on the young, who come out of their spiritual fasts and meditations and then, being young, want to drink and toke and party. "The High Holies, so Hippier than Thou, can't accept that," she spits.

At the end of the table, wavering over whether to use his real name or not, is the guy who runs the Nelson Compassion Club, supplying pot for about thirty people, some with AIDS or multiple sclerosis and some with mental illness, which is "a hard one to quantify," he admits. "I'm trying to be cautious. Recent evidence seems to show pot's not good for schizophrenics, so I don't think I'd accept a schizophrenic."

Cantwell, fresh from a "mind-wallop weekend" where he met his birth mother for the first time, tells the assembled stoners that his birth mother is Dutch and that her father grew and smoked cannabis from World War II until his death. "I didn't know anything about them, because they bullshitted on my adoption papers. But now suddenly everything fits. I'm three-quarters Dutch. No wonder those Dutch grow videos always felt like family footage." He'd gone to church with his new family, "and they hit me with the anointing oil! It was so funny! I wrote down one of the hymns. One of the hymns was called 'Garment of Praise,' and one of the verses was 'All you who mourn in Zion, I have authority to anoint unto you in Zion, oil of joy that will set you free.' Oil of joy that will set you free?! Now I only know one kind of oil that does that. Oil of joy. I was like, I got some right here, if you want to step out back. Let the anointing begin!" A few minutes later, he says, "Seriously, in this whole cannabis movement, there has to be spirituality in it or it's not going anywhere, it's just going to be a fad or a passing attraction."

Cantwell mentions that he spent the previous night arguing the merits of drug legalization with the alcohol-guzzling relatives of a friend, and Paul DeFelice, co-owner of the Holy Smoke with Cantwell, quotes The Who as if it's scripture: "They couldn't stand on two feet while they lectured about morality."

Paul is older, in his early forties, and a former ski bum whose talents can be seen in the Warren Miller ski flicks of the late 1980s. He offers to hook me up with a few outdoor growers, get me into the hills for a little crop-exhibiting walkabout. I worry that growers might not want to be seen with a reporter, especially when the local police know I'm in town and will soon know what I look like.

"The cops don't need for leads," Paul reassures me. He holds his hand a foot above the tabletop. "They have a stack of leads this high from disgruntled partners, either sexual or business. If you give any advice for growers, make it: Don't Have a Partner. Partners are always the downfall."

It was a partnership gone bad that pushed Paul to become an activist. He was a small-time grower in the 1980s. "I ran up against the inherent violence in this cozy little industry of pot growing," he remembers. "I had my little grow room, I was a ski bum, and I met this guy who is like a biker type, he's got a sophisticated grow room himself. I wanted to learn, so I was hanging with this guy and he's showing me the ropes of hydroponics and CO_2 and stuff. I get a couple of rooms going under his tutelage, and sure enough, he goes and takes all the product. I'm like, 'Where's my share?' and he's like, 'Yeah, what are you going to do about it?' Not only that—after I'd dissed him as a partner, he starts breaking into my house, to steal my stuff, steal my pot. And I'm starting to realize, Aha, here's what happens when something like this is illegal. If you've got any kind of pot or cash, and somebody knows it, and you don't have the ability to protect it, they're going to take it. I had to decide—was I going to get violent to protect what I had?"

The moment of truth came when he and a buddy caught the guy red-handed in his house with an armful of stuff. "And he's egging me on, going, 'Ah, you fucking potheads are a bunch of wimpy pussies.' He's a cokehead, that was his thing, he's more uptight in that sort of way. But he's pushing my buttons, and I'd reached a point where I'd seen this coming, so I had axe handles and baseball bats strategically placed around the house. I'm standing in one doorway, my friend is standing in the other doorway with a baseball bat, and this guy is between us, and my buddy is making me eye signs, like, 'Let's get him, let's go! Let's give it to him!' And I'm standing there like, Ahhhh, I don't know, and it's all happening too fast. All of a sudden time freezes. I'm thinking, If I grab that axe handle where am I going to hit him? Am I going to hit him in the knee? No, I'm going to hit him in the head. What happens when you hit somebody in the head? Skulls break, people bleed, people die. Am I ready to do this? This all happens in a flash, and I just say no way. I say, 'If you get out of here right now and I never see you again, it's over.' He's going, 'Yeah, yeah, you pussy.' But off he goes and I never did see him again. So it was the right thing.

"People out here will tell you the growers are all musicians, all hippies. Well, they largely are, but there's that out there too, and it sucks."

"I got very high from two puffs of that pot," I say. We've been sharing a joint.

"It's a Northern Lights-M5 cross—whatever M5 is," Paul says. He's smoked a whole fattie of it. He takes stock of his stone for a moment.

"It's quite kind," he says.

I run something past him that I was told in Grand Forks, that three groups coexist in the Kootenay marijuana world: the out-of-the-closet activists like this Holy Smoke crowd, the small-time regular-folk growers who are easy to bust—"easy to catch as seal pups on the ice," Cantwell interjects—and then that third group, identified in the public mind with bikers like the Hell's Angels, more organized, more serious, more dangerous. Everyone is complaining that the cops harvest the seal pups and leave the big boys alone. Even the cops admit it. RCMP constable Ray Watson, leader of the Kootenay "Green Team," the local pot-busting SWAT team (locals call him Rambo on account of his thick black combed-back hair and standard-issue 1980s cop mustache), told me, "Somebody who grows four or eight pounds, makes ten or twenty thousand bucks to help feed their wife and kids, do we target people like that? Yes, we target people like that. Why? So it doesn't come down to the kids. I'm a family man, got a couple of kids in the school system here. I don't want to see this marijuana come down into the school system. As far as major crime is concerned, which is multi-multi pounds, do we target that? Yes, we *want* to target that. But to be realistic, do we have the resources to target that? Sometimes we have to look at the political will, and whether we're getting the proper funding."

"The cops are afraid of the gun-toting, coke-dealing, pot-growing types, who have no scruples about what they grow, what they sell," says Paul. "They fink on each other, they market in information, that's why they don't get busted by the cops, because they'll give up everybody they know who's growing in order to keep themselves from getting busted." He names a well-known family in the valley. "Everyone is scared shitless of them because they are coked out, they are crazed, and they've got the cops' protection because they feed the cops the information they want. What do you do? It happens because of Prohibition. We're all quivering in our boots because every plant is worth its weight in gold all of a sudden. You can bet there's crooks and cops who want to take that from you."

He lets out a long sigh. "I just want to get high . . ."

✳

While Paul DeFelice says he's never been physically threatened for his activism, Brian Taylor in Grand Forks has received death threats. They seem largely to stem from misinformation about hemp, and the potential for legal hemp plants in the valley to cross-pollinate with illegal marijuana in the hills and thus ruin the pot crop. For DeFelice, running the Holy Smoke store and leading the pro-pot campaign has cost friendships. "A lot of my grower friends are keeping their distance," he says. "They don't want to associate with me when I'm this public, and there are even people I know who are out and out venomous about what I'm doing, that I'm ruining a good thing. And I'm like, 'Man, do you not realize at what cost? How many freedoms do you want to give up, how many weapons do you want to carry?' I can't agree with that. It's another form of exploitation as far as I'm concerned—you're exploiting the plant and exploiting people, using these prohibition laws. I keep telling them, 'Listen, it'll be valuable even if it's legal, it'll just have a more realistic value, it'll achieve some kind of balance, maybe around the price of coffee, and we can pay taxes on it.' I don't mind paying taxes if it goes for good stuff, for health care and education. But I don't like mafiosos and bikers.

"Actually, I take that back. I have biker friends—they're kind of a necessary counterbalance to cops when you have Prohibition going on."

✳

Down through the mountains and back on the coast, I check in with Marc Emery. On a Monday morning in a spare, phoneless downtown Vancouver office, he's ripping open a stack of mail, about sixty letters in all, hoping against hope they'll contain $14,000 worth of seed orders. He bounced a $5,000 check to his lawyer on Friday, and has had to stall on a few other payments. Slitting the envelopes and pulling out the contents results in a growing stack of money orders. Most customers spend about $150 American. Many of the accompanying letters are entertaining, some eloquent, others closer to Cheech and Chong. From Missouri: *Give me cannabis liberty or give me death!* "I don't know about the death part," Emery says. "Careful what you wish for."

Most orders call for three or four varieties, and one of the choices is invariably the strain called Burmese x Fuckin' Incredible, from Vancouver Island Seed Company, because it won the smoking test I helped judge in the winter. Number two was Blueberry, and there was a three-way tie for third between Northern Lights, Shiskaberry, and a Romulan-White Widow-Big Bud cross.

Now everyone's ordering Burmese x Fuckin' Incredible. "Everyone wants it, but we're out of it," Marc says. "The guy who grows it is very eccentric. Grows great pot, but he's not the most astute businessman. But Burmese Fuckin' Incredible will be flavor of the month all over the world in the next six months."

Another letter: *Enclosed please find 40 dollars U.S. for B.C. Afghani. What this indoor cash cropper needs is a killer high, a hammer blow to the head, no connoisseur concerns here, just two tokes and you're baked for hours.* "Just two tokes and you're baked for hours? To me that is a connoisseur concern," says Emery. He reads on: "He wants a high yield, two and a half pounds per thousand-watt lights in a Sea of Green." Sea of Green is a growing technique in which a mother plant is selected to supply clones. The clones can be cut from mom at staggered intervals, allowed to vegetate near her, then placed in another room to flower, so that the grower has a steady supply of plants ready to harvest at regular intervals. "That's extraordinarily ambitious," Marc says. "In fact, I've only ever seen that once. He's telling me he wants the best high, the hugest yield; he wants a quick maturing one, too—sixty-day flowering maximum. And he wants it all for four dollars a seed."

This order is small because in my last order only six of a hundred seeds germinated. This is my seventh order and five of the six gave me excellent results. I wonder if that one just got x-rayed in the mail?

"Well, we'll send him some extras this time. I've got plenty of spare Blueberry crosses I'm on the hook for." Emery promised a local grower he'd buy his next crop for a dollar a seed. "He picked a fabulous Blueberry male to cross with twenty-five females, and remarkably that one male produced enough pollen to totally soak all the plants. The females were five varieties—White Rhino; Mr. Nice from Sensi Seeds; the Real McCoy, which is a Haze-Skunk cross; Blueberry itself; and a pure Thai. Much to my shock, they produced seventeen thousand good usable seeds, so now I'm on the hook for seventeen thousand dollars."

✳

Across town in another rented office, Greg, a grow expert who is Emery's right-hand man, is on the phone with a customer from England. He speaks in measured, gracious tones:

"Do you have our catalogue handy?

"I didn't ask what you ordered, I asked if you have our catalogue handy.

"You're going to go get a pencil and write this down.

"Oh yeah? That's fun.

"Got your pencil?

"Mighty Mite Donkey Dick.

"Don't argue with me.

"Heh.

"Mighty Mite seeds.

"California Girl cross Durban.

"Same.

"Brenda Skunk. Brenda.

"No, they'd be mostly indica.

"That's right.

"Lovely smoke. Some of the best there is.

"You'll be thrilled by them.

"You betcha."

He hangs up the phone, takes a hit off a joint, and says, "That's where the marijuana comes in. 'Excuse me while I just smoke a joint and not fucking scream at you for being so stupid!' I've learned they don't write stuff down. They ask all these questions, you give 'em all this information, and they go, 'What were those again?'"

Greg has just returned from a tour of Australia. He loved it. To him the Aussie pot world was a refreshing change from the North American consumerist mind-set, which pollutes even our attitudes toward marijuana. "The Australians take a strain however they come across it and they'll work with it, they'll get it to grow, they'll see if it's any good, and then they'll move on," Greg says. "Whereas here, guys will throw stuff in the ground and decide they don't like it right off the bat. Well, how did you grow it?

"And everybody's looking for the best. There is no best. You need an indica to relax and a sativa to keep you awake if that's what you want, or somewhere in between. That's all the subtleties of the plant that you have to work with, really."

Greg once worked as a comedy writer in Los Angeles. He has a wry sense of humor, at times almost bitter. Thirty years of being on the wrong side of a bad law will do that. "I've read all the literature they feed our kids in school," he says. "They tell them the truth about heroin, cocaine, alcohol, and tobacco, and lie to them about marijuana. Why? Because they've been advancing their drug war, and for whatever insidious reason, they've made a big deal about marijuana. To reply to that we've had to make a big deal about it too. The hemp community makes a big deal, the medical marijuana people make a big deal about it, but it's not a big fucking deal. It's just a plant, one of thousands.

"I think we need to advance this understanding, to get it off this big-deal wagon that it's on. I've been smoking pot every day for thirty years, and I *know* it's not a big deal."

Emery has been on the phone at the second desk in the small office, but now he's listening to Greg. "This is what it comes down to," he says. "Should anyone ever be sent to jail for putting something in their body? They never explain why the American government should be allowed to create a total militarized police state to justify controlling someone's appetite. A huge police apparatus, getting bigger all the time; hundreds of thousands of officers whose basic job is diet control. That's what it is—it's one big fascist militaristic diet program!"

✳

"Come and get your goodies!"

At noon the next day Emery is handing out little keepsake mason jars, the cute kind with a tablecloth pattern on the lid. Inside are thirty prerolled spliffs, each joint labeled with a felt-tip pen to identify the strain: THN for a Thai-Hawaiian-Northern Lights cross, or CW for Chemo crossed with White Widow. The joints are thin little pinners, but potent. We're on another smoke-fest, this one on a charter boat for fifty, rented to cruise the islands on the south end of the Sunshine Coast. Now you might imagine that an oceangoing vessel loaded up with fifty stoners and fifteen hundred joints would be a wild ride. But you have to understand, this is Canada. There are no raised voices, no scenes. The daylong party is a sunny, utterly sedate affair. The only guest who seems to hold even the promise of stirring up a bit of raunchiness is Watermelon, a local comedienne and actress whose day job is selling watermelon and cannabis-laden Krazy Kannabis Kookies—"ginger snaps with extra snap"—in the nude on Wreck Beach, Vancouver's famous secluded, clothing-optional public beach.

"When I sell my cookies I always tell people, 'Don't eat it if you have anybody to impress tonight,'" she says. Good advice. Eating cannabis delivers a high quite unlike the high you get from smoking it. The cannabinoids metabolize differently because the liver gets involved, not just the lungs. In his book *Hashish!* Robert Connell Clarke suggests that THC when eaten is altered by the liver into the metabolite 11-hydroxy-THC, which may quadruple its potency. THC when smoked is carried from the lungs to the bloodstream to the brain, bypassing the liver.

"I'm doing a lot of ganja warnings this year, telling people that with food, less ganja is more," says Watermelon. "If you eat more it's not going to be a more incredible experience, it's going to be a *worse* experience. I bank on repeat business. Of course, there's going to be a variance from batch to batch, according to the strength of the pot you're using. But I bake the healthiest cookie around—I even have my own wheat grinder at home, and I grind organic whole wheat flour fresh just before I bake, I use olive oil and organic free-range eggs, I use the nicest, most expensive spices and stuff. I really go the extra mile."

For today's cruise Watermelon accessorizes her bikini with tarty high heels at times, a bad-girl look that contrasts sharply with her behavior. Turns out she's a self-labeled "litter nazi," making sure everyone cleans up after the midday organic vegetarian picnic on a pebbly beach across the strait on Keats Island: "It's one thing to take a beach by storm, it's another to leave it a shambles" is her motto. Not a Kleenex is left behind. She's the perfect poster girl for responsible pot use.

✳

Marc Emery's second marriage has ended while I've been away on my world travels. Now he has a girlfriend named Marci, an American loaded up with hard-core urban attitude. She hates the organic crap on the cruise boat. She's longing for fried chicken and fries. Marc met Marci after she sent some photos of herself to *Cannabis Culture,* face painted green, surrounded by leafy marijuana plants. They put her on the cover. "It was one of the least impressive photos of Marci, but the buds were in focus," Emery says.

"They were my plants, my plants!" Marci proclaims. "I grew them. Marc sent me the seeds, and I grew them in the closet of my little apartment in Arizona with a single thousand-watt metal halide. My parents came to visit, and I'd be like slamming the door to this closet, trying to keep the Glowing Light of God from coming out! Really, it was the most wonderful light. I loved to pluck my eyebrows in that light."

✳

From the basement of his house farther up the coast, Marc bankrolls and produces Pot TV, an Internet television station webcasting four hours of live programming a day. Dick Cowan, the Yale-educated former national director of the National Organization for the Reform of Marijuana Laws—NORML—has come north from the U.S. for a volunteer stint as anchorman on the daily 4:20 news on Pot TV.

"Canadians are a major problem for American prohibitionists," Cowan says. "They're too white to invade and too close to ignore. It's been fascinating to watch the separate process up here, which really is so much better than the United States'. The difference in the newspapers is amazing. If the *Washington Post* was a tenth the newspaper the *Ottawa Citizen* is, marijuana prohibition would have been over with."

Pot TV webcasts to the world using nine computers, a couple of consumer-quality digital cameras, and an audiovisual mixing board. Voila—a television station for about $30,000.

On this day one of the shows on air is *Burning Shiva,* hosted by Chris Bennett, author of *Green Gold the Tree of Life: Marijuana in Magic and Religion.* Bennett lives along the coast in a boat he restored and renovated, and has just finished a second book, *Sex, Drugs, Violence and the Bible.* After the show he comes up and joins us on the deck outside. One question about his work leads to many others.

"When I was researching my first book I came across the Hebrew word *kineboisin*—it's similar to the Babylonian and Assyrian words *kannab,* and it's actually the same root as our word 'cannabis'—it just means 'fragrant cane,'" he says. "Now, in Exodus

30:23, God commands Moses to make a holy anointing oil with about nine pounds of *kineboisin* and six liters of olive oil. In most Bibles it's translated as 'fragrant cane' or sometimes 'calamus' but this thing about cannabis is not something I came up with. It was verified in 1980 by Hebrew University in Israel. You can look up the Torah websites for navigating the Bible, look up Exodus 30: 23—it will list cannabis as one of the possible meanings.

"Now Moses, every time he talks to God, he goes inside the tent or the tabernacle and literally drenches himself in this holy anointing oil. THC is fat-soluble—it can pass through the skin. Now was Moses talking to God, or was Moses like a shaman, ingesting a psychoactive plant and interpreting the activity that it aroused in his brain as the voice of God?"

11 : THE CANNABIS CUP

"This is my first year being involved in the Cannabis Cup," a volunteer at the Cannabis College is telling me in Amsterdam. "I used to just sit in coffee shops and get annoyed at the courtesy vans pulling up and all these Americans unpiling. It's a monstrous big Yankee 'Buy buy buy smoke smoke smoke' kind of party. It started out as a nice little harvest festival, and grew big. After last year's downer everyone is just waiting to see what this year will be like. Will it get back to the peaceful cooperative vibe, or will it just get weirder?"

"And it's not a fair test," says Lorna, the Cannabis College manager. "Forty grams or whatever for a judge to sample in four days? It all comes down to which shop's got the nicest buffet, which shop has the women in the skimpiest outfits. The pot world is eighty percent male, even apart from the Cannabis Cup. It happens quite often I'll be in a shop and be the only woman. Everyone just standing there looking at you. It's quite uncomfortable."

Another volunteer says, "But I sympathize with the Americans. For me cannabis is just a normal thing. I just use it to sweeten my cigarettes." True to his word, he's rolling a big joint that is mostly tobacco with just a pinch of herb added. "We don't have to hide it or sneak it, or turn it into this secret mysterious event. But the Americans come over, and the freedom to smoke it makes them go crazy for a week or two!"

On the eve of the Cannabis Cup at a coffee shop named Rookies near the Leidseplein, an English couple named James and Anne Marie are "skinning up," as the English like to say—rolling tobacco and marijuana (in this case the old reliable Northern Lights) into big three-paper joints. Although smoking cannabis is of course illegal back home in Britain, the seeds are apparently legal, which I hadn't realized, and can be bought in any fish bait shop there.

James explains why: sometime after the Second World War some Frenchmen came over to compete in a famous British fishing derby. The French brought hemp seeds, which they boiled until soft, then attached to hooks. British fish went crazy for cannabis, and the Frenchmen won the Derby. "So hemp seeds were legalized in Britain," he says.

"To beat the French," adds Anne Marie.

The two cannabis lovers have visited Morocco many times, and have made good Arab friends there. Through their friends they hear tales of people being strung up and beaten in the prisons, of electroshock to the testicles used to extract confessions. In cozy Amsterdam, none of us can get a grip on how humans can inflict that kind of evil on each other.

These two Londoners have flown in especially for the Cup, which bills itself as "the world's leading convention for marijuana lovers and connoisseurs." It's a huge party in which two thousand tourists, most of them American readers of *High Times* magazine, race around Amsterdam, visiting nineteen competing coffee shops, getting their "official judges' passport" (cost: $200 U.S.) stamped. As judges they appraise the ambience of each shop while smoking and rating the unique strains of cannabis offered.

James and Anne Marie are back for the second straight year. "I'd never thought fondly of the Yanks before," says James. "But last year I found out there are no typical Americans. We met young black kids from Los Angeles, sixty-year-old Mohawk Indians from the Bronx, college professors from Kansas, retired couples from Florida. It made me realize America is just an amazing multiplicity of subgroups. Small tribes."

"And all the accents are soooo different," says Anne Marie.

✳

Cannabis Cup Central is the Pax Party House, a three-story convention space right next to a police station on Ferdinand Bolstraat. The Pax is packed with every kind of American male: young homeys moving in small posses, decked out head to toe in Oakland Raider silver and black; balding tie-dyed hippies; African-American yuppies with salon-styled dreads; and plenty of small-town guys with curved-bill ball caps looking like they just got off work at the feed mill. I ask one from Tennessee how the police treat pot smokers in his home state.

"If you don't have a lot, they sprinkle it on the ground," he says. "But if you have a lot, they crucify you to the Cross."

It's hard to imagine the Dutch wanting to crucify anyone. Tolerance in Holland is still a Christian virtue, so they allow more than zero. Listening to Soma, one of Amsterdam's finest growers, that Yoda-like Yank with Rastafarian dreadlocks down to his knees, telling a roomful of his fellow Americans how he uses ladybugs and Indian neem tree oil to organically control indoor insect problems, one needs to remember that speaker and audience had to leave their country to have this chat. If a similar seminar were held in the United States, everyone there could be charged with conspiracy to manufacture marijuana.

Most Americans come to the Cup for purely recreational reasons. A New Yorker who's made it over six years in a row tells me, "I end up just getting high and walking around looking at pretty churches. It's so progressive here, much more so than the United States. I'd call it civilized."

"It's still a controlled freedom, though," says his buddy. "The Dutch were the first country to abolish slavery. But they were also the first to use slavery, before that; they invented the slave plantation, in Sumatra. So they're always ahead of the curve. They're always inventing some new fuckery fifty years ahead of everyone else. Fifty years from now more of the world will be like Holland, and Holland will be on to something completely new." In support of his theory, the Dutch parliament is busy this week laying the legal foundations to make the country the world's first to endorse euthanasia.

✴

Last year's Cannabis Cup was marred by charges of ballot stuffing and fixed results. "Fraud at the Cannabis Cup" was played up with great amusement in the Dutch media. What had begun a dozen years earlier as a harvest festival with hippie ideals had mutated into cutthroat capitalist competition between coffee shops. Ben Dronkers told me, "If you say to them, 'I'm Brian, I want to enter the Cup,' and bring them a bag of grass to enter, you're suddenly a seed company. Silly, isn't it? But at the same time it's a game, it's a show, and I don't want to spoil the fun by nagging too much about it."

Dronkers is still taking part, whereas Eddie and Roland from Flying Dutchmen Seeds are boycotting the official competition. Roland has written, "Last year's Cup made it all clear, it's not a Cannabis contest anymore. It's just a very hard competition between coffee shops trying to gain publicity. The negative publicity caused by this is in nobody's interest; not for the organization, not for the competitors, not for the judges, and most of all not for this beautiful plant that is giving us so much."

By way of explanation, Eddie says, "In the seed competition, celebrity judges come from the States and judge the grass they are smoking. They are honest—I do believe them. But how do they know what they are smoking comes from the seeds that people claim it does?" In other words, if there is fraud at the American party, it's perpetrated by the Dutch competitors.

"If you want to have a seed contest, we told them a couple of times, start six months before," Roland adds. "For everybody who is going to compete as a seed company, one of the people from *High Times* should come to the shop and buy a packet of that seed. There are enough real good growers in Amsterdam that you could hire one to grow these seeds out and have every competitor allowed to come and check their plants once a week, to give information to the grower. 'Hey, do this, or that.' Then you know it really comes from the seeds, then it is a real competition.

"It's called the Cannabis Cup, but people don't respect it," Roland continues. "There's nothing to read about the strains. Nothing. Not where they came from, what kind of cross it is, how difficult it is to grow, what kind of smell and taste—nothing."

This year the organizers of the Cup are going out of their way to take the high road, making the competitions as transparent as possible and giving the event a high-minded theme. "Honor the Goddess" is the chosen motif, and so Cannabis Goddesses— female marijuana activists mostly—have been flown in to be feted, to give seminars, and to smoke some of the kindest herb in the world as judges of the various categories of hash and grass.

Vancouver's Watermelon, the nude cannabis cookie seller from Wreck Beach, has made it to the cover and then the centerfold of *High Times,* and been hired as official SpokesGoddess for Cup week. It's her duty to MC the evening entertainments at the famous bastion of Amsterdam counterculture, the Melkweg, introducing such acts as Patti Smith and Starship, the remnants (no Grace Slick) of Jefferson Airplane, and she takes her job seriously, wearing tasteful, classy gowns all week in a deliberate decision to dress and behave like the kind of spokesmodel who would do any straight cause proud.

"I've been to pot-legalization rallies in Vancouver where everyone is dressed like a delinquent," she says. "Pot activists are never going to get taken seriously until we show that we represent the hundreds of thousands of average users, who are mostly white-collar and blue-collar regular folks."

Part of her job is to introduce the "Cannabis Castaways," six young people chosen from a contest open to *High Times* readers, who, in the style of the TV show *Survivor,* were isolated for a week on a boathouse in Amsterdam and given huge amounts of marijuana to sample and judge, while having the whole adventure shot by a video crew. It's a pet project of *High Times* editor Steve Hagar, who personally edited the episodes. From the stage one afternoon one of the Castaways, Jeff from San Diego, who is confined to a wheelchair after a car accident in high school left him paralyzed and with limited use of his four limbs, spits bitterly into the microphone: "The government will give me Valium and Vicodin, and people die on that shit. But smoke a bong and it's time for jail."

Another Castaway interrupts to say, "Jeff's test for good pot is when he can feel his toes."

A bit later a third Castaway, DJ Nitro, who constantly wears the guaranteed heat magnet of a tight wool cap pulled low to the top of wraparound shades, announces, "I got searched twice just *leaving* my country, so I can imagine what's in store on the way back . . ."

✳

Watermelon is the most visible of a large contingent of Canadians at the Cup. One foursome of Calgary hosers sports specially made Olympic-style red and white athletic jackets with "Canadian Smoking Team" emblazoned across their backs. Another couple has arrived straight from a similar cannabis competition in Montreal. "There were eight hundred people in a rented hall," one says. "They gave you eleven varieties at the door. The smoke was so thick you couldn't even see the reggae band on the stage."

Also on hand are Hilary Black and Jill Fanthorpe of Vancouver's Compassion Club. At a seminar on medical marijuana, Hilary gives a history of the club that's exceptionally lucid, considering that as a "celebrity Goddess judge" in the hashish category she is required to smoke a mountain of high-quality hash, enough to form an opinion of each entrant and pick a winner from seventeen varieties.

At her seminar Hilary begins by describing how she worked for Emery's Hemp B.C. store on West Hastings five years ago, and found herself constantly fielding calls from people wanting to know about marijuana's purported value in alleviating chronic pain. So she educated herself. In one case she went to the house of an elderly woman with painful arthritis. After they smoked a joint together the woman was able to go to the kitchen, make herself a cup of tea, and carry it back to the living room—which may not sound like a huge accomplishment, but it was the first time in two years her hands had been pain-free enough to pull it off.

"She thought I was some angel sent to her by God," Hilary tells a packed conference room. "And as an eighteen-year-old girl, I knew I had found a calling."

The Compassion Club has twelve hundred patients, offers all kinds of free alternative therapies like Reiki massage and acupuncture, and is a registered charity. Hilary relates how a huge Vancouver police officer, after touring the club, had put a paternal hand on her shoulder and said, "You girls are doing good Christian work here." She goes on to explain that the Canadian government is on the verge of hiring a biotech company to produce "a million joints," as the newspapers like to say, for trials of medical marijuana.

"Health Minister Allan Rock is looking for a big corporation to run the show," she says. "We're trying to have some say in how corporate it's going to get, how synthetic it's going to get. Our goal is to make cannabis and other ancient herbal medicines available again."

One of the many Canadians at the Cup says to me one evening, "I hope those girls aren't being sucked in by the government." What he means is that if Canada's government decides that only the medicinal aspect of pot should be recognized, recreational users like him will continue to be denied and criminalized. There will be pot for pain relief, but not for pleasure.

When I ask Hilary about it she says, "The Compassion Club hasn't developed a direct policy on it, but my attitude is that it's one step at a time, and the first thing is to get people to accept and understand marijuana as a medicine. Once they understand it as a medicine, a lot of the lies and fears are lifted, and we've broken through a lot of the Reefer Madness–imposed stigma. Then I think it will be easier for people to understand how cannabis works as a stress reliever. Everybody knows we live in a very stressful world and that cannabis is the greatest thing to keep your stress level down—better than alcohol."

✳

At the "Smokers' Ball" Wednesday night, Mila Jansen has set up a demonstration of the Ice-o-lator. As Sasha stirs the big pail of leaves and ice water, one American tourist says to another, "Must be makin' some kinda *soup* over there."

At the Smokers' Ball there is also a "Cannasseur Self Test," which has questions like this:

> *Which of the following has no sativa in its genetic makeup?*
> *A) Warlock Haze*
> *B) AK47*
> *C) Top44*
> *D) Kali Mist*

> *Which is higher in CBD?*
> *A) Kind Bud*
> *B) Imported hashish*

I head home before the results are announced, but later I'm heartened to hear that master grower Soma only scored 76.

Soma has a booth at the Trade Expo in the Pax Party House, where he gives out samples of his homemade water hash, encouraging each recipient (he nearly always has a lineup) to observe how it bubbles merrily in the bowl of the pipe before it ignites. A young American looks on, and when the pipe is handed to him for a hit, he says, only half-jokingly, "I'm afraid. I'm afraid of the unknown."

Also admitting a certain apprehension is a speaker at one of the daily seminars held downstairs from the Expo at the Pax. "I'm a little nervous, because I'm coming out here: I'm a federal employee and I'm a pot smoker," he announces to a sympathetic audience. Not only is he a federal employee—he works in the Washington office of a Republican congressman. Here's the political advice he shares: "The Republicans are starting to figure out the drug war is a waste of money. That's the way they need to be approached. They are very conservative people in a political climate where there are only conservatives and moderates left. There are no more liberals in Washington."

Standing in the doorway of the police station beside the Pax, Jill Fanthorpe, chief cannabis buyer for the Vancouver Compassion Club, is explaining to a journalist her methodology as a Cannabis Cup hashish judge: "I take a couple of tokes and throw it out. It's basically the cleanliness test. Most of it is pretty dirty. I like organic things: fruits, vegetables, grains, and cannabis."

Just then two cops come racing out of the station, thread their way through the multitude of potheads, hop into a car, and speed away. Amsterdam cops seem to get it right, at least for the consumer. They leave the crazy Americans to smoke their reefer in peace, although they are consistently rigid in ticketing the courtesy vans that park willy-nilly up and down the street.

Keith Stroup, the founder and once again head honcho at NORML, kicks things off at the seminars one day with a speech that could only be described as lackluster, which is not surprising when you consider he's been making similar pro-pot appeals for thirty years.

"Last year there were seven hundred four thousand arrests in our country for marijuana," he declares. "Out of more than two million prisoners in American jails, four hundred thousand of them are nonviolent drug offenders. But still, ninety percent of high school seniors say marijuana is easy to get . . . We are needlessly destroying the lives and careers of hundreds of thousands of decent, honest people in this country simply because they smoke a marijuana cigarette when they relax. We've declared war on a whole generation of Americans with no cause, and it's time to move beyond the Reefer Madness stage in marijuana policy in the United States.

"Almost sixty percent of Americans agree with the core issue of what we are about, that we are not criminals. Our challenge is to translate that into action by our public officials. To them all drugs are dangerous and all use is abuse. Actually most of them don't believe that, but they believe if they challenge that, they won't get reelected. We have to demonstrate there is a significant constituency of voters out there who do not believe in arresting marijuana smokers. We have to figure out a way to get our natural supporters to come out of the closet."

This "Come out of the closet" creed is echoed by California-based Mikki Norris, coauthor of the book *Shattered Lives: Portraits from America's Drug War,* which highlights the absurd prison sentences American courts are handing down to drug offenders. Norris presents a slide show of drug war victims like Melinda George, serving ninety-nine years in Texas for the sale of one tenth of a gram of cocaine (an audience member yells out: "George W. Bush never did a line in his life smaller than that!"). She asks everyone to check out her website, potpride.com, "because we want to say, 'We're here, we're high, get used to it!'" She suggests pot users need to follow the Gay Pride model. "Gays, by coming out of the closet, made major gains in their rights, and we need to do that. Because once they see the faces of who the pot smokers really are, that we're middle-class, responsible taxpayers mostly, I don't think they're going to want to persecute us."

Coming out of the closet as a pot smoker may sound easy, but it's still a huge risk for most Americans. There are some fairly obvious undercover agents mixing in with the crowd at the Cup, like the guy with the amateur video camera pretending to tape the seminars but spending most of his time zooming in one by one on the faces of audience members. All the brave rhetoric about coming out doesn't seem to be swaying him. He's just following orders.

The only Goddess/seminar speaker who professes no interest in using cannabis herself is Nancy Lord Johnson, a Nevada lawyer and MD who in 1992 ran for vice president on the Libertarian ticket. Lord Johnson delivers a chilling speech that could be called "The Drug War and the Erosion of American Liberty."

"Kicking in your door and shooting your dog, locking your kids in another room—this is done in the name of getting the big bad drug dealer, and now they're starting to do it to everybody," she warns the crowd. She describes the sad case of an alternative therapist who had been administering liquid deprinol citrate. "Anyone know what liquid deprinol is? It's an anti-Parkinson's drug. His particular version of it was not the FDA-approved version, but it was better. He had a patient getting sick on the approved drug; the only thing that made her able to live her life and not be shaking was the liquid deprinol citrate he made available to her." Charged and convicted of supplying the unapproved drug, the therapist got thirteen years. "I got a call from a friend of mine who was saying, 'This is outrageous—this stuff never hurt anybody, it's just a vitamin, and he's being sentenced like a drug dealer!' Well, what else do we know about that never hurt anybody but causes people to get outrageously long sentences? Just because your product doesn't hurt anybody doesn't mean anymore, in the United States of America, that you are not a serious criminal!"

✳

The highlight of the Cup is intended to be the induction of Ina May Gaskin into something called the High Times Counterculture Hall of Fame. Gaskin is the founding mother of the modern American midwifery movement and author of the bible of alternative child-birthing, *Spiritual Midwifery*. At a midweek press conference, she's introduced by her husband, Stephen, who is fresh from a year spent trying to push marijuana rights within Ralph Nader's Green Party.

He says, "Ralph thinks marijuana is like a faulty windshield wiper: a consumer product that could hurt you." But Nader had eventually come to respect the view that what's happening to marijuana users in the United States is "a massive civil rights violation, on the level of a class war," says Gaskin. "Because we're a random tribe, scattered and isolated, they exploit that. I come from a country that is not as free as it was when I was a little boy."

At the press conference Ina May Gaskin relates how as a curious bookworm in the 1950s she had dug around libraries in Iowa trying to find out more about "this mysterious plant" that her jazz musician heroes like Louis Armstrong and John Coltrane smoked. Beyond that she has little to say about cannabis except that it's never done her any harm; instead she talks about childbirth as an event most women still need to reclaim. She's an advocate of natural birth, at home. "It doesn't make sense to do surgery to cut a baby out of a woman when there is a way the baby is meant to come out," she says. "Forty-one thousand obstetricians in America want women to have cesareans, and scare them into not getting second opinions." Why do doctors push for cesareans? "It seems the problem is really fear of women's sexuality, and women's creative power, and it's time to get over it," she informs a rapt audience that includes punk diva Patti Smith, who will speak glowingly of the role Gaskin's book played in the births of her own children.

Gaskin approaches birth as a sensual experience, using such touch techniques as stimulation of the nipples and kissing to harness the passions of arousal to bring forth life. "A woman can orgasm during childbirth, and most doctors don't want you to know it," she says, at which point an American woman in the audience, unable to contain herself, interrupts to say that in 1979, while giving birth to her second child, "I told my doctor, 'I think I'm having an orgasm.' And he told me I was crazy."

All these years later she's having a revelation.

✳

On the final night of the Cup, at the big party at the Melkweg, the rowdy, mostly male party-hearty crowd gets growly with impatience at the lengthy introduction of Gaskin, featuring slides of breech births and such food for thought as "lying on her back is the worst possible position for a woman giving birth." The crowd's more interested in who's going to win the annual judge's awards like the People's Cup (Barney's Breakfast Bar), or Best Coffee shop (De Rokerij, for the second year running). Hilary Black announces the winner for best hashish (the Water Hash from the Katsu Coffee shop), telling the crowd, "I look forward to the day when high-quality hashish is available all over the world." Actually, for do-it-yourselfers it already is: earlier in the evening Goddess Mila Jansen, the Dutch pot entrepreneur who invented the Ice-o-lator, that simple system of making hashish from cannabis buds, leaves, and shake using only a couple of mesh screens and a bucket of ice water, announces from the stage that her product is now used in thirty-seven countries.

And as for complaints about fairness in the judging, when all is said and done, Eddie of Flying Dutchmen, who boycotted the competition, tells me, "The right guy won. Serious Seeds. As much as we have against the process, the right grower won. Kali Mist—have you seen it around?"

His partner Roland agrees. "We respect the breeder at Serious Seeds. This is the kind of breeder he is: A year and a half ago he lost his mother plant of Bubblegum. Bubblegum is a big-selling strain, very big, and it would have been very easy for him to keep his packaging of Bubblegum and put other seeds in there—just take something similar, and call that Bubblegum. But he didn't sell Bubblegum seeds for one and a half years. First he was looking for a good mother. Now that he has the mother again, he's selling Bubblegum again. That's how you have to do it."

12 : THE UNITED STATES
OF AMERICA

One of those Cannabis Goddesses yelled it from the stage when I was in Amsterdam: "Dennis Peron is a fucking saint. He is my fucking hero!"

If a hero is a guy who's willing to risk jail time putting his principles on the line, then Dennis Peron is a fucking hero. Although Dennis Peron would say he's just living his life.

⁂

I'm trying to be an environmental purist and live without a car, which in my hometown isn't that hard. It's bus- and bicycle-friendly. But to get to California to visit Dennis Peron I need a car, so I buy a 1983 Toyota Tercel for $400 and I drive it from Canada to Northern California in a day, then sleep in the back of the car under a view of the moon on Mount Shasta. It's a beautiful, free and safe place to sleep in your car, and the rest-stop parking lot is full of people taking advantage of it.

From Mount Shasta's symmetrical snowy dome to Dennis Peron's farm is another half-day drive, south to Williams, California, then east along a winding road up into hills covered with bone-dry, dead, brilliant gold grass and scattered oak trees.

It's in this kind of country that Dennis Peron has his farm. The farm is on a gradually sloping southern exposure and has a spring-fed pond at the bottom; perfect for small-scale organic farming. It's mid-July, and in the natural amphitheater curled around the pond, four hundred marijuana plants have grown to about waist high, all in pots or in the ground, in a mixture of mushroom compost, steer manure, a bit of bat guano, and some bonemeal. They get a daily spray of a weak solution of fish emulsion, seaweed, and water.

Below the pond is a field left wild, full of tall thistles and rattlesnakes, where an ostrich patrols along paths he's stomped out for himself, an ostrich that towers over humans. He doesn't like to be petted. In fact, he seems mostly to want to rip the hair off your skull with his beak, or peck your eyes out. If you go up to the fence to the spot where his keepers feed him, he will come and throw himself ferociously against it, defending his perimeter. This big scary beast escaped once and for three days kept the entire population of humans afraid to leave the house. "It was like being stalked," says one of the farmworkers.

✳

If Dennis Peron is a saint, you could say it was apparent from childhood. When he was a kid his mother told him to finish the food on his plate, because there were starving children in China. "What? There are starving children in China?!!" At this revelation young Dennis started to bawl his eyes out, and insisted all the leftovers be packed up and sent to China by the fastest possible post. "After that I would never fill my plate," he says. "I figured the less I ate the more for others."

When he was a teenager, Dennis and his brothers experimented with drugs like cannabis and LSD. The police decided to bust the house. The cops burst in. They soon had his mother, a fifty-something homemaker and model citizen, pinned to the floor with a gun at her head.

"Where's the acid?!!! WHERE'S THE ACID???!!!!!" they're screaming at her.

Acid? She has no idea her nice sons have ever tried drugs. The only acid she can think of is the stuff in the car battery.

"In the car! In the car!" she's screaming back, hoping they'll stop hurting her arm and making her lick linoleum.

So they go to the garage and destroy the car looking for LSD that isn't there. Then they move on to the sons' bedrooms, where they eventually find a single hit in a dresser drawer, which they seem to think justifies the whole earlier exercise in terrorism against an innocent housewife.

*

Before I arrive at the farm I talk to Dennis a few times on the phone. From the first he calls me Brother, in a Bronx accent softened by decades on the West Coast, and invites me down to visit, but when I actually get there he seems surprised that I'm a journalist and not an activist, and says he's not interested in being interviewed. He's compact, lean, and muscular, and looks much younger than the photos of him from Proposition 215 rallies five years ago; farming must agree with him. He's totally welcoming, apart from interviews. I'm free to stay, hang out, and talk with him and the rest of the cast of characters who look after the growing of a crop of four hundred medical marijuana plants. He gives me a copy of his book and I sit under some cooling shade trees while the sun turns the grassy hills scorching hot. Man and beast are hiding from that sun.

The book is called *Brownie Mary's Marijuana Cookbook and Dennis Peron's Recipe for Social Change.* It follows Dennis from fighting in Vietnam ("I left a hippie and came back a hippie") to San Francisco in the early 1970s, where he created the Big Top Commune, a marijuana supermarket in a big apartment crammed day and night with beautiful young people living a trippy hippie dream. After the Big Top got busted he opened The Island restaurant, a "two-way feed, with the pot supermarket upstairs supplying customers for the restaurant downstairs. It was the only restaurant in the world where pot smoking was nearly mandatory."

By 1977 the restaurant was closed, and Big Top Two, another pot supermarket, was opened in its place. When he was busted, Dennis writes, "I based my defense on the miracle ounce. That's the ounce you can have almost legally, but you can't buy, grow, or sell it. Therefore it was a miracle that you got it, and I was a miracle worker. Considering I had two hundred pounds of pot, I would have a lot of miracles to explain." Lucky for him a cop who had shot him with a dumdum bullet at the bust started screaming at him outside the courtroom one day, saying he wished he'd killed him so there would be one less motherfucking faggot in San Francisco. The prosecution unraveled and Peron got only six months.

From jail he ran a campaign to put Proposition W on the ballot in San Francisco, calling for the legalization of marijuana. It won. We're talking 1979. On what must have felt like the brink of success, he was to see the tide turn very quickly. Dennis' friend, fellow activist, and elected San Francisco supervisor Harvey Milk, along with San Francisco mayor George Moscone, were assassinated by a right-wing politician named Dan White. When White had his sentence reduced to manslaughter through a medical defense—too much sugar in his diet—thirteen police cars were torched that night in the Castro district of San Francisco.

After that came Ronald Reagan, the War on Drugs, and the AIDS epidemic. The 1980s were grim. In 1991, Peron's lover, Jonathan West, died of AIDS. Cannabis had shown itself to be a useful appetite enhancer for AIDS sufferers; it's fair to say that for some people cannabis was the only thing keeping them alive. During a city pot drought Jonathan had dropped fifteen pounds.

Shortly before Jonathan's death he and Dennis were busted at home for having four ounces of pot on hand. When the cops saw a picture of Dennis with his slain compadre Harvey Milk in the apartment, they made sure to harangue him about how much they'd hated that fag.

In 1991 Dennis organized the placing of Proposition P on the ballot in San Francisco. It called for California to restore cannabis to the list of legal medicines in the state. It passed, with 80 percent of voters' approval. That same year he launched the Cannabis Buyers' Club out of a small apartment on Sanchez Street, supplying sick people—AIDS patients mostly—with medicinal herb. Encouraged by the passing of a resolution by the city's Board of Supervisors ("San Francisco Police and the District Attorney will place as its lowest priority, enforcement of marijuana laws that interfere with the medicinal application of this valued herb"), he opened up a larger version of the Buyers' Club at 1444 Market Street.

One former employee of the Buyers' Club said to me, "You know what it's like in Dennis' living room at the farm? All kinds of people, everyone welcome? Imagine six floors of that. It was just like hanging out at Dennis' place, only on a massive scale."

✳

The farmhouse is a low ranch-style bungalow with a large kitchen and a living room where after work people smoke, talk, and watch a gigantic TV with crappy sound. The most popular programs are top-level dog shows. It's fun to pick a favorite and hope the judges see beauty and poise the way you do.

The anarchic camaraderie of the place is like Karen's room at the Exodus collective in England. The welcome mat is out, the door is open. Open doors lead to open minds.

Arranged in the shadier corners of the grounds are clusters of camping tents for guests. "We're a white-trash village," John Entwhistle, Dennis' sidekick and manager of the farm, tells me. "It takes a trailer park to raise a village."

Since Dennis is weary of the media, Entwhistle is the one who gives me the official tour of the farm. He has a baby face, soft eyes, farmer's hands, and brown smoker's teeth. "In late 1997 we had the urge to fix the place up, to give hope to people, to show people you *can* cultivate marijuana in America. It's legal, it's open, and it's okay," he says.

In the beginning "we didn't know the names of the trees, we didn't know how to turn the weed whacker on. Now farming is where it's at. In the city, everything is paved over, you have to stay between the lines all the time, and doors are either open or closed. In the country, you're freed from that."

He takes the time to show me how to identify male from female plants as the first little nubs of sexual organs appear. These plants are all much later along in the growth cycle, though—mostly grown from clones, every plant on the farm is a female, or had better be. A rogue male could turn the crop from sensimilla to seedy.

The practice here is outdoor, pure organic, hippie-style back-to-the-land farming. One afternoon, as the sun lowers, everyone emerges from the shade for a swim in the pond. As the oak shadows lengthen and creep toward the four hundred bushy pot plants and the place takes on a dreamy, bucolic air of Eden at twilight, Dennis says, "In the city you forget that all wealth comes from the earth. Everything you need comes from the earth."

And everything you *don't* need seems to come from the sky, in the form of annoying DEA helicopters buzzing by, loud and low. Your tax dollars at work. We can only share a toke and wonder at the lopsided absurdity of America's War on Drugs. Here in Northern California, one side's got military hardware coming out their asses. The other side has some organic farming tools, an ostrich, and the support of the people, expressed democratically in the passage of Proposition 215.

✳

It was out of the Cannabis Buyers' Club that Peron organized Proposition 215, the medical marijuana initiative that was voted on and passed by the people of California in November 1996 and became the Compassionate Use Act of that state. So according to California law, anyone who obtains and uses marijuana on the recommendation of a physician "in the treatment of cancer, anorexia, AIDS, chronic fatigue, spasticity, glaucoma, arthritis, migraine, or any other illness for which marijuana provides relief" shall not be subject to criminal prosecution or sanction.

"All use is medical" is Dennis Peron's marijuana mantra. The first time he says it to me, I argue the point. As a recreational user, I appreciate it has medical value for many and spiritual value for some—

He cuts me off. "If you're smoking recreationally, just to get high, first I think you're stupid, and second, I don't have any time for you."

Dennis's "All use is medical" line doesn't fly with many patients' rights advocates, who feel that it trivializes the more pressing needs of those in chronic pain or other grave states of health. It also doesn't fly with many pot advocates. *High Times* editor Steve Hagar told me, "Dennis Peron can say all marijuana use is medical—well, that's not true. If you're just sitting watching TV and you just want to get high, that's recreational use. I don't have a problem with recreational use. But if I go to a party and I start dancing with my friends, and we start smoking marijuana, that is ritual use. When you go to a party that's a ritual, that's a ceremony. When people go to see a rock show that's a ceremony; people are tapping into the core of their spiritual being when they go see their favorite band perform. So when they smoke pot and they go to a show like that, that's religious use, no question in my mind. It doesn't matter—recreational use, medical use, religious use, it doesn't really matter. It's got all these components. Why even create the divisions in the first place?"

The Cannabis Buyers' Club in San Francisco has long been shut down, but four years later Dennis still faces potential charges, still stands accused of selling pot to federal agents who had notes from imaginary doctors. Peron was offered a deal to have the charges reduced to conspiracy to commit a public nuisance, thus avoiding a minimum nine-year sentence on the drug charges. Four other codefendants took the plea bargain, and received no jail time. Peron refused the deal. If convicted he'd be looking at that absurd minimum. Retreating to the hills was almost the only option, but Peron has managed to turn it into another defiant political act, a way to make an open, public statement about every California patient's right to grow marijuana.

Two newspaper clippings taped to the wall at Dennis's farm:

August 12—"With harvest approaching rapidly, a weekend Open House party is planned for August 16th at the Lake County Cannabis Farm on Spruce Grove Road in Lower Lake. Farm officials announced the get-together this weekend as an opportunity where, 'Everyone can experience first hand the feeling of accomplishment which permeates this garden,' according to promotional materials. 'Celebrate as our 130 legal marijuana plants, some nine feet tall, flower into medicine.'"

August 15—"It wasn't entirely a surprise Friday morning when federal agents of the DEA (Drug Enforcement Administration) in San Francisco again raided a marijuana farm near Middletown."

That was two summers ago.

"We lost a hundred pounds of marijuana we would have loved to have," says Entwhistle. "But the point was made—we are open to the public. And to show we are always ready to replant, we immediately created a greenhouse, to show visual effect: You can hit us as hard as you want, but the next day as soon as the sun comes up we're gonna be out there doing the same thing. You can't stop us unless you lock us up in jail, give us a court trial, and put us away for life. We don't believe that will happen; we don't believe these people want to do that. We don't believe the courts would affirm that.

"Last year the DEA left us alone. Now this year we're really going for it."

✳

The DEA never laid charges when they busted the farm; they just destroyed the crop and left. Charges would only cause the DEA grief, because there'd have to be a trial, and that means there'd have to be a jury. And to get a California jury to convict their fellow citizens for growing medical marijuana, which is legal under California law? Not likely.

The federal strategy has lately been to shut down medical marijuana distributors by suing them in civil court, so that the case is presented before a judge and not a jury. The day I arrive at the farm a huge legal decision comes down in a suit brought by the federal government against the Oakland Cannabis Buyers' Cooperative, one of a slew of medical marijuana outlets operating in the San Francisco Bay Area in the style of Dennis Peron's former club on Market Street. Earlier a Federal District Court judge in San Francisco had granted the feds an injunction to shut down the Oakland co-op. The Ninth Circuit of the Federal Appeals Court, which is the second-highest level of justice in the land, ruled that the lower-court judge should have considered medical necessity in his decision, and sent it back to him to rethink. It took him almost a year to come to a decision, and when he did, he acknowledged that medical necessity—the rights of patients to medical relief—in this case overrode federal laws prohibiting cannabis distribution.

From the farm, John Entwhistle tells the *New York Times* that one day marijuana "will end up in our pharmacies and grocery stores. Once you accept the underlying issue of medical necessity of marijuana, it disqualifies the federal argument against its medical use."

Hungry for news, the next day John drives to the nearest town to buy the San Francisco papers. The Hearst-owned *San*

Francisco Chronicle lives up to its long tradition of fear-mongering and Reefer Madness, burying the court's vindication of medical marijuana in the middle pages under a wimpy headline, something like "Ruling Muddles Marijuana Issue."

"When *they* win in court, it's 'Marijuana Struck Down!'" John says ruefully. "When *we* win, it's 'More Muddle.'"

The *Chronicle*'s major front-page headline is reserved for a medical story it deems more important and easier to support: "Feds Say Cancerous Animals OK To Eat." Doesn't that make you feel better?

✳

The new ruling has put the wind back in the sails, and sales, of medical marijuana clubs in the Bay Area.

At the San Francisco Patients' Resource Center on Devisadero Street, the guy at the intake desk in the storefront is reading Jack Herer's *Emperor Wears No Clothes*. "This book took me from thinking of myself as a criminal to a patriot in a single day," he says. I leave off chatting with him when a middle-aged woman brings in her cancer-riddled mother, whose chemotherapy is killing her. They've heard pot can help with the nausea and restore the appetite. The intake worker explains that she'll need a prescription from her doctor or, if she can't get one, she'll need her doctor to sign a document stating that he or she will continue to act as her primary physician should she use marijuana prescribed by another. "We need to be sure that your primary medical caregiver will remain in place," he tells her.

In the back of the building Jane Weirick, the club's director, has the tough job of finding and purchasing enough quality marijuana to meet the needs of members. What's the biggest problem? "Vendor ego. Everyone thinks they grow the greatest pot in the world," she says. "And some of them have been living on the wrong side of the law for so long they have a big fat ego about *that,* too."

Our conversation is interrupted. A woman at the pay phone is holding out the receiver like a microphone, and twenty or so club members, who've been playing cards or chatting, all begin to sing together, an energetic chorus for the benefit of a comrade who lies in the hospital at the other end of the phone connection. Twenty voices belt out the aural "Get Well" card, a song they all seem to know but that is new to me.

That done, Jane tells me that marijuana is supplied to her club by eighty-three different vendors, six of whom are reliable regulars. Jane is very fussy about what she'll buy. There's a bit of a crisis the day I'm in because a vendor has brought in some pot Jane deems to be too moldy, and he doesn't agree. They retreat behind locked doors. I'm not allowed in to watch the fireworks. Later, she says, "I'm the biggest pot snob in the world, and I see no reason no one else shouldn't be." Quality is as idiosyncratic as the eighty-three vendors. "I wish this were just like any legitimate business, and I could just get on the phone and call the supplier and say I need a hundred fifty more units of M38 by Tuesday noon, and they'd be delivered."

On the day I visit she has a couple of outdoor organic strains on the lengthy menu, a Big Sur Holy Weed and a Durban Poison. I ask her if she's ever bought pot from Dennis' farm, and she sighs heavily.

"John brought some in last year, and I asked what strain it was, and he said he didn't know. In this business we have to know. It's not all equal. The strains have differing combinations and amounts of cannabinoids, and have different effects. Some are better than others for relief of various symptoms."

Her story about John fit with the philosophy I'd seen at the farm. One day a young volunteer asked Dennis if there were any jars or labels around, as he wanted to make sure some seeds he'd found were kept in separate and distinct containers, according to variety. Some of them were already mixed up together in unlabeled plastic bags. "Do you know what these are called?" he asked hesitantly.

Dennis said, "Screw that, who cares what they're called? Make up some new names. Give them the names of the heroes of our movement!"

✳

But Dennis is a radical, a man of action, not a botanist or biochemist. And definitely not a businessman. Of the mountains of money he'd seen in a lifetime of dealing pot, he had barely hung on to a dime. "I never thought of the money as mine," he told me wistfully. "I gave it all away." At one point when the Market Street Buyers' Club was in high gear, staff were dealing with so much cash they couldn't be bothered to count the one-dollar bills. They dumped them in a box and, when it was full, gave it to AIDS charities.

"The growers always told me, 'You take care of the politics and the activism, and we'll take care of the patients,'" he said. Now he's a grower himself, charging $200 a pound to his clients. Other growers sell pot to medical marijuana clubs for only slightly less than what it brings on the recreational smoker's market: $4,000 a pound. That's a lot of money for an AIDS patient or a multiple sclerosis sufferer who's too sick to hold a job.

At the Cannabis Cup, I heard Valerie Corral of the Santa Cruz–based WoMen's Alliance for Medical Marijuana, who herself uses marijuana to control epileptic seizures caused by a car accident, make an appeal to growers: "Sure, it's great to be producing champagne-quality products, and getting top dollar, but it's also important to remember there are people living on six hundred dollars a month who need that 'champagne' for chronic pain."

Dennis Peron, growing four hundred plants for a collective of patients, might not be growing champagne-quality bud, but at least it's affordable. Dennis took it personally that so many marijuana growers remained motivated more by greed than compassion. "If pot were legal it would drop to a hundred dollars a pound," he told me on the morning I was to drive to San Francisco.

✳

In San Francisco, Fred Gardner, press officer to the city's pot-friendly district attorney Terrence Hallinan, offers his insight: "This is a case study in capitalism. Many people, unlike Dennis Peron, although they come on as hippies and say things like, 'Oh, marijuana is different, you pass the joint around, it means we're *sharing*' and other hippie blither like that, when it comes to the nitty-gritty, they are accustomed to getting four thousand dollars a pound or more, and they've gotten used to getting those new Toyotas every couple of years, and taking nice vacations.

"Many growers in Mendocino County saw Proposition 215 as a threat, a personal threat, despite a lifetime of vague talk about legalization. They don't want to get busted, but as we all know Prohibition is a form of price support for the growers.

"And on the other side, it's a rationale for law enforcement staffing levels and budgets, and overtime pay. I ride the same elevators with narcotics officers every day, and they know that legalization represents a threat to their overtime, a threat to their hundred twenty, hundred fifty thousand dollars a year. It's a threat to them big time, almost like 'End the War in Vietnam' was a threat if you were an executive at Boeing, or McDonnell Douglas, or General Dynamics in 1967. Many livelihoods depend on this prohibition."

✳

"I have an eleven-year-old with epilepsy," Fred Gardner tells me. "I understand that the component in cannabis that is an effective anticonvulsant and sedative is called cannabidiol, or CBD. The cannabis that growers in California have been breeding for many generations is very high in THC and low in CBD; they've almost bred it out. So we need to do research. We are at the very beginning of a scientific movement to understand this plant."

It rankles Gardner fiercely that European companies are far in advance of Americans now in cannabis research. The British company GW Pharmaceuticals has merged with Hortapharm BV, an Amsterdam cannabis research company with the world's finest living library of cannabis seed strains. With the full approval of the British government, GW is working toward developing viable, marketable, herbal cannabis extracts. "They have defined six different cannabinoids of interest," Gardner says. "They have a computer-controlled greenhouse, state-of-the-art equipment; they turn out ten thousand plants per crop, six crops per year where there is quality control."

A trip to a GW-founded website, www.medicinal-cannabis. org, will fill you in on the world of cannabinoids, which it refers to as a "family of chemically related 21-carbon alkaloids found uniquely in the cannabis plant." They're very busy in Britain these days looking for answers from those sixty thousand plants a year. "Scientists have identified more than sixty different cannabinoids, but for years research focused on THC," the website proclaims. "Only quite recently have scientists begun studying whether additional, nonpsychoactive cannabinoids may also hold medicinal value. For example, preliminary research indicates that CBD works as an anticonvulsant and antioxidant, cannabichromine (CBC) is anti-inflammatory, and cannabinol (CBN) may have tumor-reducing properties. The amounts and proportions of these and other cannabinoids vary from strain to strain and may be adjusted by breeding."

"We in California want to be doing that research," says Fred Gardner. "We started this movement; the five point seven million Californians who voted for Proposition 215 are indirectly responsible for GW Pharmaceuticals' interest in this subject. We started it, and now we are *waaaay* behind because of the oppressive federal government here."

13 : TWO JUSTICES

Shortly after I leave California the U.S. Attorney General's Office announces that it will appeal its civil case against the Oakland Cannabis Buyers' Co-operative to the Supreme Court of the United States, hoping to reverse the Ninth Circuit Court decision that allows the co-op to plead a defense of medical necessity when it breaks federal law to supply relief to people in pain. In the short term, the appeal will prevent the co-op from operating.

In the long term, who can say for certain how the Supreme Court will rule?

I'm excited. I'm thinking, Finally medical marijuana will have its day in the highest court, in the pure court of pure ideas, where justice takes precedence over the shallow legal gambits of politics or the innuendo of bad science.

And I've been watching what's been going on up here in Canada, a country with a legal system not terribly different from that of the United States. Both are based in English Common Law. The Court of Appeal for Ontario, the highest court in Canada's most populous province, has just rendered a verdict in the case of a medical marijuana user named Terry Parker.

"Concerning the constitutionality of the marihuana prohibition . . . of the Controlled Drugs and Substances Act" was how the justices framed the legal question. Their unanimous decision, written by Justice Marc Rosenberg, begins:

"It has been known for centuries that, in addition to its intoxicating or psychoactive effect, marihuana has medicinal value. The active ingredients in marihuana are known as cannabinoids.

The cannabinoid that gives marihuana its psychoactive effect is tetrahydrocannabinol (THC). While less is known about the other cannabinoids, the scientific evidence is overwhelming that some of them may have anti-seizure properties. The most promising of these is cannabidiol (CBD). Smoking marihuana is one way to obtain the benefit of CBD and other cannabinoids with anti-seizure properties.

"The respondent Terrance Parker has suffered from a very severe form of epilepsy since he was a young child. For close to 40 years he has experienced frequent serious and potentially life-threatening seizures. He has attempted to control these seizures through surgery and conventional medication. The surgery was a failure and the conventional medication only moderately successful. He has found that by smoking marihuana he can substantially reduce the incidence of seizures . . ."

Justice Rosenberg notes that Section 7 of the Canadian Charter of Rights and Freedoms "guarantees that everyone has the right to life, liberty and the security of the person." He continues: "Put simply, Parker claims that he needs to grow and smoke marihuana as medicine to control his epilepsy. Because Parliament has made cultivation and possession of marihuana illegal, he faces the threat of imprisonment to keep his health. Parker argues that a statute that has this effect does not comport with fundamental justice."

The decision: "I have concluded that forcing Parker to choose between his health and imprisonment violates his right to liberty and security of the person . . . I would declare the prohibition of marihuana in the Controlled Drugs and Substances Act to be of no force and effect."

The court has granted the Canadian government a year to rewrite the law to allow medical marijuana to those who need it. As I write, the Canadian government's foot-dragging politicians and their bureaucratic mandarins have come up with some absurd regulations that make marijuana infinitely more difficult to obtain from a physician than opiates or cocaine. But to its credit, the government has paid a private company, Prairie Plant Systems, to grow up to nine hundred pounds of pot a year for five years (indoors, a thousand feet underground in an abandoned mine in northern Manitoba), which it intends to distribute to medical marijuana patients in clinical trials.

*

If that's not enough, on Canada's west coast, British Columbia's highest court recently reached a split decision on the issue of a person's right to use marijuana recreationally, in the case of one David Malmo-Levine.

You may remember David Malmo-Levine from a brief appearance in Brian Taylor's hillside trailer in Chapter 10 of this book, where like a TV pitchman he extolled the virtues of Hempty, the relaxing CBD-heavy hemp tea. I first met David in 1997 in Vancouver, where he'd recently been busted for openly, publicly selling marijuana at a business he called the Harm Reduction Club. I still have a copy of the *Guide to Safer, Smarter Smoking* he handed out to every member. On the cover a cartoon character named Sammy Sweetleaf offers helpful hints: "Don't Drive Impaired—Use a Glass Pipe or a Bong—Save your Lungs—Grow Pot and make Ganga Butter—Wait 5 hours Between Hoots to Avoid Burnout. Remember, Pot Is Less Harmful Than Caffeine! Your Rulers Want You to Feel Ashamed of Smoking, Growing and Dealing So They Can Control You. Don't Let Them—Come Out of Your Closet and Puff Tough!"

*

I can't say that at the time I took David too seriously. He was twenty-five, his neo-hippie hair was dyed green one day, purple the next, he had a conspiracy theory for every occasion, and he was given to muttering things like "They'll be banning chocolate next!"

But David Malmo-Levine took it upon himself to learn the law, learn his rights, and learn how to make an argument that the law didn't respect his rights. He fought his marijuana possession and trafficking charge with a defense based on the harm principle: namely, that for something to be declared a crime, it has to be clearly shown that harm has been caused an individual, a group, or society. David Malmo-Levine felt that his actions—trying to supply organic marijuana and to educate consumers on how best to enjoy it—actually reduced harm.

*

In the B.C. Court of Appeal the judge's decision quotes at length the nineteenth-century British philosopher John Stuart Mill, the originator of the harm principle. The key concept:

"The only purpose for which power can be rightfully exercised over any member of a civilized community, against his will, is to prevent harm to others. His own good, either physical or moral, is not a sufficient warrant . . . Over himself, over his own mind and body, the individual is sovereign."

Let's hear it for personal sovereignty.

Malmo-Levine shared his appeal with another marijuana possession case. In that case the lower-court judge's findings of fact included:

"Assuming current rates of consumption remain stable, the health related costs of marihuana use are very, very small in comparison with those costs associated with tobacco and alcohol consumption."

The Appeal Court justices accepted this and other findings of fact, then knuckled down to the nitty-gritty, taking on questions like, "Is the Deprivation of the Appellant's Liberty in Accordance with the Principles of Fundamental Justice?" and "Does the [Canadian Drug Law] Strike the Right Balance Between the Individual and the State?"

Two ruled for the state, but one of the three justices ruled, "In my view, the evidence does not establish that simple possession of marijuana presents a reasoned risk of serious, substantial or significant harm to either the individual or society or others."

Because the highest court in British Columbia was split, these same issues will be heard by the Supreme Court of Canada in the near future.

✳

Now, since American justice is based broadly on the same traditions as Canadian justice, and an open mind trying to reach a judgment is the same north or south of the border, you can understand why I was heartened when I heard that the U.S. Supreme Court had agreed to hear arguments in a case regarding patients using marijuana out of medical necessity. Terry Parker's case forced the Canadian government to accept that marijuana is medicine. Faced with similar evidence in *United States v. Oakland Cannabis Buyers' Co-operative,* surely the Supreme Court would make the same judgment.

I mean, even if the Court ignored Canadian evidence, it would have to consider American evidence, like this 1988 decision from the Drug Enforcement Administration's own administrative law judge, the last time that organization considered whether marijuana should be reclassified under the law so that it could be used medicinally. Judge Francis L. Young wrote: "The evidence in this record clearly shows that cannabis has been accepted as capable of relieving distress from great numbers of very ill people, and doing so with safety under medical supervision. It would be unreasonable, arbitrary, and capricious for the DEA to continue to stand between those sufferers and the benefits of this substance in light of the evidence in this record.

"The administrative law judge recommends that the Administrator conclude that the cannabis plant considered as a whole has a currently accepted medical use in treatment in the United

States, that there is no lack of accepted safety for use of it under medical supervision, and that it may be lawfully transferred from Schedule I to Schedule II. The judge recommends that the Administrator transfer cannabis from Schedule I to Schedule II."

✳

Have you ever read a transcript of oral arguments at the Supreme Court? It's not a long document—each side gets only half an hour. And it's not lawyers presenting their best arguments—it's lawyers trying to dodge an almost immediate barrage of questions from the justices, who come across mostly as confused and cranky old farts.

United States v. Oakland Cannabis Buyers' Co-operative is heard on the morning of March 28, 2001. Barbara Underwood, the acting solicitor general, lays out the government's case: Congress has determined, "There is no currently acceptable use for the drug, and it has a high potential for abuse." Plus, there is a procedure in place to reclassify marijuana if our lawmakers' assertion of its medical worthlessness should ever be proven false. This leaves no room for the Oakland Cannabis Buyers' Co-op to decide that marijuana is useful, because it undermines the ability of the Controlled Substances Act "to protect the public from hazardous drugs."

She continues: Necessity is not a defense here because Congress "has already balanced the harms and come to a different conclusion." Furthermore, the Buyers' Co-op members have "alternatives" to marijuana, "other medications including a synthetic form of the active ingredient of marijuana." She means Marinol, a synthetic form of THC.

✳

Didn't we hear a Canadian court rule that the active ingredient in marijuana when it comes to controlling seizures is not THC, but

CBD? Actually that's a little simplistic; what's involved is really a little-understood interrelationship between half a dozen or more of the cannabinoids. Sorry for this bit of an aside, but that's okay—Underwood is about to lose her train of thought anyway, thanks to her first interruption.

"May I ask one question on that subject, Ms. Underwood?" It's Justice David Souter. "You have a footnote in your brief, footnote 11, that describes some of the situations there that give the impression that this whole cause is a sham, that it's really just a front for using marijuana—and your argument you're just making now suggests there are always alternatives. Do you think we should take the case on the assumption that there really are some people for whom this is a medical necessity or should we assume there are no such people?"

He's asking, Should we believe these epileptics and AIDS patients and MS sufferers? Or should we assume they're all shameless fakers who just want to get high?

My first reaction when I read this was, Why would Supreme Court justices want to *assume* anything? Why wouldn't they want the truth?

Underwood almost stumbles. "The—on the assumption that there are no such people," she tells him. "Because the Food and Drug Administration charged with evaluating the medical—the scientific information and the DEA, that is the agency that reports to the Attorney General and Secretary of Health and Human Resources, having evaluated the claims of medical use, have found that there is no accepted medical use, that some of the claims of medical use are simply wrong—"

Note that she says "some of the claims," not all. If only some are wrong, that would make some right. Justice Ruth Bader Ginsburg interrupts here, and seems to be steering toward that conclusion.

"May I just stop you there because, take one of the examples that was in the brief, the one about the man who was constantly vomiting and the only thing that calmed him down, he had a lymphoma or something like that, that is not an uncommon experience, and what surprised me about this case was, that kind of thing has been going on, individual doctors prescribing marijuana just to prevent that kind of extreme suffering . . . Am I wrong in thinking that there has been quite a bit of this going on in the medical profession?

Underwood responds, "The record doesn't reflect and I don't know how much of it has been going on." She mentions Marinol again, and says, "Efforts are being made to find other methods of administering the pure substance."

Another question: "Ms. Underwood, these judgments made by the federal agencies, the FDA and the DEA . . . I'm not sure they have come to the conclusion that marijuana would never ever, ever be helpful to someone who's in extreme pain. Could you really say that there has been a determination by the federal government that marijuana is never medically useful?"

Time for Underwood to bob and weave: "Well, the determination that's been made is that the medical utility of it has not been established, which is a slightly different way of putting it."

Jesus Christ. Woman just dodged a direct question from the Supreme Court! Don't they make 'em swear on the Bible anymore?

✳

The justices go rough on the Buyers' Co-op's lawyer, Gerald Uelman. They seem to think that a necessity defense is for emergencies only—like, climbing into someone's boat can't be trespassing if you're drowning; necessity can't be thousands of people coming to a dispensary for medication. Very late in the proceedings, after the little white light has gone on to show him he has only five minutes left, Uelman, a law professor at Santa Clara University, starts to riff on the cornerstone of the Co-op's argument, the federal government's own Compassionate Investigative New Drug program.

Federal authorities themselves established and still oversee a medical marijuana program for sick people. At its peak in the 1980s the Compassionate IND program supplied seventy-eight patients with medical marijuana grown on a government farm in Mississippi. In 1992, before medical marijuana had shown up on the radar screen of the American mainstream, President George Bush cut off the application process to the program. There have been no new patients accepted since, but the eight patients still alive today continue to accept a government ration of mediocre mid-grade pot.

Uelman's argument is that when the federal government created the Compassionate IND program and started handing out marijuana to sick people, it did so, as it explained to Congress, "because of compassion and because of the therapeutics."

He raises a case from the 1980s, *United States v. Burton,* in which a patient was charged with marijuana cultivation and pled a medical necessity defense. The defense was ruled invalid because the Compassionate IND program, in place and accepting patients at that time, gave the defendant an alternative to growing his own. After his conviction Burton successfully sued the federal government for the right to be placed on the Compassionate IND program. He received marijuana from the government.

With two minutes left of his allotted time, tripping over his words against the ticking clock, Uelman says, "A patient with glaucoma comes into court, asserts a medical necessity defense. The court says you have a reasonable alternative, and that patient then goes to the government and they put him on the Compassionate IND program, and provide him with cannabis. Well, now the government decides we're not going to operate that program anymore, and *we* say if you're not going to do it then *we* can, because the only justification *you* had to do it was this medical necessity concept!"

Pretty good argument: The government says the stuff has no medical value, and yet down on a farm in Mississippi at this very moment they're growing it themselves to give to eight patients. Isn't that catching them in a lie?

The court decision comes down six weeks later. It's written by Clarence Thomas, reputedly the only justice to have tried marijuana, just to be cool at Yale Law School.

"In this case," Thomas writes, "to resolve the question presented, we need only recognize that a medical necessity exception is at odds with the terms of the Controlled Substances Act." Because the act says marijuana has "no currently accepted medical use," no medical use can be tolerated.

"There is no medical necessity exception to the prohibitions at issue, even when the patient is 'seriously ill' and lacks alternative avenues for relief." It's like rubbing salt in the wound.

Not once in his fifteen-page decision, or in a concurring decision written by Justice John Paul Stevens, is mention made of the Compassionate IND program.

I spoke to Gerald Uelman the other day. He's sixty years old, and comes across on the phone as a soft-spoken, avuncular professor. I asked him, "You made the point that the government is already growing medical marijuana, so how can they deny it has any medical value? If this is the strongest argument you made, how can the Court not even mention it in their decision?"

"That's an excellent question," said Uelman. "I think it's a dishonest decision for that very reason. My definition of an honest decision is one that evaluates the arguments and accepts or rejects them. When the Court just ignores an argument there is something else going on.

"My take, and I've been following and studying drug laws for thirty years, is that this is not an area of public policy that is governed by rational weighing of evidence. It's governed by politics, and the reality is that the reluctance of any politician to stick their neck out on this issue, for fear of being labeled soft on drugs or soft on crime, has just skewed the whole issue so that rational consideration is no longer a factor even.

"One would have hoped that this wouldn't come into play at the level of the U.S. Supreme Court, but it's pretty clear that the Supreme Court isn't isolated from these kinds of political considerations."

14 : POT POLEMIC

Psychedelics were the question, not the answer. The CIA, and the even deeper placed Illuminati, heard the question, and their answer to the question was NO. Ever since then, everything that has happened in Babylon (that welter of images and media we believe to be history)—every "event" and all "power" must be situated in the cognitive space created by that NO. It is as if the word were a spell, or an anti-drug with its own flood of anti-hallucinations, anti-insights, anti-"vibes." It's the BIG NO concept.
—Hakim Bey, from the Foreword of
Psychedelics Reimagined

Marijuana was an even older question, to which Louis Armstrong and others had said yes decades earlier, and it seemed to make him a mellow fellow, and it led to a beautiful music called jazz. And jazz led to black people and white people playing together for the first time in integrated orchestras and combos, making music in an atmosphere of peace, love, and brotherhood. But even then, way back when, before their hysteria to exterminate psychedelics, the warriors of the BIG NO concept had declared sweet herbal God-given marijuana flowers taboo, fit only to be crushed under the boots of their BIG NO storm troopers.

This party line made Al Gore in 2000 afraid of the truth of his own life and youth: Did I smoke dope in college? Well, in my day I took many more than a toke or two and it didn't seem to do me any harm, but now I've gotta ride the bandwagon and raise the false alarm, for I am older, conservative, now I preach that the pot, and the speed, and the LSD, the heroin and the coke should all be illegal, and even if it were true that the one I had a soft spot for, sweet Mary Jane, might deserve to be rehabilitated, to be given the status of alcohol, celebrated like the beer in commercials during Sunday football games, and left to the individual to learn to respect, well, that would send the wrong message to kids about the other, nastier drugs out there. And that would only make it harder to control our kids.

A MESSAGE TO THE KIDS OF AMERICA

There is a substance called marijuana that millions of grown-ups like to smoke; it's one of those goofy adult things like booze and sex. Nice with wine by the fireplace on a cold winter's night. Nice with a margarita on a warm summer beach. Nice by itself on a hike in the woods, or a stroll around a CD store. In and of itself, it's not that big a deal. But pretty soon you're going to realize The State has made it into a very big deal called a Criminal Offense. And if you've tried it, and liked it, it's going to make you wonder why all those people go to jail for it, and it might just make you wonder what other injustices are going on in The Land.

I hope so.

If you do like smoking pot, when you grow up you will realize that 85 or 90 percent of the population prefers alcohol to reefer. A word of advice: don't choose your friends entirely according to the substances they are fond of or willing to use; you'll limit yourself. Some of my best friends never smoke pot. Most of them. Don't be swayed and don't try to sway others. This is difficult when you are young and pot pleases you and you want to share your amazement at what it does to your head with everyone you know.

Now if you try pot and like it, you may also start thinking that those dopey DARE scare programs they made you sit through in school must have lied to you about other drugs like cocaine or heroin. Actually, they didn't. Just because they were wrong about marijuana doesn't mean they are wrong about every drug. Some drugs are addictive, serious shit. As you grow up you'll notice that 1 or 2 percent of the population can't seem to get enough alcohol, reefer, coke, speed, heroin, or double-fudge chocolate ice cream to ease their pain. Watching sick people overdrug themselves is not pretty, but it's the price to be paid for a free and open society.

Marijuana does have value as a medicine, but your government would rather put sick people, people in pain, people in wheelchairs, into prisons than allow these people access to marijuana to ease their suffering. Why? Because to admit that marijuana has therapeutic value is to admit that they are wrong. And that's very hard for any government to do.

If you grow up to be a thinking person, you will eventually figure out this basic truth: In order to win an imaginary war against "drug dealers," your government is willing to lock away thousands of your fellow Americans, who are guilty of no other crime than wanting, and in some cases desperately needing for the sake of their health, to be left alone to smoke a herb. Boys and girls, you are living in strange times.

Where are the prison guard parades? Where are the "Proud to Be a Prison Guard" T-shirts?

How would you feel if your child told you, "I want to be a prison guard when I grow up"?

I am a supporter of marijuana, homemade beer, the Vancouver Canucks, the Hamilton Tiger Cats, the Montreal Expos, the Tampa Bay Buccaneers, and the right to ingest anything I see fit into my body. Wine sometimes gives me a headache, a rye and ginger can be nice in moderation, beer is good while cutting the lawn, and I love the occasional evening of Scotch or good Russian vodka. I've already ruled out certain harder substances, like heroin (did nothing but make me vomit) and cocaine (twenty minutes of feeling like hot shit, then back to being a needy bastard, needing more coke).

While I respect the new generation of sincere young psychonauts, my days of experimenting with new substances are over. I didn't get very far. Cannabis, coke, weak doses of LSD, some amazing mescaline, mushrooms were nice. I'll never know the pleasures, mysteries, wisdom, or horrors granted by new and old compounds like DMT, GHB, 2-CB, ayahuasca, or ibogaine. I'll even pass on peyote, or maybe I'm saving it for when I'm old and gray and can't deny that my earthly body is dying. But unless you're doing it with the proper sense of ritual, and preparedness, why bother?

*

Americans, get up off your asses and go see how people walk the earth, how they get life from it, how removed you are from it. When I came back to North America from my travels it seemed like all the TV ads were about day trading, sitting on your fat ass in front of a computer screen all day making money from money, contributing nothing real to the planet, in fact making money off its betrayal. Are there certain people in America (they're usually thirtyish white guys in the ads) turning into online misers, counting their money instantly, daily, hourly, to the minute, to the second? It's sad. And it's spreading—I saw the same type of TV ads (for etrade.es) on a screen up in the corner of that pot-friendly bar in Barcelona.

What's the point of making money off money? Once you have enough to be comfortable, wouldn't it be better to help others get there? It's a global village, and global warming is the global warning: a new swimming pool in Houston is not unconnected to drought in the Sudan. People ripping up the planet to get rich selling oil for the gas-guzzling toys of hydrocarbon junkies, then rewarding themselves with pleasures rather than helping solve the problems of the poor? What kind of a world is that?

What's more likely to destroy the earth, pot or pollution?
And there's a war on pot?

❊

I have no illusions that the legalization of marijuana would change
the world much. If marijuana were suddenly legal on a global scale,
then America would be the world's preeminent marijuana-producing
nation, just as it is now with caffeine, booze, and tobacco. Coca-
Cola, Budweiser, and Marlboros would be joined in global domi-
nance by another fine product, some mass-produced California
sensimilla that's trusted to be consistently okay, not great but not
too expensive, like a Gallo Brothers wine.

We've created a culture of people who by and large finish
their workday so stressed and exhausted that all they want to do
when they get home is flop in front of the tube and veg, allow the
great tit of television to tell them what they can buy to make their
weekend fun. If pot were legal, how many people would simply add
it to that formula? Get home and get high. Pot can be a great stress
reliever, sure, but it would be a shame if people used a new freedom only to anesthetize themselves.

The plant has things to teach us, if we approach every experience of it as a lesson. But America at rest, America at leisure,
is not a meditative culture. It's party time! Get me shit-faced, make
me forget. It's all about self-gratification. Self-annihilation.

❊

When I was young I actually thought it was cool that marijuana
was illegal. It added to the mystique; it gave us something to bond
over, to be clandestine and secretive about. A Utrecht coffee shop
owner said to me, "You get higher in America because of Prohibition—there's a kick to the rush, a kinkiness to it. And Prohibition creates more of a border between those who are 'in' and
those who are 'out.' Here in Holland you can smoke it and not

have to choose your friends carefully, or think about who you can tell or not."

Now that I am quite suddenly feeling middle-aged and domesticated, I'm not interested anymore in who's in or who's out, who's hip and who's not. I've gone from wanting to be cutting edge to wanting to cut the hedge. In a larger sense I want unity of purpose, and (and this is going to make me sound like a beauty pageant contestant) I want everyone to have a shared sense of belonging to a good and just society.

There are socially acceptable ways to indulge your inner adolescent, like caring desperately if your pro sports team wins the playoffs. But there is nothing worse than being made to feel adolescent when you don't feel you deserve it, as when you indulge in a pastime that a mature citizen can do responsibly and sensibly, like marijuana smoking. In other words, I'm sick of having to sneak around like a schoolkid just to score some herb.

✳

For the sake of this book I traveled to twelve countries, and found marijuana for the most part easily obtained and widely enjoyed. For much of the research and most of the writing of this book, I was high on marijuana. Now then—it can't be *that* amotivating.

I was talking in Amsterdam with Ben Dronkers, the founder of Sensi Seed Bank, in his coffee shop near the Hash Marihuana Hemp Museum. History is the struggle between democrats and aristocrats, he was saying. "We still have a Queen here in Holland, but in America in politics you see the same thing: Bush becomes Son of Bush, they become aristocrats, like our Queen. I'm very left-wing oriented, and you see the right wing there. And we will end up in the middle, because there is no other way. The world will be one, don't you think so? Because there is no other way."

I wish I could be as optimistic. But in America the right keeps right on winning.

✴

They win even while losing. Look at the War on Drugs. Immune from the thrall of gung ho American patriotism, foreigners have an easier time seeing it for what it is. On that cannabis cruise among the islands of the Sunshine Coast last summer, Marc Emery's grow expert Greg reminded me that when the drug war was launched in the 1980s, "The American government was buying cocaine in Panama, then selling it and buying guns for the Contras in Nicaragua. But Americans just didn't get it: they never seemed to make the connection that the coke that was going up their kids' noses was bought by fucking Ollie North."

Do you really think anything has changed? Nothing has changed. The supply lines established by American covert operations are still bringing cocaine and heroin north. The war on these drugs continues to be lost, and it's reflected in the market prices for them, which have never been lower.

And down in Colombia the American military is getting set to play with a whole new batch of toys. Our government has decided on our behalf that the best way to solve our drug problem is to teach some foreigners to kill some other foreigners. The only way it could get better for our military supply industries is if we could get both sides buying our weapons.

✴

Through a series of odd jobs arranged by his father, George W. Bush worked his way up to the title of President of the United States.

[283]

George II's second favorite book after the Bible is *The Dream and the Nightmare: The Sixties' Legacy to the Underclass,* by Myron Magnet. When he was governor of Texas, the book was required reading for Bush's staff.

Magnet argues that the sixties witnessed a huge cultural revolution that preached the liberation of the individual through sex and drugs, which was okay, or at least not personally damaging, for the great masses of middle-class boomers who bought into it as young people. The sixties: Tune in, turn on, get out of college, and get offered a good job anyway.

But for some young people, then and since, particularly minorities on the economic margins, the message of the sixties has been fatal. An underclass teenage boy indulging a drug habit, or a teenage girl who gets pregnant, both of them without middle-class safety nets, are doomed to fail. The undereducated addict will need more money than an unskilled job flipping burgers can provide. He'll turn to crime. The teenage mom will turn to welfare dependency.

I've seen it in my own family: a niece smoking her brains out starting at fourteen as a way of avoiding learning the work habits that high school requires, using marijuana to justify truancy and pure laziness. If it hadn't been pot it would have been something else—alcohol or harder drugs, either of which would likely have been more catastrophic. But she's a middle-class kid, at twenty years old starting to realize it's now or never as far as getting her shit together. She'll be given every chance to get it right, until she gets it right. But a girl from a less affluent, or structured, or nurturing environment might have been on the streets at fourteen, and at twenty a single mom on welfare, too overwhelmed by her brats to think about going back to school.

I can guess what Magnet would say to middle-class whiners like me, demanding my freedom to smoke my pot, but protected by affluence from the consequences a pot habit can inflict on more economically vulnerable folk. He'd say I'm setting a terrible example for the uneducated poor, for the underclass, for people who are one bad habit away from a life of crime or welfare. Whereas I can handle pot, and I can handle life, they can't. They don't have the tools.

This is the best of the arguments "compassionate conservatives" make, and it needs to be addressed. It's true: marginal people, people with the deck stacked against them, aren't helped by the prevailing wisdom of our popular culture, which tells us that an individual pleasure like smoking marijuana all day is heaven on earth, and that partying by the pool like the rappers in the video is the ultimate goal.

Sure, if you're a Louis Armstrong or even a Wyclef Jean, smoking chronic all day is fabulous, the best; the late great Satchmo did it, and Clef and loads of other young stars still do. But when it comes down to you, if you ain't a musical genius or a can't-miss sports star, you better get out that door, get to school, and learn how to do something productive and legit five days a week like the rest of us. Or create a viable alternative for yourself.

Everyone needs to take responsibility for his or her own life; everyone has a responsibility to the larger society to contribute as much as he or she takes. And anyway, those who contribute feel happier than those who just medicate.

I like what New Mexico governor Gary Johnson said when *Playboy* magazine, playing the devil's advocate, said to him: If cigarettes and alcohol are bigger killers than drugs, maybe these things should be illegal too. Johnson replied, "It doesn't work. Look at Prohibition. We live in America. We live in a free society where we are able to make choices. America is about allowing choice. It's about giving individuals freedoms and holding them accountable for those freedoms."

✻

I'm not interested in living in the strongest country in the world. I want to live in the freest.

What your government is saying to you is, We deny you the liberty to grow a plant that humans have grown for thousands of years, because we don't trust you to use it as responsibly as the ancients did.

How do you fight that?

Use marijuana responsibly. Show respect to your neighbors, the planet, the plant. Live clean and let your works be seen.

EPILOGUE

Just after I finished this book some sick fucks decided the best way to solve the world's problems was to crash airplanes into buildings and kill innocent people. For a while it seemed history had been changed forever by nineteen guys with box cutters and one demented Saudi millionaire.

In the meantime there have been some quiet changes on the world pot front. In Switzerland approval for Dutch-style coffee shops is moving smoothly through the legislative process. Belgium and Portugal have decriminalized personal possession. In Britain, Tony of Tony's Hemp Corner admitted publicly to supplying medical marijuana to 250 patients, and was promptly busted. GW Pharmaceuticals announced that a cannabis-based prescription spray, applied under the tongue, would be market-ready by 2004. The value of GW shares shot up after Tony Blair's government rescheduled cannabis from a class B to a class C drug, disarming police of the power to arrest for pot possession. Whether this proves to be a liberalization remains to be seen: Chris Sanders tells me police street seizures of personal stashes are on the increase, because the cops now just write a ticket as if it's a parking fine, and avoid the time, money, and paperwork a court date would have consumed under the old system. But Blair's about-face suggests to me that to fight the new War on Terrorism British police will at least siphon some resources from the pot part of the unwinnable War on Drugs.

I wish I could say the same process was under way in America. Unfortunately, on October 25, 2001, thirty DEA agents invaded the

Los Angeles Cannabis Resource Center in West Hollywood, destroying four hundred growing plants and seizing the medical records of 960 members. Protestors outside were joined by the mayor and city council of West Hollywood, which had cosigned the Center's mortgage and helped it gain membership in the local chamber of commerce.

The DEA action reminds me of that old joke about the pope's response on seeing Christ Himself coming to the door: "Quick, look busy!" Priorities in the Justice Department may be rearranged to fight a War on Terrorism, but the DEA has served notice they're not prepared to surrender a cent of the hefty chunk of cash marijuana accounts for in their drug war budget. When the DEA decides the most important thing is to look busy, pity the chemotherapy-wracked cancer cases using an herb to keep from vomiting, or the multiple sclerosis sufferers who find pot the best antispasmodic. Thanks to bin Laden, they may not be Public Enemy Number One anymore. But they're still sitting ducks for a misdirected police action.

In the last chapter I urged people to get more international, to get up off their asses and see the world. I meant it, and I still do. Everywhere in the world, and that includes Muslim countries, when strangers meet face-to-face, they put aside larger disputes and judge one another as individuals. We need to remind one another we are all individuals sharing a planet. Call me a naïve pothead if you like, but I know for a fact that the vast majority of people on this planet are peace loving. The worst thing Americans can do now is send only the warriors abroad, and hide at home nurturing insularity, mistrust, and fear of the other. Peace lovers, fun seekers, get out there and greet your foreign counterparts. Roll one up and find the shared pleasure of that smoky communion.

Then roll another one for me.

ACKNOWLEDGMENTS

A great big thank you to the many kind people who helped me along the way, particularly Gary and Paris in Nimbin, Russell, Katie, and Chris in London, and a certain sweet family in the Dutch countryside.

Thanks to the folks at *Cannabis Culture* magazine and their excellent website, and likewise to those at the Media Awareness Project site. And to Gabe Moses at *High Times.*

Grow guru Ed Rosenthal, the Ann Landers of pot, helped me get over my "smirk factor" and answered many questions, from basic horticulture to complicated politics.

And finally, thanks to Max, Anne, and Bunu, who all three, I'm certain, wish they could have supported this project with more enthusiasm, but supported me nonetheless.